Colección Támesis

SERIE A: MONOGRAFÍAS, 360

A COMPANION TO MIGUEL DE UNAMUNO

A COMPANION TO
MIGUEL DE UNAMUNO

Edited by

JULIA BIGGANE

and

†JOHN MACKLIN

TAMESIS

First published 2016
Tamesis, Woodbridge

ISBN 978 1 85566 300 8

Tamesis is an imprint of Boydell & Brewer Ltd
PO Box 9, Woodbridge, Suffolk IP12 3DF, UK
and of Boydell & Brewer Inc.
668 Mt. Hope Avenue, Rochester NY 14620–2731, USA
website: www.boydellandbrewer.com

A CIP record for this title is available
from the British Library

This publication is printed on acid-free paper

Typeset by
www.thewordservice.com

Contents

* *Translated by Julia Biggane*

Contributors

Julia Biggane was senior lecturer in Hispanic Studies at the University of Aberdeen; she now works at the London School of Economics. She has published on Unamuno's narrative and drama, and has translated, with a critical introduction, *La tía Tula* into English.

Sandro Borzoni teaches the history of philosophy in Italy. He studied the relations between Unamuno and Italian culture during his PhD in Salamanca, and translated Unamuno's *Nuevo Mundo* into Italian. He has also edited *De la desesperación religiosa moderna*, a collection of Unamuno's previously unpublished essays.

J.A. Garrido Ardila is Professor of Modern Spanish and Comparative Literature at the University of Edinburgh and Funcionario Docente de Carrera with the Spanish Ministry of Education. He has published on the literature and history of the Spanish Golden Age and 20th century, and on 18th-century English literature and Scandinavian modernism. In 2010-12 he was the Principal Investigator of a Leverhulme International Network on 'Unamuno's Literature and Politics'.

Ramón F. Llorens García lectures at the Universidad de Alicante. He is the author of several scholarly publications on the works of Unamuno and José Martínez Ruiz («Azorín»).

C. Alex Longhurst is Emeritus Professor of the University of Leeds. He is the author of *Unamuno's Theory of the Novel* (Oxford: Legenda, 2014).

John Macklin was, until his retirement, Professor of Hispanic Studies and Head of the School of Modern Languages and Cultures at the University of Glasgow. He published research on Pérez de Ayala and Spanish modernist literature, and translated narrative fiction by Unamuno and Cervantes into English.

Jean-Claude Rabaté is Emeritus Professor of the Université Sorbonne-Nouvelle, and is author (with Colette Rabaté) of an edition of Unamuno's correspondence in exile (*Cartas del destierro* : Universidad de Salamanca, 2012) and of a biography of Unamuno (Madrid, Taurus, 2009).

Pedro Ribas Ribas is Professor of Philosophy at the Universidad Autónoma de Madrid. His publications have focused on the history of Spanish and Latin-American Marxism, on Unamuno, and on philosophers exiled after the Spanish Civil War.

Stephen Roberts is Associate Professor and Reader in Modern Spanish Literature and Intellectual History at the University of Nottingham. His research interests include the emergence of the modern intellectual in Spain and the literature, thought and political activities of Miguel de Unamuno and his contemporaries.

Alison Sinclair is Professor of Modern Spanish Literature and Intellectual History (emerita) at the University of Cambridge. She specializes in nineteenth and twentieth-century Spanish literature, culture and intellectual history, the history of sexuality in Spain, psychoanalytic approaches to fiction, comparative literature, and the spread of cultural ideas in Europe. Her most recent work has been on the AHRC-funded project 'Wrongdoing in Spain 1800-1936' (2011–2014).

Gareth Wood is senior lecturer in Modern Spanish Literature at University College London. He has published research on the reception of English literature among a range of Spanish writers including Galdós, Javier Marías, and Unamuno.

Acknowledgements

Julia Biggane would like to thank C. Alex Longhurst, Stephen Roberts and Alison Sinclair for their kindness, support and advice during the preparation of this volume. She would also like to thank Syrithe Pugh for her help with translation from Latin. She is deeply grateful to Scott Mahler for his immense patience and unfailing encouragement throughout. She would also like to thank Morna, John, Eric and Mary Biggane for their constant support and love.

Foreword

JULIA BIGGANE

This *Companion* offers a survey of the enormous body of work produced by Miguel de Unamuno (1864-1936) in various genres over the course of almost half a century, from the 1890s to the eve of the Spanish Civil War. No single-volume study could hope to be exhaustive in its study of such a prolific writer, yet at the same time, because Unamuno's work explored fairly constantly certain themes and certain fundamental questions about existence and identity (both individual and national) over many years, the risk of repetition in tracing its trajectory is always present. This *Companion* attempts to address both challenges by dividing its study of Unamuno's work into two parts: the first charts Unamuno's work chronologically, analysing major developments and turning points or breaks as well as continuities; the second part studies selected central themes and pre-occupations in his writing.

Because Unamuno's fundamental concerns were examined across a range of media, the second part of the volume mostly eschews a genre-based approach, focusing instead on a different key aspect of Unamuno's thought or creative practice across a range of his works. Sandro Borzoni examines Unamuno's existentialism and his complex views on religious faith; C. Alex Longhurst explores Unamuno's linguistic philosophy, and his views on language and its relation both to community and to the individual self; Alison Sinclair focuses on the ethical dimensions of Unamuno's work; Gareth Wood examines the painfully intertwined ontology of self and other in Unamuno's fiction and drama; Julia Biggane's chapter analyses the changing representation of gender and sexuality in his work during a period of important social change in Spain and beyond; J.A.G Garrido Ardila and Julia Biggane's chapter focuses on the enduring intertextual engagement with Don Quixote in Unamuno's essays, fiction and drama. Dividing the volume into two parts in this way aims to help the reader acquire a more comprehensive and substantial sense of the fundamental continuities and changes in Unamuno's thought and creative work than a purely chronological, or genre-based approach would allow. The only exception to this approach is the final chapter, in which Ramón Llorens focuses on Unamuno's travel writing—a much neglected aspect of Unamuno's *oeuvre*. Broadly speaking, the study privileges his narrative fiction over other literary genres, as this has proved to offer the most substantial, nuanced and varied, enduring vehicle for the exploration of his key preoccupations. There is, nevertheless, substantial coverage of his major essays and dramatic works too.

A further major challenge faces any serious reader of Unamuno: in addition to the daunting quantity of his own work is the vast amount of critical study it has attracted over the years. A journal devoted exclusively to the study of his work has been in existence since 1948; scores of monographs and many hundreds of articles have been published since his death. Indeed, Unamuno criticism has its own history, and has constructed many different – at times contradictory – Unamunos. Of course this is a phenomenon affecting many prolific authors with long careers, but is perhaps particularly marked in Unamuno's case because his thought drew on such a vast and eclectic range of philosophical, theological, political and literary sources, and because his political beliefs and affiliations shifted profoundly over the course of his career. A concentration on the Hegelian aspects of Unamuno's thought and literary production (as explored in Regalado García's 1968 monograph, for example, or in parts of Wyers' 1976 study), risks underplaying the irrationalist, anti-systemic elements of his thinking. Conversely, an emphasis on Kierkegaard and Cervantes as influences on his work can overshadow Unamuno's sustained engagement both with contemporaneous developments in the natural and social sciences, both of which also played a part in his understanding of individual existence (see, for example, Sinclair (2000) or Johnson (1989)).

Anyone studying Unamuno's work would be well-advised to keep uppermost in his or her mind Unamuno's own description of his position on many issues: 'alterutralidad' [alterutrality], which sought not the distortions of a smoothly synthetic or superficially coherent neutrality or middle ground between polar differences, but sought to keep opposing positions in dynamic, constructive tension, avoiding complete identification with any one of them. It is in this way that we should understand his most fundamental thinking as laid out in *Del sentimiento trágico de la vida*: Unamuno is not a confident atheist, detached agnostic or untroubled believer, but sought ways of living with the uncertainties that the rejection of all these positions entailed. It is in this manner that we should understand his post-1897 political thought too. His brief support for the military uprising against the Second Republic in 1936 must be set against his previous sustained opposition to the proto-fascist Primo de Rivera dictatorship just a few years before, for example, rather than being seen as the simple culmination of a shift to the right after his earlier socialist campaigning. His views on the Castilian language can smack of cultural imperialism, particularly to contemporary readers, but should be considered within a broader context of his enduring opposition to the various imperialisms (cultural and military) of institutions such as the Church and armed forces, and to the more conservative elements of the post-1875 Restoration regime. Nor should the irreducibility of Unamuno's position on most matters of substance to any single easily identifiable philosophical or ideological position be confused with simple contrarianism, for all that he, at times, succumbed to polemicising; Unamuno was genuinely and consistently concerned to find ways of productively thinking through and living with uncertainty and multivalence. It is this quality of his work that continues to makes Unamuno 'good to think with', even for readers who disagree profoundly with some of his assumptions and conclusions.

In an attempt to avoid offering a reductive or monolithic view of a complex and rich body of thought and literary production, this *Companion* invited contributions from a range of distinguished scholars with very different approaches to and views on Unamuno's work: even when texts or themes are discussed in more than one chapter, varied perspectives are brought to bear upon them. All authors have aimed to offer not just incisive analysis of the texts or topics studied, but also a balanced overview of issues and debates arising in Unamuno studies. The further reading recommended at the end of each chapter attempts to offer additional guidance through the very dense thicket of scholarship on Unamuno, but ultimately, the reader will have to exercise his or her own critical judgment about the more ambivalent, ambiguous or otherwise challenging aspects of his work. Unamuno, would, of course, approve: so much of his work, fictional and non-fictional, aimed precisely to create critical, engaged, *active* readers.

This *Companion* aims to be accessible and useful to advanced undergraduates, graduate students and scholars in Hispanic Studies and other disciplines across the humanities. All Spanish quotations and terms are followed by a parenthetical English translation except in a very few instances where the Spanish is immediately comprehensible even to those not versed in the language. In many cases where the precise formulation/diction of the Spanish is not germane to the analysis, only the English translation is supplied, but references to the two established *Obras completas* editions are provided to allow consultation of the Spanish if desired. Published English translations are referenced where feasible. In order to avoid excessive repetition between chapters, the titles of Unamuno's major works referenced in this volume are not translated in-text; translations are provided in the 'Note on editions used and translations of Unamuno's works' at the beginning of the volume.

This foreword must end on a deeply sad personal note: John Macklin was not able to contribute to this volume in the way he wished to before his untimely death in 2014. This *Companion* would not have existed without him, and it is to his memory that the volume is dedicated.

Note on editions used
and translations of Unamuno's works

Although an edition of Unamuno's *Obras completas* [Complete Works] was published by the Biblioteca Castro from 1995 onwards, it has not yet been completed, and is not widely institutionally available. The most accessible editions remain those published by Afrodisio Aguado (Madrid/Barcelona: 1958) and Escelicer (Madrid: 1966), both edited by Manuel García Blanco: one or the other is usually found in most major university/institutional libraries. All in-text references are to both editions and are given parenthetically as OCE (Escelicer) and OCA (Afrodisio Aguado), followed by the respective volume and page number.

An author: date reference below after the English indicates a published translation (whose details are given in the Bibliography at the end of the volume).

Novels, novellas and short-story collections

Nuevo mundo [New World]
Paz en la guerra [Peace in War] (Unamuno: 1983)
Amor y pedagogía [Love and Pedagogy]
El espejo de la muerte [The Mirror of Death]
Niebla [Mist] (Unamuno: 2014)
Abel Sánchez [Abel Sánchez] (Unamuno: 2009)
Tres novelas ejemplares y un prólogo [Three Exemplary Novels and a Prologue]
    Dos madres [Two Mothers]
    El marqués de Lumbría [The Marquis of Lumbría]
    Nada menos que todo un hombre [Every Inch a Man]
Tulio Montalbán y Julio Macedo [Tulio Montalbán and Julio Macedo]
La tía Tula [Aunt Tula] (Unamuno: 2013)
Cómo se hace una novela [How a Novel is Written]
La novela de Don Sandalio, jugador de ajedrez [The Novel of Don Sandalio, Chess-player]
Un pobre hombre rico [A Poor Rich Man]
El sentido cómico de la vida [The Comic Sense of Life]
San Manuel Bueno, mártir [St Manuel Bueno, Martyr] (Unamuno: 2007)

Plays

La esfinge [The Sphinx]
La venda [The Bandage]
La princesa Doña Lambra [Princess Lambra]
La difunta [The Deceased Woman]
Fedra [Phaedra]
El pasado que vuelve [The Return of the Past]
Soledad [Loneliness (also the given name of the female protagonist)]
Raquel encadenada [Raquel in Chains]
Sombras de sueño [Shadows of a Dream]
El otro [The Other]
El hermano Juan o el mundo es teatro [Brother Juan (a play on Don Juan), or All the World is a Stage]
Medea [Medea]

Essays

'La regeneración del teatro español' [The Regeneration of the Spanish Theatre]
'¡Adentro!' [Within!]
'Mi fe' [My Faith]
'La ideocracia' [Ideocracy]
En torno al casticismo [On the Essence of Spanishness]
Vida de Don Quijote y Sancho [Life of Don Quixote and Sancho]. Translated as part of *Our Lord Don Quixote* (Unamuno: 1976b).
Del sentimiento trágico de la vida en los hombres y en los pueblos [Tragic Sense of Life] (Unamuno: 1954)
La agonía del cristianismo [The Agony of Christianity] (Unamuno: 1974)
Manual de Quijotismo [Manual of Quixotism]
Alrededor del estilo [On Style]
El resentimiento trágico de la vida [On the Tragic *Ressentiment* of Life]

Poems/Poetry Collections

El Cristo de Velázquez [Velázquez's Christ]
Cancionero [Miscellany]
Romancero del destierro [Exile Ballads]

Travel Writing

Paisajes [Landscapes]
Por tierras de Portugal y España [Through the Lands of Spain and Portugal]
De mi país: descripciones, relatos y artículos de costumbres [On/From my Country: Descriptions, Tales and Studies of Customs]
Paisajes del alma [Landscapes of the Soul]
Andanzas y visiones españolas [Spanish Adventures and Visions]

Life-writing

Diario íntimo [Intimate Diary]. Translated as part of the volume *The Private World*
   (Unamuno: 1985)
Recuerdos de niñez y mocedad [Memories of Childhood and Young Adulthood]
De mi vida [On My Life]

Introduction

JULIA BIGGANE

As a novelist, dramatist, essayist, poet and public intellectual, Miguel de Unamuno (1864–1936) is a towering figure in twentieth-century Spanish cultural and political life. He was a strikingly energetic and prolific writer, producing five novels, seven novellas, eleven plays, scores of short stories, dozens of essays – major and minor – many hundreds of poems, an extensive body of travel writing and several memoirs. He also wrote a vast quantity of articles on diverse subjects for a wide range of newspapers and journals in Spain, wider Europe and Latin America. Widely recognised and translated during his lifetime, he was an inescapably canonical figure on university syllabi across Europe and the Americas for many years after his death, and still appears on many curricula, though his work may be framed rather differently. He still makes occasional appearances in contemporary Hispanic literature, sometimes in unexpected places – Roberto Bolaño's short story 'Una aventura literaria', (Bolaño 1997: 54) for example, or, less surprisingly, in Jon Juaristi's 2007 novel *La caza salvaje*.

Unamuno's literary fame rests principally on his novels, novellas and later drama. Unsurprisingly, the thematic and stylistic emphases of his prose fiction changed significantly over the course of an almost fifty-year writing career: the realism and preoccupation with national history in his first novel *Paz en la guerra* (1897) gave way to playful anti-realism and subversion of the conventional third-person narrator in subsequent novels such as *Amor y pedagogía* (1902) and *Niebla* (1914), and then to sober character studies such as *Abel Sánchez* (1917), *La tía Tula* (1921) and *San Manuel Bueno, mártir* (1930). Nevertheless, after *Paz en la guerra*, there are important continuities across his fiction: his characters are lonely, alienated or conflicted figures, assailed by profound doubts about the nature and purpose of their existence; they all hunger after some form of immortality and are anxious to leave a lasting mark – reproduction (whether spiritual or biological) is a major concern. His characters perceive themselves as vulnerable to destruction or annihilating absorption by a threatening 'other' – be that the author-figure himself in *Niebla*, an envied rival in *Abel Sánchez*, or even a much-loved figure in *San Manuel Bueno, mártir* and *La tía Tula*. Across most of his fiction, temporal settings and locations are sketchy or only loosely defined, so giving the impression that the novelist is concerned more with broad human experience than specific circumstance or period.

Certainly the travails of Unamuno's protagonists are consonant with his reflections on the human condition as laid out in his most famous essay, *Del sentimiento trágico de la vida*. This 1912 work, which sets out Unamuno's philosophy of existence, is central to his thought. It draws eclectically and idiosyncratically on disparate sources, but his starting point is the early-Enlightenment Dutch philosopher Baruch Spinoza's premise that what essentially defines the living being is its effort to survive indefinitely. For Unamuno, in humans, this entails a yearning for personal immortality, which is one of the conditions giving rise to religious faith. But if a longing for eternal life is an essential part of the human condition, so is reason, because without it, mankind cannot perceive, reflect or communicate. Yet a reason depending upon sceptical enquiry is not, in Unamuno's representation, compatible with religious faith, or with life as it is actually lived and experienced. Human subjects are, then, for Unamuno, fundamentally riven by the competing but interdependent claims of reason, faith and life: a hunger for immortality is not rational, and cannot be assuaged or extinguished by arguments from reason, but nor can it be understood or expressed without the reflective, communicative capacities lent by reason; reason may operate on the basis of sceptical enquiry, yet its scepticism can never be absolute (otherwise, Unamuno argues, the thinking subject would have to doubt his or her own existence), so it can only sustain itself by leaning upon faith, even if only upon faith in reason. And lived experience often runs counter to reason and faith. That humans must live with this constant, irreconcilable conflict is, for Unamuno, what makes them tragic.

Of course the relation between reason and faith is a hoary question in theology and philosophy: what is distinctive about Unamuno's representation of the problem is the deeply combative yet intimate dynamism of faith and reason's interdependence, and the insistence that concrete individual lived experience not be factored out of any philosophy of human existence nor subordinated to the spiritual or immaterial in any religious conception of life. Though in Unamuno's eyes tragic, the uncertainty about life after death arising from this conflictive relationship should form the basis not of despairing inertia, but, on the contrary, a vigorous personal ethics. Unamuno summarises this ethics by citing from the French essayist Senancour's early nineteenth-century novel *Obermann*: 'Man may very well be perishable. But let us resist such a possibility, and, if nothingness is what really awaits us, let us make it an injustice' (Unamuno

1954: 263; OCE VII, 264; OCA XVI, 387). For Unamuno, in order that death be an injustice, the individual must pursue a vocation in life (whether a calling, or an imposed or accidental path) with such commitment and passion that he becomes irreplaceable. In terms of interpersonal relations and collective co-existence, the essay advocates an ethics of 'mutual imposition': Unamuno adapts the Christian biblical command to 'love thy neighbour', and argues that 'it is by imposing my ideas upon my neighbour that I become the recipient of his ideas. My endeavour to impose myself upon another – to be and live in him, and by him, to make him mine (which is the same as making myself his) – is what gives religious meaning to human collectivity, to human solidarity' (Unamuno 1954: 279; OCE VII, 272–3; OCA XVI, 402). Once again the basis of human existence is represented by Unamuno as intimate combat and struggle – both with oneself and with others.

It should be clear that Unamuno's preoccupation with religious uncertainty, with reproduction (and the questions about gender and sexuality it throws up), as well as the presence of a potentially threatening but necessary and intimate 'other', cannot be read solely in terms of a timeless philosophy of existence. The struggles undergone by his tragic philosophical subject, or his fictional protagonists, are not easily abstracted from the dramatic material shifts in gender roles and relations taking place across European and American societies in the early years of the twentieth century, nor from contemporaneous debates about secularism and the entrenchment both of explicitly atheist political philosophies or movements and reactionary religious politics in the Spain of the time. And the potentially usurping or dominating 'other' may be read as a figure obliquely representative of any number of emerging threats to the established socio-economic, cultural or political order in Spain during the early part of the twentieth century. Even though an explicit, detailed social context may be absent, it is impossible, then, to remove Unamuno's tragically uncertain philosophical subject, or his lonely, ambivalent characters, from the prevailing social, scientific/technological and philosophical dislocations of late modernity. It is not just his experimental or avant-garde novels *Amor y pedagogía* and *Niebla* that deserve a place in the Spanish modernist archive, and his thought, for all its eclecticism, idiosyncrasy and ultimately theological ground, is also very much of its moment, sharing with or anticipating the preoccupations of philosophers such as William James, Henri Bergson, Edmund Husserl and Martin Heidegger.

Unamuno's significance is certainly not limited to his fictional output or his philosophy of existence: he was amongst Spain's first modern intellectuals, and took his role as a public commentator very seriously. In addition to his responsibilities as professor and rector at Salamanca – Spain's oldest university – he was a prolific newspaper essayist, and occupied a prominent position in the early twentieth-century political sphere. His own allegiances shifted over the course of his life: an early sympathy for Basque autonomous rights (Unamuno had been born and raised in Bilbao, and had lived through the siege of that city in the final Carlist War) was supplanted by membership of the socialist party for a period in the 1890s; thereafter, his politics were that of a broadly liberal republicanism containing both progressive and conservative elements. He could be mordantly critical of the post-1875 monarchical regime, and particularly of King Alfonso XIII: his criticism of regime and king led to his removal from the rectorship of Salamanca in 1914. Further criticism of the King and of Primo de Rivera's proto-fascist military dictatorship after 1923 earned Unamuno internal exile to the Canary Islands in 1924. He escaped to France, and was pardoned by the regime, but, on principle, remained in exile until the dictatorship collapsed in 1930. Unamuno then briefly became a member of the Spanish parliament as part of the Republican-Socialist coalition in the new Second Republic, but he soon became disenchanted with the Republic, and later, his hostility to the broad-left Popular Front coalition government led him initially to support the military coup mounted against it in July 1936, a coup which triggered the Civil War. Unamuno recanted shortly afterwards, condemning the ideological poverty and the savage repression of the Nationalist rebels. He died, unreconciled to either the Republican or Nationalist side, at the very end of the same year.

Unamuno's social and political writings tackled some of the deepest fault lines of Spanish society in the period leading up to the Civil War: he wrote on Spanish nationhood and nationalism, was critical of the powers of the Catholic Church and the military, and was excoriating about the imperial ambitions and political meddling of Alfonso XIII. He wrote controversially on the politics of language – particularly the status of Castilian Spanish in relation to Spain's other languages. Although at times his analyses were not entirely coherent, or were characterised by polemical provocation rather than nuanced enquiry, all his political writing demonstrated a deep, sustained and intimately-felt engagement with some of the most sensitive issues in national life. No serious study of the history and literature of the first half of the twentieth century in Spain can afford to ignore his contribution to Spanish culture, thought and public life.

I

The Development of Unamuno's Work

1

Unamuno before 1902:
Writing Nation, History, Politics

JEAN-CLAUDE RABATÉ

Unamuno's thought and writing underwent considerable change between the late 1880s and the early 1900s; at the same time, some elements of his youthful intellectual production remained constant throughout his life. This chapter traces the lines of evolution and continuity in his early work, from an initial preoccupation with Basque identity and culture, through an extended examination of Spanishness, Spain's history, and its relationship with Europe, to the beginnings of his 'intimate dramas'—literary texts unconcerned with place or nation.

From Romantic Foralism in Bilbao to Positivism in Madrid

On 21 July 1876, a political event took place that had immensely significant consequences for the Basque provinces: the prime minister, Antonio Cánovas del Castillo, announced the abolition of the Basque *fueros* or customary laws.[1] It could not have left indifferent the young Miguel de Unamuno, who had just finished the first year of his baccalaureate studies. Reading the Catalan federalist and libertarian socialist Francisco Pi y Margall's *Las nacionalidades* [Nationalities] a few months after the *fueros* were abolished made a huge impact on the young Miguel. His romantic interest in the question of nationhood, fed by ancient Basque legends, found an echo and a doctrinal base in Margall's nationalism, whose ideology derived in part from Pierre-Joseph Proudhon. Unamuno later commented that he and his friends regarded Pi y Margall's book as a kind of holy scripture when they gathered regularly to discuss federalism. Their discussions took place:

---

1 The *fueros* were fiscal and other exemptions and privileges enjoyed by the historic Basque lands since the medieval period.

'always with a view to the redemption of our Basque lands [...] which we
thought of as another Ireland, Hungary or Poland. Because at that time, for
us boys in 1879, these three countries were models of political slavery'
(OCE VIII, 340; OCA X, 305).

On 27 December 1879, shortly before he left the Basque country to begin his
university studies in Madrid, Unamuno published his first article, anonymously,
in the *Noticiero Bilbaíno*. Entitled 'Strength through Union', the fifteen-year-old
Unamuno expressed a political desire shared by many: the grouping of Basque
parties into a Basque-Navarrese Union, concerned exclusively with overturning
what they saw as the abusive 1876 law. The abolition of the *fueros* fomented the
development of a romantic Basque *fuerismo* [foralism] (a position of support for
the *fueros*, and, according to Urrutia (1997: 19), widely acknowledged as a form
of proto-nationalism) and Miguel and his friends were caught up in this atmosphere
of what Unamuno would later describe in *De mi vida* as sentimental 'Basqueism',
'a romantic blast of anti-urbanism and even disdain for the refinements of
civilisation!!!!' (OCE VIII, 249; OCA X, 168). He read authors such as Amiel
and Rousseau, and, in his own words, wept like Ossian over what he saw as the
prostration and decadence of the Basque people (OCE VIII, 143; OCA I, 308).
The young Miguel and his friends would vent romantically against the city—a
seat of vice—against progress, and the construction of the railways; they took
refuge instead in the purity of the countryside. As was normal for a member of
the urban bourgeoisie, Unamuno was not a native Basque speaker, but his interest
in Basque culture drove him to learn the language, making notes and lexicons
(this was in the period before Basque was standardised).

His interest in language was broadened and deepened when he went to the
Universidad Central in Madrid in 1880 to pursue a degree in Filosofía y Letras.
The curriculum included study of Ancient Greek, Latin, Hebrew and Arabic,
literature and history (both that of Spain and the wider world), and philosophy
(metaphysics). Unamuno read voraciously, and, outside the classroom, was an
assiduous attender of the Ateneo, one of the country's most prominent fora for
the discussion of new and progressive intellectual currents. During his time in
Madrid, Unamuno was introduced to Krausist thought, and to the work of figures
as influential and diverse such as Kant, Hegel, Nietzsche, Darwin, Taine and
Spencer. The rationalist and positivist currents to which he was exposed
challenged both his romantic tendencies and his religious faith. Although
Unamuno disliked Madrid and was homesick for his native Bilbao, his family
and his fiancée Concha Lizárraga, his experiences as an undergraduate led to
a profound change in his intellectual development.

This change, as well as his continued interest in Basque culture and language,
is visible in his doctoral studies, which he took up immediately after his graduation

in 1883. His thesis title was 'Critique of the Problem concerning the Origin and Prehistory of the Basque People', and his approach placed him very much at odds with traditionalist and romantic theories of Basque history. Urrutia describes his position as one of 'radical scepticism' (1997: 25), and Unamuno drew on rationalist, positivist theories and the influential philological thought of Humboldt and Schleicher to conclude that what had been hypothesised up until that point about the origins of the Basque people, and about the kinship of Basque with other languages, lacked scientific basis, and that almost nothing was known for certain about Basque prehistoric culture (OCE IV, 118; OCA VI, 139–140). The field of Basque history and research was dominated by mythologising, and, as Unamuno argued, although such creations of the imagination 'could be pleasing, even enchanting, they did not, unfortunately, satisfy the intelligence' (cited in Urrutia 1997: 26). There is also more than a hint of Unamuno's Hegelian readings in his assertion that 'the Basque people would eventually be assimilated, lost like a stream in the great currents of the wide river' (OCE IV, 88; OCA VI, 91).

Having successfully defended his thesis in June 1884, Unamuno returned to Bilbao and began the arduous task of preparation for an academic post, which could only be secured by the extremely demanding nationwide competitive examinations known as *oposiciones*. This proved to be a *via crucis* for Unamuno lasting several years. He competed unsuccessfully for Chairs in Latin and Castilian, Psychology, Logic and Ethics, and Metaphysics in various different areas of the Spain. Although his lack of success was dispiriting, as Urrutia notes, the wide reading his preparation required further broadened his already impressive intellectual reach (1997: 27).

To support himself, he taught at secondary-school level, and offered private tuition in Spanish. He also turned to journalism, and the titles of two of the journals he contributed to – *Socialismo* and *Ensayos de cuestiones económica acerca del socialismo* [Essays on Economic Questions Pertaining to Socialism] – give an indication of how far his political sympathies had changed since his early romantic foralism.[2] At the end of the 1880s, Unamuno was finally successful in the *oposiciones* examination, and took up the Chair in Ancient Greek at the University of Salamanca in 1891.

Culture, Society and Politics in Unamuno's Early Work (1895–1902)

It was during his early years in Salamanca that Unamuno wrote a series of essays for the prestigious cosmopolitan Madrid journal *La España Moderna* in 1895: these were subsequently collected as published as a single volume

---

entitled *En torno al casticismo* (1902). These essays have to be placed in the context of an end-of-century crisis in Spain. The factors behind the crisis were several: the Restoration political settlement and its institutions were becoming increasingly obviously moribund; the long decline of Spain's political and economic position within the world was being accelerated by independence movements in colonial Cuba and the Philippines, and by the rise of more industrialised nations in Europe and the Americas; calls for political, economic and cultural modernisation of the country were met by powerful, militant defences of throne and altar. The economic dimensions of the crisis were not at the forefront of debate; discourse centred instead on moral crisis and ideological fracture, as Tuñón de Lara (1974) has demonstrated.

In order to carry out an examination of the 'national conscience', then, intellectuals such as the young Unamuno came to the fore and took part in a notable attempt at critical renewal. It was thanks to them – or they were to blame for – turning Spain into a problem: while other more traditionalist forces continued to dream of its past, they criticised Spain, called it into question, and imagined its future. Like those of some other intellectuals and writers, Unamuno's writings demonstrate that the 'crisis' was already sharply present in a decomposing society well before the so-called 'Disaster' of defeat in the Spanish-American War and consequent imperial loss in 1898. Even as Unamuno was busy burying myths about Spain, other more conservative thinkers were enthusiastically disinterring them. The Church hierarchy was particularly active in its resistance to change. In spite of threats of excommunication and removal from office, Unamuno bravely and lucidly re-opened polemics about pure or essential Spanishness (*casticismo*) inherited from the eighteenth century. For all the force of the debate between modernisers and traditionalists though, it has to be said that it remained alien to the vast majority of the population.

In the vein of Clarín before him, and Joaquín Costa after him, in *En torno al casticismo*, Unamuno called for new winds to blow across the plains of Spain: he was in search of new ideas, texts and writers capable of helping him to discover alternative ideals. In order to counter the 'purism' that manufactured nationalist myths, recuperated historical and literary glories and appropriated a code of honour inherited from the so-called Golden Age of seventeenth-century drama, and to counter the lingering after-effects of the Inquisition, Unamuno created rich, fertile neologisms and concepts to frame the debate about Spain's past, present and future in new terms. The essays imposed no truth: they were instead a call for debate and tolerance against prejudice, and an invitation to reflect on and search for a national identity which might lead to the fusion of European culture with Spain's most intimate and profound historical and cultural existence.

En torno al casticismo is far from a systematic analysis of Spain's problems and possibilities: as Thomas Mermall notes, the essays are indicative of a budding intellectual testing his newly acquired ideas, and display a striking profusion of languages: 'philosophy, religion, science and its various branches— biology, geology, psychology, evolution—interact promiscuously with descriptive, lyrical, and argumentative discourse' to make up a 'heterogeneous, complex text' (1993: 281). In its engagement with some of the most famous ideological debates of the nineteenth century – science versus religion, Krausism versus Catholicism and traditionalism versus Europeanising modernisation – the volume represents an awkward combination of contradictory readings: those of the Krausists (Sanz del Río, Giner de los Ríos, Amiel, Azcárate), of positivists (Comte, Spencer, Darwin and Taine), and of the famous European philosophers, writing at a moment in which European thought was in crisis.

Casticismo

The object of the essays' analysis—the concept of *casticismo* [purity/authenticity, deriving ultimately from the Latin *casticeus/casta*]—had long lain at the heart of debates about the essence of Spanishness, and what should – or should not – define national culture. Unamuno lays out his own position on the very first page. Noting that the adjective *casto* is ordinarily used to describe 'pure' animal species, and that it is held to be an excellent and advantageous quality, Unamuno argues that the term itself:

> entrenches an ancient prejudice, the source of myriad errors and much harm: the belief that so-called 'pure' breeds are superior to cross- or mixed breeds, when it is proven, both through experiments on domestic animal breeds and also by history, that [...] crossbreeding is a source of new vigour and progress, so long as the differences between breeds do not outweigh what they have in common
>
> (OCA III, 169; OCE I, 784).

For Unamuno, this example can serve as an analogy for Spain and Spanish culture, and encapsulates one of the volume's key arguments: the country must open itself more to 'crossbreeding' with European ideas, cultures and practices in order to modernise and make progress; those *casticistas* who had historically attempted to seal off Spain from foreign currents such as the Reformation, or who promoted a chauvinistic account of Spanish intellectual and cultural achievements were, in effect, producing a pernicious inbreeding, leading to the decline of the country. In Unamuno's view, crossbreeding would not dilute existing native culture; on the contrary, 'Cosquilleos de fuera despiertan lo que duerme en el seno de nuestra conciencia' [Stimulation from the outside awakens what lies dormant in the heart of our consciousness] (OCE I, 853; OCA III, 278). In other words, Spain must both open itself to outside influences and also delve into its own depths as a nation.

Indeed, the relationship between exterior and interior, surface and depth, is the central theme of the whole volume, particularly in relation to the way that the history of Spain had been written. As Blanco Aguinaga rightly noted, 'The controversy about *casticismo*, which was so violent from the eighteenth century onwards, has never been in Spain a byzantine discussion between disinterested scholars, but rather a theological and political battle (1954: 53); one of the aims of *En torno al casticismo* was to correct the hitherto dominant historiography of Spain as a nation. In order to do so, Unamuno proposed a distinction between *historia* [history] and *intrahistory* [intrahistory]. Traditional historiography had concerned itself only with *historia,* the stuff of political events and forces, institutions and elites.

Historically speaking, Castile had dominated Spain from the end of the fifteenth century, and the particularity of its institutions, and shaping forces – the uniquely close relationship between monarchy and Church for example, especially in relation to the Inquisition, and the zeal in excluding perceived threats from without, from the Reformation onwards – was inevitably intimately tied up with the concept of *casticismo*. In the second essay of the volume, 'La casta histórica Castilla' [Pure Historic Castile], Unamuno wrote:

> However it came about, Castile placed itself at the head of the united monarchies, and then set the tone and guided the spirit of the monarchy; the Castilian is, in the last instance, the castizo [...] Castilian *casticismo* is what we must examine [...]
>
> (OCE I, 805; OCA III, 204)

In this reading, *casticismo* is measured in terms of its fidelity to the values of Castilian Catholic monarchy and scholastic thought, to the championing of the alliance of throne and altar.

Casticismo and Castilian Literature
Unamuno continued his analysis of traditionalist Castilian *casticismo* in the third chapter of the volume, 'El espíritu castellano' [The Castilian Spirit], which surveys Castilian cultural production. He here criticises the playwright most mythologised by *casticista* literary history, Pedro Calderón de la Barca. Calderón's theatre is reproached for its incongruous juxtapositions, its artificial episodes detracting from the main plot and for the representation of a reality that constantly takes the form of violent, Manichean contrasts. Unamuno laments the presence of overly conventional unsubtly drawn protagonists, and regrets the absence of any *chiaroscuro* where the truth of life and psychological profundity might be located. For Unamuno, it is entirely understandable that Calderón should have triumphed in the writing of *autos sacramentales* (seventeenth-century allegorical

religious plays) and in the creation of allegorical characters while he failed in the study of souls. In a kind of accusatory counterpoint, Unamuno contrasts Calderón with the older early-modern English playwright William Shakespeare, whose drama, for Unamuno, embodied all humanity, and demonstrated nuance and *nimbo*.[3] Unamuno's criticism of Calderón had a particular contemporary dimension: the tercentenary of the playwright's death had been celebrated not long after Unamuno had begun his university studies, and the chapter should be read as an attack on those late nineteenth-century traditionalists who had appropriated this anniversary for their own reactionary purposes. Included within this number is one of Unamuno's own university teachers, the renowned *casticista* historian, critic and champion of Calderón, Marcelino Menéndez y Pelayo.

These were the same figures who, in the 1890s, had also celebrated the honour code as represented in early-modern plays by Calderón and, for example, Guillén de Castro, author of *Las mocedades del Cid*, an account of the legendary medieval Castilian noble warrior Rodrigo Díaz de Vivar. As part of his criticism of this concept cherished by traditionalists, Unamuno argues that, far from being essentially or exclusively Spanish, the systematisation of the concept of honour into a gentlemanly code had its origins in medieval French literature (OCE I, 834; OCA III, 249). Its values were later applied anachronistically by *casticistas* to the foreign policy of Spain during the late nineteenth-century colonial wars in Cuba. Between 1896 and 1900, Unamuno used the socialist and anarchist press to denounce this appropriation of the concept of honour, whether individual or national, arguing that it was responsible for the doomed attempt to retain Cuba in the face of the might of the United States, and the resultant deaths of so many young Spanish men. Referring to *Las mocedades del Cid* in the article, 'El Reinado social de Jesucristo' [Christ's Social Kingdom], Unamuno argued that:

'There is a vulgar phrase that expresses [one of the crucial verses of the play]: "better a martyr than one who has to confess to not defending his honour". This is what is happening with the Spanish nation in the wretched matter of the stupid and brutal war in Cuba. Every time that someone speaks of autonomy or other liberties, the chauvinists and every kind of reactionary agitator make a big noise and find a thousand different ways to say that this is not the moment for concessions, and that what needs to be done is to smash the insurrectionists to pieces'.

(OCE IX, 658).[4]

---

3   *Nimbo* may be translated as 'nimbus', and is one of the many metaphors and similes of the volume derived from the natural world, an indication of the lingering positivistic influences in Unamuno's thought at this time. Thomas Mermall defines the Unamunian concept of *nimbo* as 'an aura that fuses differences and endows ideas with a sense of continuity and cohesion' (1993: 282).

4   This article is not collected in the Aguilar *Obras completas*.

The more aggressive, direct tone of this article published in the socialist press contrasts notably with the more circumspect, polished language of the essays that made up *En torno al casticismo*.

Unamuno's early work also engaged repeatedly with one of the most famous examples of Castilian literature, Cervantes's *El ingenioso hidalgo Don Quixote de la Mancha* [Don Quixote]. For Unamuno, Don Quixote stood as a symbol of Spain's historical follies. Unamuno instead championed Alonso Quijano, the modest, sane *hidalgo* who only became Don Quixote after having been driven mad by his reading of chivalric romances:

> In the sublime ending to his *Don Quixote,* Cervantes shows our country—the Spain of today—the way forward: its regeneration in Alonso Quijano el Bueno [...] that divine last chapter must become our gospel for national regeneration
> (OCE I, 791–2; OCA III, 183).

He had been calling for the death of the myth of Don Quixote years before the famous exclamation of his 1898 article [...] '¡Muera don Quijote!' [Death to Don Quixote!] and its accompanying call for the resurrection of this character in the form of Alonso Quijano el Bueno (OCE, VII, 1194–1196; OCA V, 712–716). In turn-of-the-century Spain, Miguel de Unamuno was attempting to influence and modify the course of Spanish history. In the summer of 1901, he told his fellow *Bilbaínos*, in the face of the rise of peripheral regionalisms that he had foreseen:

> Spanish history has come off its hinges: it needs to be turned in a different direction. For centuries it has followed a centrifugal course; now it has to be centripetal
> (OCE: IV, 241–2; OCA VI, 333).

For Unamuno, such a change of direction must give rise to reflection and self-criticism, because defeat in the 1898 Spanish-American War put an end to any hopes of the centrifugal and imperialist politics of *casticista* Spain. The search for a new cultural identity involved an examination of conscience. For Unamuno, the analogy between a defeated, maltreated Don Quixote's return to his village and the humiliatingly defeated nation was perfect: a Castile now besieged by peripheral Spain could be conquered by it tomorrow:

> When Spain had vast overseas dominions, Castile was predominant, and had to be predominant. Castile was populated by the most central, unified and most imposing, yes, but also the least egoistic people. Don Quixote went abroad to impose his faith. [...] But was left in a bad way by his bruising encounter with Robinson [Crusoe], was crushed and saddened. [...] He will have to be cured,

and cured by being shut in; the periphery is pressing on the centre, encircling
it, invading it bit by bit, subduing it.

(OCE IV, 241; OCA VI, 333–34).

The medical metaphor of the 'cure' for Spain's ills is here inscribed within the
broader discursive framework of psychoanalysis: 'The disinterested knowledge of
its history gives a people courage, knowledge of themselves, in order that we might
shed the detritus of disassociation which weighs collective life down' (OCE I, 800;
OCA III, 196). When Don Quixote died, his madness died with him, and the
healthy strengths of Alonso Quijano el Bueno are a model for Spain's regeneration.

The tragic end of empire, and the conflict which brought it about in 1898,
prompted Unamuno to reflect further on this literary myth. An exchange of
letters with his friend Ganivet reviewed matters covered in previous essays in
order to attune them to the new political situation after the colonial war. Unamuno
stressed once more the idea that Don Quixote and the destiny of the Spanish
nation had identical dénouements. The similarities between the repeated failure
of Don Quxjote's adventures and Spain's humiliating confrontation with the
US took on their full tragic significance with the 'suicide' of the Spanish fleet
under Admiral Cervera in 1898. In an atmosphere of febrile nationalism, the
writer wanted to liberate the Spanish people from a past that was oppressing
and suffocating them, while the national and local press – conservative, liberal
or republican, the 'criminal press' in Unamuno's words – was dedicating new
hymns to past glories, trying to compensate for the military disaster. The
hardline attitude of many Spaniards recalled what, for Unamuno, was the
barbarous and *castizo* honour code forged in the dramas of Guillén de Castro
and Calderón, and embodied in the emblematic figure of Don Quixote.

Ultimately, the obvious anti-Quixotism of *En torno al casticismo* is tightly
tied to the evolution of the colonial wars, and it became increasingly aggressive
before culminating in the double exclamation 'Death to Don Quixote!' and
'Long Live Alonso Quijano el Bueno' over the summer of 1898. In contrast to
Ganivet, Unamuno exalted the figure of Robinson Crusoe, and pilloried that
of Don Quixote. His was an original reading of the figure of Don Quixote and
was much misunderstood by his compatriots. The supposedly anti-patriotic
Unamuno, accused of being a 'separatist' or a 'filibusterer' proclaimed the
superiority of Robinson Crusoe, an anonymous working man who succeeded
in creating with his own hands a material civilisation. Unamuno placed him
far above Don Quixote, whereas for Angel Ganivet, Crusoe was mere *escudero*
(page) to the Knight Errant.

Unamuno's position towards Don Quixote changed after 1902, and his 1905
essay, *Vida de Don Quijote y Sancho Panza* exalts an ethical Quixotism,
apparently bracketed off from contemporaneous ideological conflicts.

Intrahistoria

In order to combat the pernicious effects of reactionary *casticismo* and the scholarly historiographical concentration on major events, the state and its institutions, and on elites, Unamuno created a suggestive counter-concept, as vague and ultimately indefinable as it was fecund and suggestive: *intrahistoria*. It became a key idea in Unamuno's thought between 1895 and 1902, and even though explicit discussion of the concept disappeared after that point, implicit traces of *intrahistoria* continued to appear in his subsequent work. In contrast to traditional *historia*, which privileges, for example, the lives of heroes, the din of battle and the grandeur of powerful institutions, the object of study of *intrahistoria* is the anonymous people of the countryside, the lives of millions of ordinary people living silent, obscure lives. Unamuno privileged these lives and the everyday labour of countless Spaniards, describing them as calm, immutable forces recalling the depths of the ocean, in contradistinction to the ephemeral storms of the choppy surface waters and waves of the sea, whipped up by the clamour of events (OCE I, 793; OCA III, 185).

The anonymous protagonists of *intrahistoria* would have to be studied through their speech, folklore and stock of common knowledge. Eighteen months after the original publication of the essay 'La tradición eterna' in *La España Moderna*, Unamuno gave a public lecture in Seville's Ateneo [Athenaeum] on 'The Cultivation of the Demotic' (OCE IX, 47–59; OCA VII, 473–492), expanding on this idea. Vigorously opposing a history conceptualised in terms of 'knowledge as mere ornament', the result of a 'historicist eruditionism', he defended 'demotics' – the study of folklore, an academic field still in its infancy. As he notes in the final essay of *En torno al casticismo*. The rural masses were the only possessors of an unknown popular culture, of a forgotten but still living *infraliteratura* [Infraliterature]:

> The very existence of a plebeian literature has been forgotten, and no-one stops to listen to the songs of the blind, or the chapbooks or cheap serialised novels which nourish those who don't know to read and so have them read aloud to them. No-one asks which books become grimy from being thumbed in farmhouse kitchens or which are read out amongst groups of farmworkers. And whilst some import superficial exotic artefacts and others cultivate bookish literary 'purity', the people feed their fantasies with the old Breton and Carolingian cycle legends, with heroes who have travelled the world, and which mix the derring-do of [...] Valdovinos or Tirant le Blanc with the beauties of José María and with heroic acts from our civil wars
>
> (OCE I, 866–867; OCA III, 298–299)

Investigating demotics involved a search for the 'soul of the people', equivalent to the German *Volksgeist*, the collective spirit. In his Seville lecture, Unamuno argued that 'Legend is history made flesh from the thinking of the people, transfigured until it attains eternal poetic truth' (OCE IX, 49; OCA VII, 481). Unamuno also urged his readers to participate actively in the discovery of Castile, to seek in its current geography the traces of a living but silent past and to traverse its bare, uniform plains. In creating the concept of *intrahistoria*, he was searching for a new way of studying the geographical reality of Castile and wider Spain. In his description of the environment – climate, relief patterns, vegetation in the majestic pages of the second essay of *En torno al casticismo*, 'La casta histórica Castilla' – Unamuno attempted to rehabilitate a Castilian landscape that until relatively recently beforehand had been largely disdained.[5] Ultimately, though, Unamuno was in part seeking the universal underlying the local and specific: he was interested in the spirit of *intracasticismo* (OCE I, 869; OCA III, 303).

For Unamuno, *intrahistoria* was 'eternal tradition', the title of *En torno al casticismo*'s first essay. It is very clearly a challenge to the vision of the *casticistas* 'who celebrated the 'venerable tradition of our elders, the alliance of church and throne and the glorious victories of Numancia, las Navas, Granada, Lepanto, Otumba and Bailén'' [key battles against various 'Others', both within the Peninsula and without] (OCE I 785; OCA III, 173). In his correspondence with Angel Ganivet over the summer of 1898, Unamuno voiced his ideas about the irrelevance of war to the majority of the population. Referring to the defeat of Spain at Cavite in the Spanish-American War, he argued:

> I am sure that there were many many [...] more people in Spain working silently, worrying only about putting food on the table, than there were people preoccupied with public events
>
> (OCE III, 660; OCA 987–988).

Unamuno also disdained the Restoration of the monarchy in 1875. Citing Antonio Cánovas de Castillo, for whom 'the Restoration was the renewal of the history of Spain', Unamuno asserts:

> It was not the Restoration [...] that renewed the history of Spain; it was the millions of men who carried on doing what they had been doing before, those millions for whom the sun that shone before 29 September 1898 was the same as the sun that shone afterwards, and the jobs that they had to do were just the same too.
>
> (OCE I, 793; OCA III, 186)

5   The rehabilitation had started with Giner and his students, at the Instituto de Libre Enseñanza: see Ramón F. Llorens García's chapter in this volume for further detail on the ILE and Unamuno's writings on the Castilian landscape.

But Unamuno did not just set the *intrahistoria* of the silent masses against the Restoration and its parliament (a 'temple of mendacity' in his view); he also denigrated events such as the 'Sexenio'—the six-year republican period following the uprising of 1868 (the so-called 'Gloriosa') that put to an end the long reign of Isabel II and interrupted the Bourbon monarchy. The 'Sexenio' was considered a period of hope by progressives, but Unamuno mocked the speeches of General Prim, their leading light. And it is hard to assimilate smoothly Unamuno's poetic vision of the silent, apolitical masses as representing 'eternal tradition' entirely to a progressive position, however much the study of 'demotics' is championed, or however universal the ultimate object of study is.

This, of course, is partly the point: *intrahistoria* is neither entirely progressive nor conservative. Designed to avoid simplistic binary opposites, it was coined precisely to counter the radical ideologies of both tendencies. It is, above all, an ambiguous attempt at ideological synthesis, a crucible in which the influences of the prolific, contradictory readings of the young Unamuno, his memories of debates and 'wars of ideas' and the last civil war of the nineteenth century were all fused. Although informed partly by Unamuno's humanist socialism, this concept of *intrahistoria* translates the vacillations of someone searching for another type of historiography, set apart from erudite specialists, Marxists and traditionalists who glorified 'pure' or 'authentic' Spain. Its central defining metaphor—the deep sea waters as opposed to the waves on the surface of *historia* —is intended to be a flexible way of allowing a passage between *intrahistoria* and *historia*, which are both made of the same substance. Ultimately, though, the reader cannot help but notice the limits of this metaphorical language, which suggests much more than it delineates, something that Unamuno himself acknowledges in the last essay of the volume, 'Sobre el marasmo actual de España' [On Spain's Current Stagnation] (OCE I, 867; OCE III, 300).

This final essay undertakes some substantial score-settling with Restoration society and its defects. As Cerezo Galán notes (1996: 178), it may be seen as a perfect example of Regenerationist thought, but Unamuno would soon enough distance himself from such thinking. Although the preceding abstract, theoretical essays succeeded in masking their important political dimension, this last essay, in particular, is consonant with Unamuno's commitment as an active socialist and assiduous contributor to *La Lucha de clases* [Class Struggle], the periodical of the Basque socialists. Unamuno here stressed another vicious effect of the climate created by the various Spanish 'traditionalisms/purities' with the expressions 'latent Inquisition' and 'immanent Inquisition', which he used to characterise the atmosphere of the Restoration period, comparing it with a tombstone weighing down on the country, or with the oppressiveness of a stormy night. Unamuno here recalls the tragic work of the Inquisition which had strangled at birth any chance of penetration of Reformation thought into the Peninsula (OCE I, 865–9; OCA III, 296–303).

For Unamuno, the isolation of Spain had favoured individualism, intolerance, sectarianism, extreme and overly rigid character, facilitating the creation of the radically dissociated soul and the power of the Inquisition. The Inquisition forged an enforced 'purity' in the image of an extreme climate and terrain, a harsh and rocky plain, without features or ambience that might soften it, leaving its mark on heroes as different as Cervantes or Calderón. The speech Unamuno gave at Cartagena in August 1902 during the Juegos Florales festival in the city, is, to some extent, a repetition and prolongation of the themes of the 1895 essays, but also foreshadowed the turn towards Unamuno's new conception of politics, a conception informed by religion even as it distinguished itself from it: Unamuno likened the speech to a 'lay sermon' at a moment when, seduced by German liberal Protestantism, he proclaimed the need for Spain to undergo a 'secular, popular and indigenous reformation' (OCE III, 724; OCA IV, 1085).

Between Literature and History, 1897–1902

Carlism and Intrahistoria

Growing up in Bilbao, Unamuno had witnessed the last of the Carlist wars while he was still a boy, and the events left an indelible mark on him. Carlism is difficult to summarise in a few words: it was not just a dynastic dispute, but the crucible and synthesis of the ideological conflicts of the nineteenth century; in the judgement of the distinguished historian of Spain, Pierre Vilar, it was at once reactionary *and* progressive, its protagonist the rural northern people. For Vilar, Carlism was a rejection of individualistic liberal capitalism in the name of communitarian moral and religious traditions; it was a type of reactionary political populism, undeniably of the people. Carlism, like anarchism, interested Unamuno because for him, it was one of the intimate and genuine manifestations of the collective spirit of the Spanish people.

Unamuno felt that Carlism had not been sufficiently or disinterestedly studied. Carlist ideals had been misrepresented, too narrowly co-opted and made too programmatic: as a consequence, they had lost their intrahistorical force. Carlism had been misunderstood, as Unamuno noted in the last essay of *En torno al casticismo*: 'Why continue to write about an intrahistorical movement which we see only through historical prejudice? Let such a written account remain for another occasion' (OCE I, 868; OCA III, 302). A few years later, in the prologue to *En torno al casticismo* (1902), the author expanded on his thoughts and offered an answer to the question above:

'The other occasion came with my novel *Paz en la guerra*, but as this was neither a polemic nor a propagandistic work, it could not have the desired effect and its outcome was not what I had envisaged. So an account of this most authentic [castiza] stirring of the soul of our people must once again remain for another occasion'

(OCE, I, 781–782; OCA III, 168).

Unamuno had been wounded by criticisms from some of his friends that *Paz en la guerra*—his first published novel—had been too sympathetic and understanding of the Carlist movement. He argued that such sympathy was explained by the long years of historical research (1889–1896) that he had undertaken in order to write it:

There were those who labelled me a Carlist because instead of intemperately cursing the supporters of Carlos VII, and speaking of the crimes of Carlism and other such nonsense, my intention had been to explore and demonstrate in unheated terms what lay at the heart of Carlism, and how useful and powerful a force it is

(OCE, I, 781; OCA III, 167).

His correspondence over the summer of 1898 with Angel Ganivet gave him the opportunity to discuss further what he saw as what was 'authentic' or 'popular' about Carlism:

Popular Carlism, which I have studied a little, is ineffable, by which I mean inexpressible in speeches and manifestos; it is not 'oratable'. And popular Carlism, with its socialist, and even anarchist base, is one of the most intimate expressions of the Spanish people

(OCE, III, 662; OCA IV, 991).

For Unamuno, there were two types of Carlism: the popular Carlism to which he felt an attraction; and historical, or 'party' Carlism and its leaders, which he criticised for fomenting ultra-conservative religious fundamentalism.

Paz en la guerra: Eternal Tradition and Childhood Memories

Published in 1897, *Paz en la guerra* is set during the Carlist war of 1872–1876, the final armed struggle in a long ideological confrontation between 'liberalism' and 'traditionalism' in nineteenth-century Spain. The novel has an important autobiographical aspect, as Unamuno later acknowledged:

Here in this book—the book of who I was—I invested more than twelve years of work: here I gathered in the flower and fruit of my experience of childhood and adolescence. It contains the echo, and perhaps the perfume

of the most profound memories of my life, and of the life of the town where
I was born and raised
(Unamuno 1983: 5; OCE II, 91; OCA II, 73).[6]

We should note that *En torno al casticismo*'s first essay, 'La tradición eterna'
– in which Unamuno coined the fundamental concept of *intrahistoria* – was
written at around the same time as *Paz en la guerra,* and the novel's closing
section breathes life into the concept through the fictional rendering of the
famous siege of Bilbao. In addition, the title of the novel, which obviously recalls
Tolstoy's *War and Peace*, tells us that the very foundation of this work is the
dialectical alliance between two terms that are mutually antagonistic but are
nevertheless linked in an indissoluble manner. The title alone prefigures the
final dialectical reflexion of Pachico Zabalbide, a mouthpiece for Unamuno,
about these two contraries.

But exactly how is the fictional tale infused by the theoretical essay dedicated
to 'eternal tradition'? During the siege of Bilbao, the inhabitants of the city
gradually discover the virtues of their forebears. In the midst of their pain and
suffering, these city-dwellers resemble the humble and silent folk of the country.
This is where the true unity of the story lies: the inhabitants of Bilbao discover
the serenity and tranquillity of the depths of eternal tradition at the very moment
at which they are plunged into the most tumultuous and noisy currents of their
lives. The metaphor of a loom, repeated several times over the course of the
narration of the siege symbolises access to the deepest life of *intrahistoria*:

> The jolt of the siege brought out what lay behind and beneath ordinary daily
> life, and they could all hear the slow weaving of the infinite pattern of fate.
> [...]. And these elderly men calmly walking the on police duty, shouldering
> their useless weapons, were the living symbols of peace, for they awakened
> memories and lent a sense of calm. They were a living symbol of that peace
> which weaves its infinite pattern beneath the superficial embroilments of war
> (Unamuno 1983: 210–213; OCE II, 204–5; OCA II, 258–261)

The elderly, and women and children are the true heroes of the siege of Bilbao;
they belong to the same family as the humble and silent peasants of the theoretical
pages of 'La tradición eterna'.

---

6   There are certainly traces of Unamuno's childhood vision of the war in the novel. In a besieged
Bilbao, some inhabitants such as Don Miguel Arana, the liberal businessman, discover simple
happiness: during a pilgrimage, he is inundated with memories of the country and of his childhood.
Amidst the bombings, the inhabitants of the city become intoxicated by the noise, and in the festivities
and dances: they are ways of denying and exorcising the war, which becomes a game that the
inhabitants take part in as if they were children. Their childlike vision of the war is also Unamuno's.

Aside from the siege of Bilbao, the novel offers us two more intrahistoric moments: one after the death of Ignacio on the Somorrostro battlefield, when his father is deeply moved as he witnesses the oath of fidelity to the foral laws sworn by King Carlos himself underneath the sacred oak tree at Guernica; the other in the denouement of the novel, which extends the story in an atemporal way with the appearance of Pachico Zabalbide, a reflection of the author himself. If Ignacio embodies archaic Carlism, Pachico looks towards the future and takes it upon himself to transmit eternal tradition to new generations.

Paz en la guerra's representation of the chronology of war does not correspond to the historical chronicle. Unamuno does not divide history in the manner of a professional historian, and the reader quickly realises that the novel's rhythm is very different from that of history. The novelist amplifies certain events in the war, rejecting any 'total' historical view, and privileging one moment of the war: the siege of Bilbao. He used schematisation and stylisation to give the siege a fundamental position in the narrative and, in the representation of the besieged city, he concentrates on the life of the 'silent' people, those who leave no trace in history. *Paz en la guerra* is, then, the novelistic transposition of Unamuno's propagandistic essays, those militant essays that had their origins in Unamuno's affiliation to the socialist grouping of Bilbao in 1894. Through Pedro Antonio Iturriondo and his family and friends, Unamuno's ideological project is to search out the people of *intrahistoria* during the crucial moment of the siege of Bilbao. In spite of the terminal damage inflicted on the Carlist cause, and the death of Ignacio, Pachico continues to search for a new Spain, but always within the bounds of 'eternal tradition'.

Pedro Antonio, ex-combatant of earlier Carlist wars, embodies an entire tradition; his son, who inherits a past lived in close solidarity with his father, participates also in the key event of the war. The weight of the legacy is demonstrated during the regular evening gatherings above Pedro Antonio's shop. The participants have no psychological depth or coherence as human figures: they simply react to the military events of yesteryear and the present, and to the Carlist cause they are defending. They are not rounded novelistic characters, but instead elemental beings who evoke memories of a history simplified by its obscurantism and manichean thinking as they warm themselves by the heat of the fireside during the long Basque winter evenings.

The young Ignacio, rather than embodying a regenerated Carlism, is as anachronistic as all those around him. Profoundly influenced by the traditionalist education inculcated by his uncle Pascual, a 'fundamentalist' priest, the family's spiritual director, and devotee of the 'liberalism is a sin' school of Catholicism, Ignacio takes in the Carlist myths of his relatives and, embracing a lost cause, he becomes a worthy heir to the values of his father. Without any intellectual formation or education and incapable of political reflection, his vacuousness is astonishing. He lives and acts less as a novelistic character than as a representative of the people. Two parenthetical moments in the novel are fundamental for Ignacio. He visits his parents' village twice, discovering there the land of his forebears, and as he immerses himself in their lives, seems to shed his own self: 'Little by little, everything became darker; Ignacio without any awareness of self, allowed himself to be penetrated by the voices of the valley.' (Unamuno 1983: 49; OCE II, 115–6; OCA II, 113)

Thus, Ignacio disappears as an individual hero in order to symbolise a complete adherence to the permanence of a land and a people: he flees from the city and distances himself from what is his present time. He is a completely uncultured young man, reading only chapbooks that allow him to enter the depths of intrahistory, of popular consciousness:

> They were the poetic sediment of the centuries. After having nourished the songs and stories that have consoled the lives of so many generations of men, going from mouth to ear and ear to mouth, told and retold beside comforting fires, they now lived on through the good offices of blind streetpeddlars in the evergreen fantasy of the populace.
>
> (Unamuno 1983: 32; OCE II, 107; OCA II, 98).

The sentence recalls fragments of *En torno al casticismo,* particularly the last pages of 'Sobre el marasmo de España' [On the Stagnation of Spain], but also parts of the lecture Unamuno had given on 'Demotics' in which he had praised the wealth of customs, legends, stories, refrains, songs and ballads of a secular folklore belonging to rural people. He urged Spaniards to discover a traditional culture to counter the effects of the vulgar and the routine.

Another function of Ignacio is to downplay the importance of *historia,* highlighting the trivial nature of the 'historical' present. Pedro Antonio's son flees the scene to fade into the anonymity of the unknown soldier, into the monotony of the grey misty and drizzly days, while the narrator is constantly describing the marches and countermarches of a platoon compared to a flock of sheep wandering through the mountainous terrain of Vizcaya. In order to get to the *intrahistoria,* Unamuno criticises and caricatures the trifling nature of present events, representing the war as a puppet play. Ignacio loses his personality as novelistic hero inasmuch as he disappears and is replaced by the besieged city of Bilbao and by the Basque people: 'This is not a novel; it is an entire people', says Unamuno at the end of a prologue to the novel he wrote in 1923 (Unamuno 1983: 6, OCE II, 92; OCA II, 74). Ignacio reappears twice more in the story but, permanently uneasy, he seems merely to be subsisting; thus he heads towards the end of his aimless existence at the battle of Somorrostro, where Unamuno puts an end to the life of his character.

The young Ignacio remains passive in the face of events, wandering like a sleepwalker through a dark fog of ideas and leading an existence without a *raison d'etre*. His death, therefore, when it comes, is natural and fortuitous: curious, he looks out from his trench and is killed by a stray bullet. Ignacio's death is described without indulgence, compassion or novelistic rhetoric (OCE II, 250–251; OCA II, 334). It is the opposite of the heroic death, that key moment of the traditional nineteenth-century novel. Ignacio is relieved of the dead weight of his life, and in parallel to this slow annihilation, Unamuno desacralises the myth of the Carlist war. The writer does not resort to the technique of simultaneous narration, moving between the besiegers and the besieged: he focuses his gaze on the siege in Bilbao and on the life of its inhabitants in a long parenthesis of over a hundred pages which breaks the continuity and the logic of the narration of the war in the countryside. The coherence of the work, then, is not novelistic but ideological; at its deepest level, the plot is concerned to relate the discovery of values and the permanence of a people, laid out in the first two chapters, with the siege of Bilbao, drawing out the lesson and significance of the event. Instead of seeing, as historians did, a confrontation between two sides, he intuits that in the future, victors and losers will discover the same serenity and peace, true life, thanks to the rebirth of the ancestral virtues of the rural Basque people.

Paz en la guerra does not end with Ignacio's death, but continues for a good seventy pages more. It is Pachico Zabalbide who is the protagonist of this strange novel's denouement. A double of Unamuno himself, and originally conceived as the antithesis of Ignacio, Pachico is a pure intellectual, the cerebral, sceptical victim of disenchantment: he himself doubts, and he sows doubts and questions in others, disdaining political parties. The opposition between both characters is clear: Ignacio's physical vitality is opposed to the weak and sickly Pachico. While the former lives by the ingenuous faith of the simple and pure-hearted, Pachico reasons and reflects on his faith, like the young Unamuno in the Madrid of the 1880s, who had come under the influence of Krausism, and combined novel thinking, liberating rationalism and desire for moral purity. Pachico becomes a young man who reasons, playing with ideas, commenting on Hegel and positivism (Unamuno 1983: 69; OCE II, 127; 78; OCA II, 131–2). In politics, he opposes Ignacio on the grounds that he is a pure spectator, one who rejects any commitment: 'he was not a Carlist, nor a Liberal, nor a monarchist, nor a Republican—and [...] was all of them at once [...]. A political party is nonsense' (Unamuno 1983: 74; OCE II, 129; OCA II, 135).

Nevertheless, Pachico intervenes in an overly episodic way, and his views are too partial to represent, by themselves, the ideas of the narrator. Neither is he simply the inverted image of Ignacio, as some links exist between the two boys. Ignacio's fidelity is to the past, whereas Pachico's is to the future: after Ignacio's death, Pachico is charged with overcoming the contradiction and with projecting eternal tradition towards the future. At the end of the conflict he is invested with a mission: to transmit the ancestral values that he has discovered during his visits to the country. To some extent, he is a reincarnation of Ignacio and, like him, submerges himself in the contemplation of the landscape. From the summit of Pagasarri, facing the Cantabrian sea, he discovers the deep intricacies of his friend's life, and Unamuno's prose here has recourse to the same sea metaphors used in the pages of *En torno al casticismo* and other contemporaneous articles. Pachico is the indispensable complement of Ignacio, who is reborn in his friend. Pachico asks himself:

> A life lost? Lost...for whom? Lost to him, the victim, poor Ignacio...But such lives are the spiritual atmosphere of a whole nation of people, lives that we take in with every breath, lives which sustain and spiritualize us all
> (Unamuno 1983: 287; OCE II, 266 OCA II, 360).

At the end of the novel, he walks back down the mountain to go and preach, 'to unleash his sermons' on the peninsula, like a secular St John of the Cross.[7]

The *nivolas*, or the crisis of the narrator and history

At the same time as Unamuno was finishing *Paz en la guerra* in the autumn of 1896, he was also drafting a short, partly autobiographical novel unpublished during his lifetime, which is, perhaps, the prolongation of the spiritual itinerary of Pachico Zabalbide.[8] The adventures of its protagonist, the young Eugenio Rodero, are those of the Miguel de Unamuno that arrived in Madrid in 1880 to pursue his university studies and experienced the same religious and ideological crises as Pachico. From a very early age, like Pachico and Eugenio, Miguel de Unamuno struggled constantly against any form of dogmatism. Eugenio dreams of becoming a saint who, in the future, would pronounce his 'lay' sermons throughout the peninsula. The purely autobiographical tale of *Nuevo mundo* gave him the opportunity to demonstrate the cultural and political intentions initially laid out in *En torno al casticismo*. After having fled the conventions of old Europe, Eugenio Rodero returns from America, defeated by the resistance of 'the barbarians'—his uncultured, ignorant readers—and tired of 'battling for the blessed truth' in the middle of a cultural desert and amidst the 'stagnation of Spain'. In this respect, Pedro Cerezo Galán argues that:

---

7 For further discussion of *Paz en la guerra*, see Chapter 8 in this volume.
8 The novel was eventually published as *Nuevo mundo*: see Unamuno (1994).

The new double [of Unamuno], Eugenio Rodero, could well be the final
reconciliation of Unamuno's two souls in *Paz en la guerra*, Pachico and
Eugenio, integrated into a replete character, with an intense interior life and
a strong idealism, which makes him into a lay apostle of the new pacifist
ideals (1996: 220).

But why kill off this double? Perhaps to reveal to us his spiritual testament,
that of a profound utopian, mystical anarchist and victim of a repressed
sexuality. Eugenio Rodero is not a viable character: he is too complex, too
much a prisoner of his own contradictions. But from this failure and death
are born other works, such as *Amor y pedagogía* or *Niebla*, which assert a
new theory of the novel and a coherence imposed by the political-cultural
mission of the writer.

    Disillusioned that *Paz en la guerra* had passed largely unnoticed, and
conscious of its defects—he noted the work's excessive ponderousness and
documenting of detail as well as its extensive digressions—Unamuno outlined
the subsequent evolution of his novelistic itinerary in a 1923 prologue to *Paz
en la guerra*, drawing attention to the abandonment of temporal and spatial
references, descriptions of nature, and stating his intention to limit the digressions
that had damaged the unity of *Paz en la guerra*'s story in order to produce
instead 'dramas íntimos' [intimate dramas] (Unamuno 1983: 6; OCA II, 74;
OCE II, 91). Numerous studies of Unamuno's prose fiction also stress that *Paz
en la guerra* is very different from his subsequent novels: *Amor y pedagogía*,
for example, published in 1902 but begun in 1900, and *Niebla*, published in
1914 but drafted seven years previously.

    Literature and political commitment do not become divorced in Unamuno's
novel-writing after 1897. His literary output continued to be fuelled by political
articles, essays and childhood memories; he was an attentive and always critical
witness of the events of public life. In spite of some undeniable differences
between *Paz en la guerra* and the subsequent novels, which Unamuno christened
nivolas ['nivols' rather than 'novels'],[9] the final section of this chapter will try
and indicate the constancy of themes across a body of fiction that fuses fiction,
intimate confession and political concern.

    Unamuno wanted to challenge the nature of the traditional nineteenth-century
novelistic character as embodied, for example, in the works of Benito Pérez
Galdós. Well-constructed intrigue and the *fabula* had to be banished: the absence
of intrigue, and of plot would be instead be the meat of the writing, and the
highly individualised traditional hero whose psychology and behaviour the
novelist delighted in portraying from cradle to grave would also disappear. With

---

[9]   The *nivola* is discussed in greater detail in Chapter 2 of this volume.

the creation of the concept of the *nivola*, Unamuno substituted the 'objective' tale of the novel with the 'interior' story, and, from 1900, when he began to write *Amor y pedagogía,* this preoccupation with interiority is also visible in various major essays such as '¡Adentro!', which, as it its exclamatory title suggests, incites the reader to explore the most secret and intimate nooks and crannies of the soul.

In novel after novel, we discover the same elements, the same conception of existence, the same struggle for truth in both surface reality and deep inner life that characterised his earlier work. In an almost imperceptible way, we move from the rains, fog and cloudy Basque landscapes or the sacred places of Carlism to the 'landscapes of the soul', the mists of the unconscious; the intrahistory of the Basque people has become the 'infraconsciousness' of the characters of the *nivolas*. The unconsciousness portrayed in *Paz en la guerra* prefigures that of Augusto Pérez, always enveloped in the spiritual mists of everyday existence, in the midst of an existential anguish which feeds the intimate drama that the demiurge-narrator tries to capture. The metaphor of weaving is also repeated from one novel to another, and the weeping of Pedro Antonio grieving for his dead son and the failure of the Carlist cause is mirrored in *Niebla* in the tears of Augusto Pérez, who goes to pray and cry in a church after having been rejected by his fiancée Eugenia. In the church, the refuge of mortal man, Augusto runs into the ex-atheist Avito Carrascal, the protagonist of *Amor y pedagogía*, who now lives only for the cult of remembrance of his son, who has committed suicide.

The multiple speeches, public lectures, essays or articles that Unamuno published in the Salamancan, national or foreign press, designed to shake his fellow countrymen out of their apathy, invaded both the early novels and the later *nivolas*. The traditional novel was challenged by Unamuno's ideological and political intentions, and he carried within himself a 'civil' war in favour of culture and civilisation; but the people of *intrahistoria* portrayed in *Paz en la guerra* do not seem capable of taking on a political role in the future. And the dogmatic or aboulic characters of the *nivolas*, such as don Avito Carrascal or Augusto Pérez are the comic and tragic representatives of a provincial petty bourgeoisie that was passive in the face of history.

Three years before the outbreak of the Civil War, and his death later that same year, Unamuno argued in an article entitled 'Paz en la guerra' (OCE VIII, 1192–1194; OCA X, 980–984) that ever since the publication of his first novel, thirty-six years previously, he had followed one single itinerary, whose path had followed the contours and vicissitudes of a 'thinking in movement'. He uneasily repeated the words of Pachico Zabalbide in a Republican Spain that did not understand them. Such words sought to justify his commitment as an intellectual, and gave meaning to his life and coherence to his work:

Only in the refuge of true and profound peace is war understood and justified. It is here that sacred vows are made to go to war for truth, which is the only eternal consolation. It is here that war proposes to be transformed into holy work. Not outside war, but within it, in its very heart, peace must be sought: peace in war itself

(Unamuno 1983: 383; OCE II, 301; OCA II, 417).

Further Reading

Blanco Aguinaga (1978), Rabaté (2001), Round (1989), Unamuno (2005c), Urrutia (1997).

2

Writing Vital Struggle:
Unamuno's Narrative Fiction 1902–1923

JULIA BIGGANE

This chapter traces the changes in Unamuno's narrative after the appearance of his first published novel, *Paz en la guerra*, until shortly before he was sent into exile. It deals, then, with much of the mature fiction for which Unamuno has become best known in Spain and beyond, and covers a period in which the evolving effects of a recent major turn in Unamuno's personal, intellectual and political preoccupations were played out in his literary and essayistic production. The chapter examines the two heavily metafictional, experimental novels *Amor y pedagogía* (1902) and *Niebla* (1914); the starker and structurally simpler novels *Abel Sánchez* (1917) and *La tía Tula* (1921), and the shorter texts (*Nada menos que todo un hombre, El marqués de Lumbría* and *Tulio Montalbán y Julio Macedo*), originally published in popular novella collections, with the first two republished, along with a new text, *Dos madres*, in the 1920 volume *Tres novelas ejemplares y un prólogo*. This volume contains an important critique of realism in fiction and provides an explanation of Unamuno's narrative practices throughout the period under study, so deserves careful examination. As *La tía Tula* is discussed in some detail in the chapter on gender and sexuality, and elsewhere in this volume, its treatment here is relatively brief.[1] The present chapter will also discuss the major 1912 essay *Del sentimiento trágico de la vida en los hombres y los pueblos*. This text explored a fundamental question for Unamuno: if, as Spinoza had proposed, our essence as living beings is distinguished by the will to persist indefinitely in our being, how do we live—and how should we live—if we cannot know whether our hunger for immortality will be satisfied? Engagement with this question informed all Unamuno's post-1897 thought, and an appreciation of it is essential for an understanding of his literary texts.

---

[1]   See Chapter 9 of this volume, and also Alison Sinclair's discussion in Chapter 7.

As the above summary implies, the chapter will concentrate on explaining the philosophy guiding Unamuno's narrative production over the period: without an understanding of his thought at this time, his fiction can seem strange, at times schematic, and difficult to contextualise. Narrative form and technique are discussed in detail insofar as they embody Unamuno's central ideas. The vast amount of critical literature on Unamuno's fiction during this time cannot be given adequate coverage in a single chapter. Some key studies are addressed briefly, and the 'Further Reading' recommendations at the end of the chapter attempt to guide the reader who wants to continue exploring the critical reception of particular texts, or of Unamuno's work as a whole over this period.

The Post-1897 Turn in Unamuno's Thought

As Jean-Claude Rabaté details in his chapter in this volume, Unamuno's childhood faith and religious practice had been undermined during his early student years in Madrid as he came into contact with a range of secular or atheistic schools of thought, thinkers and political movements. The major change visible in Unamuno's work after 1897 is often explained in terms of a spiritual crisis he underwent as he endeavoured to regain his faith. To be sure, his contemporaneous private writings leave us in no doubt that he suffered an acute and deeply painful reassessment of his position towards religion, life and his identity at this time, in part, it seems, prompted by the death of his profoundly disabled young son Raimundín. And it is certainly true that a preoccupation with the nature of individual being, spiritual existence and (im) mortality lie at the heart of Unamuno's thought after this point. Pedro Cerezo Galán deftly characterises Unamuno's major concerns after 1897 as centring on the dual question of destiny – '¿Qué será de mí [después de mi muerte]?' [What will become of me (after my death?)] – and personality – '¿Quién soy?' [Who am I?] (1996: 571). Consideration for the needs of the human heart and will (as opposed to the intellect) become prominent in his writing. This turn towards the personal and spiritual did not replace the interest that Unamuno had previously shown in social, political and national problems in essays such as *En torno al casticismo* and the articles he regularly published in broadly left-wing or liberal journals and newspapers, but it did mean that consideration of the individual was now a necessary precedent to any consideration of the collective. And although introspection, along with knowledge and awareness of the individual self were also now crucial starting points for any substantial enquiry or enterprise, for Unamuno this concern did not represent a subjectivist retreat from the world. In the diary he kept of his painful struggle with faith this time, he argues that:

The idea of death, and the beyond, and nothingness woke me from my dreams: it was a call to eternal egoism. But it also prompted me to think, not just in relation to myself but also, for charity's sake, everyone else, that the question of whether we are destined or not to have eternal life is the central axis of our lives and our conduct. An egoism that is universalised is no longer an egoism of the type we usually understand by that term

(Unamuno 1998: 125).

Self-examination, self-questioning and development of the soul were not solipsistic activities, then: they entailed interaction with others, and would ideally encourage spiritual and self-awareness on their part.[2] Stephen Roberts characterises this new 'yo' [self] as a 'yo-para-los-demás' [a self-for-others] (2007: 74).

It was in 1897 also that, though professing continued sympathy for some socialist ideals, Unamuno resigned his membership of the Bilbao branch of the socialist party, and while he did not repudiate the importance of the economic as a primordial motor of historical development, he now insisted on the religious as a crucial dual driver (see, for example, 'Nicodemo el fariseo' [Nicodemus the Pharisee] OCE VII, 365–385; OCA III, 123). Critical of rationalist thought for treating man as if he were a machine (Unamuno 1998: 65), Unamuno became scathingly hostile towards 'intellectualism': that is, any kind of learning that did not engage with the knotty questions of life—those concerning the heart and will. Referring to intellectualism as a terrible disease, Unamuno deemed it 'as bad as idiocy' (Unamuno 1998: 70). The last remnants of positivism, visible in essays in such as *En torno al casticismo*, also disappeared during this time.[3]

It would be a mistake, though, to see this marked and definitive change in Unamuno's thought in terms solely of an acute personal religious crisis. Elements of it were already burgeoning or visible in his work before 1897: Blanco Aguinaga notes that Unamuno had begun to conceive of socialism in religious terms before 1897 (cited in Inman Fox 1976: 222); Zubizarreta (1958) and Urrutia (1997: 57) date to 1895 certain religious and intellectual preoccupations indicative of Unamuno's later concerns. Although we cannot know their specific interplay, personal, intellectual and political factors all played a part in Unamuno's intense reassessment of his thought and belief over much of 1897. Moreover, the existing tensions, questions and incoherence in his thought[4] that came to a head in 1897 can also be

2   Unamuno's 1900 essay '¡Adentro!' is an incisive, vivid manifesto of this new 'egoism' (OCE I, 947–953; OCA III, 418–427).
3   For example the Tainean geographical determinism of the second essay, 'La casta histórica Castilla'.
4   Unamuno was well aware of the contradictions in his thought before 1897: see, for example, his comments in *En torno al casticismo*'s opening essay, 'La tradición eterna' (OCE I, 783–4; OCA 170–171).

seen as symptoms of broader cultural changes and conditioning forces in intellectual production in Spain. Roberta Johnson characterises the final decades of the nineteenth century thus: 'Spain telescoped two and a half centuries of European thought into thirty years', arguing that since the Counter-Reformation, the enduring power of the Church in Spain had inhibited the development of philosophy and did much to prevent the entry of modern thought from abroad. When more conducive circumstances were finally established in the mid-nineteenth century, measured assimilation and evolution of different phases and orientations of particular schools of thought could not take place in such circumstances: they clashed without resolution, or produced unsustainable attempted syntheses, producing at the end of the century ideological malaise and a growing scepticism about the efficacy of any kind of philosophical thinking (Johnson 1993: 2–3). While it may seem a little stark, this summary is not inaccurate, as other studies of the intellectual period attest (see, for example, Cerezo Galán [2003] and Storm [2001]).

Certainly the trajectory of Unamuno's thought after 1897 is not radically at odds with that of other writers of his generation: his shift away from formal commitment to organised or radical Left causes towards a more individualist conception of his task as an intellectual and writer was paralleled by other writers of the Generation of 1898, as was his embracing of irrationalist thought, and, later, aspects of vitalism and a tragic conception of life.[5] Moreover, the turn to irrationalism towards the end of the nineteenth century was certainly not confined to Spain, as the work of thinkers as diverse as Nietzsche, Bergson and Henry James attest; similarly internationally influential from the 1890s onwards was the perception, in James McFarlane's nice formulation, that 'the custody of life's integrities began to pass to the individual from society' (1991: 82).

Major elements of the turn in Unamuno's thought at this time were, then, clearly not just idiosyncratic or exclusive to him; they were also part of a wider constellation of ideas and cultural tendencies within and beyond Spain. Limitations of space mean that this chapter will concentrate on the specific and distinctive forms they took in Unamuno's narrative work, but, at the risk of labouring the point, it is crucial to keep in mind that, although, as Shaw has observed, Unamuno's preoccupations were theological rather than philosophical in origin (1975: 72), Unamuno was in significant ways not outside the European mainstream of thought and literary production, even if his and his contemporaries' positions are still to be adequately mapped on comparative cartographies of late nineteenth- and early twentieth-century culture.[6]

---

    [5]   For helpful accounts of the Generation of 1898, and Unamuno's place within it, see Shaw (1975), Blanco Aguinaga (1978) and Inman Fox (1976).
    [6]   As Gayle Rogers notes, despite important recent scholarship, Spanish modernism is still 'widely viewed by critics in Europe and the Americas as an object of study distinct from (and

The Tragi-Comic Sense of Life: Authority and Uncertainty in *Amor y pedagogía* and *Niebla*

Amor y pedagogía was the first long prose-fiction text that Unamuno wrote after 1897. He had written two earlier plays shortly after the turn of that year: *La esfinge* (1898) and *La venda* (1899). Both plays thematise the more painful aspects of Unamuno's 1897 turn, particularly the unsuccessful struggle to regain his earlier religious faith. *La venda* concerns a woman blind since birth who gains sight only to want to return to her previous familiar blindness; an analogy with Unamuno's desire in 1897 to turn away from the more rationalist and materialist aspects of the intellectual insights he had gained since adolescence – insights that undermined his childhood faith – will be evident to anyone who has read his *Diario íntimo*. *La esfinge* appears even more rawly autobiographical: it focuses on a writer and political campaigner who turns away from collective action in order to pursue change and renewal on an individual basis through the attempted recapturing of his childhood faith.[7] Perhaps it was partly the benefit of time that allowed Unamuno in *Amor y pedagogía* to distance himself a little from the more painful aspects of the shift he had earlier undergone: published a full five years after 1897, the novel exhibits none of the anguish of the plays, though it is no less personal, and no less intensely concerned with the crucial changes that had taken place in Unamuno's thought and sensibilities in the intervening period.

There are three major ways in which the text narrativises the consequences of the 1897 turn. The most prominent is the central anecdote of the text, which concerns a young man, Avito Carrascal, who initially believes that, by relying on hyper-rationality and inductive logic, if he makes the correct biological choice when marrying, and if he follows the latest scientific pedagogical theories, he will be able to raise his son to be a genius. His plans fail because he is unable to adhere to his inhumanly logical programme: he marries the woman he is most attracted to, rather than the one he believes to be most suitable for his scheme, and she counters the scientific discipline of his pedagogy with indulgent maternal love and Catholic faith; he also places his trust in a philosopher,

---

too often, belated, secondary, or derivative with regard to) its [international] counterparts and as bounded essentially by the Spanish nation and the discipline of Hispanic Studies' (2012: 10). And when Unamuno is mentioned in comparative or international studies of modernism, he is too easily seen as an entirely exceptional or idiosyncratic figure simply because his contemporaries Azorín, Baroja and Maeztu are even less well known outside Spain. In the Penguin *Modernism: a Guide to European Literature 1890–1930*, for example, he is the only Spanish prose-fiction writer to merit a brief biographical entry (Bradbury and McFarlane 1991: 637–638).

[7]   This is not to suggest that an autobiographical reading exhausts the significance of either play. For fuller readings, consult, for example, Zavala (1963) and Franco (1971).

Fulgencio Entreambosmares, who is preparing a grand systematic unifying 'philosophy of everything' far removed from Avito's positivist thought. Avito's son grows up not to be a logical genius but a lost and confused failed poet who, love-lorn, commits suicide. In the final episode of this tale, Avito's wife offers her husband tender maternal comfort as he grieves for his son, and it does not seem difficult to extract the moral of the story: intellectualism is laid bare in all its pernicious obtuseness; while it lies in ruins, the vital qualities of the heart—the compassionate love of Avito's wife—remain. Moreover, the story suggests that the religious instinct is inescapable, however Avito might try to defeat it: he treats science with devotional reverence, building a shrine to it in his home (OCE II, 331; OCA II, 459), and an inner voice, which he refers to as his 'demonio familiar' [familiar demon] (OCE II, 334; OCE II, 464) repeatedly tells him he has 'fallen' when he errs from his pursuit of scientific knowledge (see, for example, OCE II, 326; OCA II, 451).[8]

This stark plot summary might suggest that *Amor y pedagogía* shares the tragic impetus of *La venda* or *La esfinge*. But until its final pages, the caricatural representation of its main figures, and the bathos surrounding the execution of Avito's plans mean that the tale is closer to humour than tragedy. In addition, the story of Avito is just one component in a multi-stranded text: the accompanying prologue, lengthy epilogue and appendix all counter the melancholic denouement of its plot.[9] The novel is, then, most accurately described as a tragicomedy. Moreover, both the structure of the novel and the humorous content of the paratexts all further embody the values that Unamuno's post-1897 literature attempts to champion. The humour in the text is evident from its very beginning. The dedicatory page reads:

> Al lector
> Dedica esta obra
> El Autor
>
> [To the reader
> the Author
> dedicates this work]
>   (OCE II, 303; OCA II, 419)

This gentle guying is continued in the prologue, where an unidentified prologuist warns the reader immediately that 'there are those who think—and

---

8   His religious impulse is later further underlined in *Niebla* where Augusto Pérez comes across him in church where he regularly now prays.
9   A further 'Prologue/Epilogue', and Appendix were added to the second edition published in 1934.

perhaps with reason—that this work is a deeply regrettable mistake on the part of its author' (OCE II, 305; OCA II, 421). The dedication contains a serious point alongside the whimsy: as the unusual syntax above suggests, it is each single reader that is given sovereign importance, in line with Unamuno's new concentration on the individual—after the 1897 turn, he is insistent that Spain is a pueblo of 'yos' rather than a homogenous collective to be instrumentalised by those with power in society (OCE III, 1175; OCA V, 421). The humorous subversion of literary convention continues in the epilogue where, at the publisher's request, the author pads out the novel with extraneous material so that it might conform to the length of other novels in the series;[10] appended to the text is a solemn treatise by Fulgencio Entreambosmanos on the origins and ontology of origami birds. These features, along with the criticism of the author contained in the prologue, are designed to provoke the reader into adopting a constructively sceptical attitude to the novel as a whole, and can be assimilated to Unamuno's post-1897 desire, in Shaw's phrase, to 'spread spiritual awareness' amongst his readers (1975: 48).[11] Nevertheless, it goes further than merely promoting an active readerly attitude: as the epiloguist notes, the comic is the realm of emancipation from the logical (OCE II, 407; OCA II, 580), and this aspect of the novel further undermines rationalist or 'intellectualist' approaches.

The very structure of the novel also humorously undermines the sovereignty of reason. Unamuno refers to the tripartite division of the text in terms of its *prólogo*, *epílogo* and *logo* (OCE II, 397; OCA II, 563); by making the prologue and epilogue (as well as Don Fulgencio's treatise) integral to the meaning of the text overall, the *logo* as Logos (that is, the source of reason and meaning) is cut down to size. The Logos as authoritative word or meaning is yet further undercut by the polyphonic nature of the text: the presence of at times disjunctive accounts by a prologuist, Unamuno as implied author of the fifteen chapters of the novel along with its epilogue, and Don Fulgencio means that there is no single certain centre of textual authority. Once again, this can be assimilated to the desire to promote active, enquiring readership. But it may also rehearse a theme that became a central preoccupation of some of Unamuno's most significant post-1897 works: the relation between literary character as fictional creation and the human being as creature (i.e creation) of a divine being, along with the questions of autonomy/heteronomy that such a proposed correspondence throws up.

---

10   This was not an invention of Unamuno's: his publisher, Santiago Valentí Camp, did ask him to expand the text for this reason: see Unamuno 2002: 458–459.

11   It may well be that there is an element of defensiveness or pre-emption in the criticism of the author. See Ribbans 1971: 89

It is Don Fulgencio who proposes an analogy between fiction and life. As more than one critic has pointed out, although Fulgencio is a figure of fun because of his intellectualism, he also shares important traits with Unamuno himself (Gullón 1964: 66; Ribbans 1971: 99). Fulgencio tells Avito that although man is expected to follow the 'script' provided for him by what he refers to as the Supreme Being [el Ser Supremo], there will always be a moment when he can insert his own improvised material (the *morcilla*, as it is referred to in Spanish theatre) (OCE II, 340; OCA II, 474); there is, then, a chance to resist what is imposed and to be free, even if within limits. Fulgencio also urges Apolodoro to 'Be you, be yourself, unique and irreplaceable' (OCE II, 361; OCA II, 507). Despite the control that Avito (who endows scientific knowledge with the status of a religious Supreme Being, as the shrine he mounts to it in the family home indicates) has attempted to exercise over Apolodoro's upbringing to make him a rational genius, his son's decision to take his own life over an affair of the heart suggests that he cannot be fully determined. His suicide also contravenes the religious values which his mother has, surreptitiously, tried to inculcate in him. Apolodoro's suicide seems, then, to substantiate Fulgencio's theory of the *morcilla* as the limited autonomy available to fictional and human creatures. He wins his freedom, even though it is a tragic freedom.

Towards the end of the text, the epiloguist asserts boldly that 'Art's principal purpose is to emancipate us from determinism' (OCE II, 400; OCA II, 568), and *Amor y pedagogía* certainly seems driven by a liberatory impulse, seeking freedom both from what it represents as the lifelessness of abstract rationalist/intellectualist thought and the stifling Logos of realist literary convention: Unamuno elsewhere compares the realist author to a controlling puppet master (OCE II, 972; OCA IX, 415). Critical readings of *Amor y pedagogía* tend to see it principally as a precursor of *Niebla* (this includes the perceptive and illuminating studies by Ribbans 1971: 87; Marías 1966: 88); to be sure, *Niebla* does take up and elaborate on some of its themes. But *Amor y pedagogía* is a clever and interesting work in own right: its wealth of ideas, its structural audacity and wit make it deserving of a more prominent place in the Unamuno canon, and readers who are unfamiliar with it are urged to explore this at once deeply serious and playful text.[12]

* * *

Amor y pedagogía set out to puncture the certainties claimed by rigidly rationalist or intellectualist thought, and, through its plotting, polyphonic

---

[12]   For further discussion of *Amor y pedagogía*, see Chapter 7 in this volume.

structure and analogising of fictional and human creatures, sought playfully to suggest that life and will would always challenge the limits of determining authority, be it parenthood, pedagogy, fictional or even divine creation. Adopting a similar tragi-comic register, Unamuno's next novel, *Niebla*, published nine years later in 1914, again focused on questions of uncertainty, and fictional/divine authority, but in an even more radical, ambitious way. Using three simple (if not all conventionally realist) plotlines—a young man's friendship with an aspiring novelist, his pursuit of a young woman's hand in marriage, and a visit he makes to Miguel de Unamuno to ask advice about suicide when his marriage plans end in humiliating failure—*Niebla* proposes nothing less than a tragic theory of human existence, and of how we acquire consciousness of that existence. Although it draws substantially on ideas that Unamuno laid out in his 1912 essay *Del sentimiento trágico de la vida*—and indeed is not fully comprehensible unless the reader has some knowledge of that text—it is not a thinly novelised philosophical treatise, or mere allegory of a coming to awareness of the tragic sense of life; it is an ingenious narrative *tour-de-force*, proposing a relation between fictional creation and human creature not of analogy, as suggested in *Amor y pedagogía*, but of indistinguishability, if not identity. It is also a frustrating text: as Alex Longhurst has observed, even though it has been 'pored over and analysed to death by the community of Unamunistas, there are still too many questions [in it] that resist hermeneutical subjugation' (2014: 90). This necessarily limited study will concentrate on the main themes of *Niebla*, glossing the arguments in *El sentimiento trágico de la vida* that feed into the novel, and will attempt to give some sense of the novel's ingenuity and importance.

The central narrative of the novel traces the development of Augusto Pérez: the early chapters represent him as a young man who enjoys the aesthetic contemplation of objects in their unused, pristine state (OCE II, 557, 558; OCA II, 804, 806). In a way, his own life is unused too, or at least experienced at a remove from high emotion or vital engagement. It is also distanced from the practical: financially comfortable, Augusto spends his days playing chess with his novelist friend Víctor Goti or card games with his loyal and affectionate servants. He assumes that others live like him, sheltered from unmediated emotion:

> 'Mankind does not succumb to great sorrows or joys because these sorrows and joys come to us enveloped in an immense mist of minor incidents. And this is what life is: mist. Life is a nebula'
>
> (OCE II, 561; OCA II, 810).

Although he lives in the comfortable family house, Augusto considers himself homeless after the recent death of his mother (OCE II, 560, 562; OCA II, 809,

811) (his father had died several years before), and he has no sense of any design or purpose to life, believing that 'chance is the intimate rhythm of the world' (OCE II, 561; OCA II, 810). As a result, he has only a weak sense of his own agency, and is wont to question or reverse accepted causality. When he first becomes attracted to a young piano teacher, Eugenia, he initially encountered during a walk through his city's streets, he muses:

> When one discovers an apparition one has been searching for, isn't it actually the case that the apparition, moved by one's search, comes out to encounter one? Didn't America come out to find Columbus? Hasn't Eugenia come out to find me?
>
> (OCE II, 561; OCA II, 810–11).

Although he understands that games cannot be endlessly provisional or reversible – players cannot replay their hands until the desired outcome is achieved – he is unsure whether the same rule applies to life, and, if so, why that should be. Augusto is similarly ingenuously questioning of language, wondering, for example, why Eugenia's surname, Domingo, is not Dominga: Augusto wants the linguistic signifier to correspond to an underlying signified – Eugenia the female person (OCE II, OCA II, 806).

As the examples above suggest, Augusto is not just bewildered by the linguistic referent's being adrift from its signifier: his life more generally clearly lacks a final 'signified' or anchor-point to finalise meaning and purpose, fix causality, cure his 'homelessness' and dispel the mist of anaesthetising everyday minor incidents. It at first seems that his romantic love for Eugenia might provide all this: the challenge of winning her love enlarges his world and intensifies life for him (OCE II, 583; OCA II, 844); the narrator notes that 'Empezaba a conocer el mundo' (OCE II, 583; OCA II, 844). He feels that he now has a purpose in life (OCE II, 586; OCA II, 849). It is not just Augusto's existential awareness – adapting Descartes' *cogito*, he proclaims 'Amo ergo sum' (OCE II, OCA II, 837) – and worldly knowledge that seems to grow as a result of his love; his self-confidence and sense of autonomy also develop, even after Eugenia has refused his advances and he fears he may have been played by her. He acknowledges that it is owing to her that his 'facultad amorosa' [capacity for love] has been awakened, but, now that it has been brought to life, Eugenia herself is superfluous:

> Conmigo no juega nadie, y menos una mujer. ¡Yo soy yo! [...] Y sintiendo en esta exaltación de su yo como si éste se le fuera hinchando, hinchando y la casa le viniera estrecha, salió a la calle para darle espacio y desahogo. [I'm no-one's plaything, and still less a woman's! I am my own person!

And his sense of self grew in intensity and size, as if it were swelling and swelling, as if the house were becoming too small to contain it, so he went out in order to give it some space and relief.

(OCE II, 623; OCA II, 907)

But as also becomes apparent, the Eugenia he falls in love with is his own ideal creation: he more than once unwittingly walks past her in the street at precisely the moment he is conjuring her image in his mind (OCE II, 562–3 and 566; OCA II, 812–3 and 818). And when he leaves the house to give the buoyant *yo* described above some space, finding himself in a crowded street where no-one notices his presence, 'aquel yo del «¡Yo soy yo!» se le iba achicando, achicando, y se le replegaba en el cuerpo' [that 'I' of 'I am my own person' shrank and shrank, folding back into his body] (OCE II, 623; OCA II, 908). Augusto's sense of self, then, depends on the acknowledgement or recognition of the Other (whether a privileged other such as the beloved, or, failing that, others more generally).

So it is not surprising that, when humiliatingly deceived and belittled by Eugenia, acting in concert with Augusto's rival for her hand, Augusto should contemplate suicide. It is here that the novel transforms itself from the conventional – if slightly schematic and undisciplined – tale, narrated largely in a whimsical or humorous register, of a jilted idealist who has placed too much weight on romantic love, into something more curious and more radical: Augusto decides to consult the writer Miguel de Unamuno about his plans. The significance of this metalepsis can be explained more easily after a summary of the episode: Unamuno explains to Augusto that he cannot kill himself because, as a fictional character, he is not alive or real in the first place; he is the merely the product of his author's and his reader's fantasies (OCE II, 666; OCA II, 975): his existence, then, is dependent on and determined by his author. But Augusto counters by pointing out that as Unamuno had previously claimed that Don Quixote and Sancho, products of Cervantes's and his readers' fantasies, were not just *as* real but *more* real than Cervantes (in the sense that any recognition or existence he now had was dependent on them, rather than *vice versa*), it was conceivable that he, Augusto, was more real than Unamuno. As with Augusto's earlier chiastic musings about Columbus and America, if there is no ontological anchor point or final cause, then propositions are infinitely reversible. Augusto continues to challenge Unamuno's omnipotence and independent existence until the author, angered, decides that he will demonstrate his sovereignty by making Augusto die as soon as he returns home. This death sentence inculcates an immediate and desperate desire on the part of Augusto to continue to live, but Unamuno is implacable. Augusto's ambiguous final words to Unamuno are a resigned/ defiant 'A morir, pues!' [To die, then!] (OCE II, 670; OCA II, 982). After the encounter, Unamuno notes of Augusto:

His life had recently been extremely sad and painful, but it was much sadder and more painful for him to think that it had all been a dream, and not his own dream, but mine [i.e. Unamuno's]. Nothingness seemed much more frightening than pain. 'To dream that one exists is one thing, but to be the dream of another...'

(OCE II, 671; OCA II, 983).

Augusto does subsequently wonder whether, even if he is a product of Unamuno's imagination, he does not also live in the imaginations of those who read the story of his life; if so, 'isn't what is in the fantasies of various people, rather than just one person, real?' (OCE II, 671; OCA II, 983). Augusto dies shortly afterwards, but it is not clear whether the death results from his own willed actions (extreme over-eating), or Unamuno's desires. Further ambiguity is stoked before the narrative proper has even begun: in the prologue, Augusto's friend Víctor Goti, casts doubt over the nature of his death as represented in the novel; Goti's views are then curtly countered by Unamuno in a post-prologue which threatens Goti with the same fate he claimed to have meted out to Augusto.

The most obvious way to read this denouement, coupled with the introductory, conflicting paratexts, is as a witty (if ultimately disconcerting) illustration that it is not just Augusto who lacks a final signified or ontological anchor point; Unamuno as author-figure is similarly bereft. He cannot guarantee final meaning of the denouement or have the final say on Augusto's death either (literally—the final paratext is an epilogue in the form of a funeral oration to Augusto given by his pet dog Orfeo). Indeed, given the chiasmic/reversible dynamic claimed by Augusto in relation to his creator regarding their respective realities/ fictionalities, it is possible that the closing words of Unamuno the author-figure—'And here is the story of Augusto Pérez' (OCE II, 678; OCA 994)— demonstrate that he is actually obeying the wishes of Augusto, who had earlier suggested that Unamuno might exist only as a pretext for allowing Augusto's story to be made public (OCE II, 666; OCA II, 975). It is also possible that Víctor Goti the novelist, not Unamuno the author-figure, is actually the author of *Niebla*: certainly the *nivola* he describes in Chapter XVII resembles the text we are reading as *Niebla*.[13]

Read in this way, *Niebla* can be seen as a novel about the absence of any ultimate guarantor of being, knowledge or meaning. By irresolvably blurring the distinction between fiction and reality, the metaleptical elements in the tale underline this

---

[13]   The term that Víctor coins for his work, *nivola* came to be used by critics to refer not just to *Niebla* itself, but to other post-1897 long narrative by Unamuno. The *nivola* as genre, and Unamuno's irritation at its being widely misunderstood, is discussed in more detail below, in the section on *Tres novelas ejemplares y un prólogo*, as are other concepts that Unamuno used when explaining his fictional practice such as oviparous/viviparous writing and writing *a lo que salga*.

existential uncertainty. It is this broad aspect of the novel that most critical readings emphasise (see, for example, Marías (1966), Ribbans (1971), Olson (1984), Spires (1986 & 1988), Johnson (1993) and Cerezo Galán (1996)) and it is certainly possible to see how the text has been assimilated into the modernist canon: the focus on the subjectivity of its protagonist (expressed not infrequently through interior monologue), the anti-realist elements, which produce an open play of signification, the novel's polyphony and undercutting of any centre of narrative authority are all consonant with the effects of a collapse in traditional certainties and consequent sceptical introversion often characteristic of modernist literary production. Important aspects of the novel are also consonant with the *fin-de-siècle*/proto-modernist qualities of the Generation of 1898 novel, most notably the failure of human love to provide ultimate satisfaction and fulfilment (see Shaw 1975: 56).

But there is another, more specific aspect of *Niebla* that also deserves attention: its fictionalisation of themes central to Unamuno's essay (and personal manifesto) *Del sentimiento trágico de la vida*. The ontological and epistemological uncertainties of *Niebla* are not solely philosophical; they are theological too – the novel's absent/uncertain transcendental signified or final cause may be read as God. This aspect of the text is not forced on the reader, but it is present throughout, and some parts of the novel are hard to explain without reference to the essay. Augusto, for example, may be read for most of the novel as a character representative not just of ingenuous idealism; he also, specifically, lacks a sense of his own *mortality* until his encounter with Unamuno the author-figure. Before that point, he seems to have a serene (or perhaps superficial), unquestioning religious faith (OCE II, 557; OCA II, 804), and even has an – again untroubled – inkling that he lacks a soul (which Unamuno defines in *El sentimiento trágico* as consciousness of one's personal and concrete immortality [Unamuno 1954; 12; OCE VII, 116; OCA XVI, 139]). But it is not until Unamuno the author-figure tells him that he will die that he acquires tragic wisdom about what is important in life:

> I swear to you, Sr Unamuno, that I will not kill myself, I won't take this life that you or God have given me [...] now that you want to kill me, I want to live, to live, to live [...] even if I am made a figure of fun again, even if Eugenia [...] breaks my heart into tiny pieces. I want to live, to live, to live...
>
> (OCE II, 669; OCA II, 981)

His desire speaks to what Unamuno defines in *Del sentimiento trágico de la vida* as:

> 'The only real vital problem, the problem that strikes at the very root of our being [is] the problem of our individual and personal destiny, of the

immortality of the soul [...] your essence, reader, mine, [...] and that of
every man who is a man, is nothing but the endeavour, the effort, which he
makes to continue to be a man, not to die
                    (Unamuno 1954: 4, 7; OCE VII, 111, 112; OCA XVI, 130, 133).

It is only after his realisation of this fundamental vital problem that Augusto
corrects his previous Cartesian idealism[14], inverting it to a formulation that
emphasises the precedence of the mortal flesh and bone[15] and consciousness of
material being over the products of the mind: 'Soy, luego pienso' [I am, therefore
I think] (OCE II, 672; OCA II, 984). This is also the formulation that Unamuno
lays out in *Del sentimiento trágico* when defining the starting point for all
philosophy not perverted by intellectualism (Unamuno 1954: 35–36; OCE VII,
130; OCA XVI, 162–3).

More than once, Unamuno comes close to suggesting in *Del sentimiento
trágico* that man is the cause of God rather than vice versa (because of man's
hunger for immortality—see, for example, Unamuno 1954: 178, 217; OCE VII,
213–4, 237; OCA XVI, 304, 343); this suggestion is mirrored in *Niebla* when
Augusto proposes to Unamuno the author-figure that, far from being Augusto's
omnipotent determining creator, he may exist as a vehicle to allow Augusto to
exist in the imagination of his readers. As the quotation from Augusto above
suggests, there is an interchangeability between God and Unamuno the author-
figure in the text, and as the open-ended conclusion to the novel indicates,
Unamuno the author-figure's status as final 'cause' of Augusto is far from
guaranteed. Moreover, the metafictional play in the novel may, in addition to
the reading suggested above, also relate to one of the assertions made in *Del
sentimiento trágico*: laying out a vision of humanity defined by its hunger for
immortality, Unamuno affirms that 'Nothing is real that is not eternal' (Unamuno
1954:39; OCE VII, 132; OCA XVI, 166); this may explain the ontological
indistinguishability between author and character suggested by *Niebla*: if neither
is guaranteed to be eternal, neither is real.

In addition to (or indeed perhaps instead of) being seen as a ludic modernist
parable of ontological insecurity, *Niebla*, then, may be read as an allegory of the
painful agnosticism that, for Unamuno, defined life for those who reflected
carefully (and both *Niebla* and *Del sentimento trágico* were intended precisely

---

[14] We think, for example, of Augusto's playful tweaking of 'cogito ergo sum' to 'amo ergo
sum' in Chapter VII (referenced above), and the insistence on the ideal nature of his love for
Eugenia, nicely encapsulated in the episode where, because he is so busy summoning her up in
his mind, he walks past her in the street (OCE II, 562; OCA II, 812).
[15] 'El hombre de carne y hueso' [the man of flesh and bone] is Unamuno's preferred phrase
for mortal man; its origins seem to be biblical. It is also the title of *Del sentimiento trágico de
la vida*'s opening chapter.

to prompt careful reflection about such matters, as Víctor Goti's prologue suggests, even as it pokes gentle fun at Unamuno). Its inconclusiveness means that, like *Amor y pedagogía*, it is, ultimately a tragi-comic text rather than a tragic one, but the existential stakes being wagered are much higher in this later text.

Tragic Unrecognition: *Abel Sánchez*

In comparison with the polyphonic *Niebla*, whose main narrative was supplemented with crucial paratexts, generously interlarded with parables or anecdotes, whose characterisation was schematic when not caricatural, and whose register was often humorous or whimsical,[16] the structure of *Abel Sánchez* (1917) is starkly simple, and its tone unremittingly sober. Despite the absence of metafictional ludism, it is still recognisably a modernist text in its concentration on the interior life of its protagonist, Joaquín Monegro; although the novel is narrated mostly in the third person, events and other characters are focalised through his perspective.

   In the words of its narrator, it is the story of a 'sombría pasión' [a sombre passion] (OCE II, 683; OCA II, 1001). Joaquín's Monegro's life has been blighted since childhood by his schoolfriend Abel Sánchez, who was always effortlessly popular, preferred to Joaquín and who became more publicly successful than him. Although in adulthood Joaquín becomes a highly competent and well-regarded doctor, he continues to feel overshadowed by the fame and plaudits that Abel--an artist--achieves. Joaquín is even bested by Abel in love: the woman with whom Joaquín is infatuated as a young man also prefers Abel and marries him. As the title and this plot summary suggests, the biblical story of Cain and Abel hovers over the tale, becoming an explicit part of events when Abel makes it the subject of one of his paintings which, as if to stoke Joaquín's resentment even further, goes on to win a national prize. Eventually, in a moment of rage, Joaquín indirectly causes Abel's death. As Ricardo Gullón notes, this incident may be seen as a kind of symbolic Cainite homicide (1964: 142). Unsurprisingly, the text is most often read as a case study in envy, though, as Julián Marías has pointed out, is not the psychology of envy that interests Unamuno (1966: 44);[17] nor, as Nicholas Round notes, does the novel examine envy in terms of its

---

[16]   See, for example, the prologue, where Víctor Goti gently mocks Unamuno the author-figure for his preoccupation with the hunger for immortality (OCE II, 545–6; OCA II, 787), the representation of Fermín, Eugenia's anarchist uncle, exchanges between Víctor and Augusto such as that in chapter X (OCE II, 588; OCA II, 851) and the response of Orfeo to Augusto' musings in chapter VII (OCE II, 578–9; OCA II, 837).

[17]   This is not to say that the novel's detailed study of envy is without psychological acuity; it has certainly lent itself to penetrating psychoanalytic readings: see, for example Alison Sinclair's (2001: 170–190).

immorality (1974: 51): it is as an existential condition that the novel approaches the topic. Ultimately, though, envy is the vector of a wider theme linking the novel back to the concerns of *Del sentimiento trágico de la vida* and *Niebla*, even if, generally speaking, this aspect of the text has been under-examined in critical readings: *Abel Sánchez*, like *Niebla*, lays out one of the possible consequences of living without assured ontological security. As Nicholas Round points out, for Unamuno, such security could only have one source: 'a God who loves, forgives and preserves his creatures, and whose own absolute and eternal being guarantees theirs' (1974: 26).

In *Del sentimiento trágico de la vida*, Unamuno lays out various responses to this problematic uncertainty: procreation, in order to assure that one lives on in some form in others, and artistic creation, which may assure a metaphorical afterlife for one's name and work (Unamuno 1954: 55; OCE VII, 141–2; OCA XVI, 182). These are generally constructive, benign responses, even if always inadequate to the hunger for immortality that, for, Unamuno is the very essence of human existence (Unamuno 1954: 38–57). There are other, less edifying responses too: herostratism, for example (Unamuno 1954: 56; OCE VII, 142; OCA XVI, 183). Certainly Joaquín Monegro's character may be read in this way: he notes in the written confession that he leaves for his daughter that 'I did not seek truth and knowledge, but instead sought prizes and fame, and to be more than him [i.e.Abel]' (OCE II, 713; OCA II, 1046). Joaquín also projects the same qualities onto his rival, telling Abel 'you are horribly ambitious [...] for glory, fame, renown...You always were; you were born ambitious' (OCE II, 691; OCA II, 1009). Although *Del sentimiento trágico de la vida* does not dwell on herostratism, its underlying mechanism is a fundamental theme in Unamuno's thought and fiction: one's sense of self and existence depends upon the recognition of an Other: 'The murder of Abel by his brother Cain was not a struggle for bread—it was a struggle to survive in God, in the divine memory. Envy is [...] spiritual hunger (Unamuno 1954: 55; OCE VII, 142; OCA XVI, 182–3)'. If this Other cannot guarantee eternal survival or memory, then human others and memories must substitute for it.[18] This belief explains the attraction of the Cain narrative for Unamuno: God's turning away from Cain's offering analogises the lack of any guaranteed eternal recognition or memory. Underlying Joaquín's envy is an even more basic feeling: what he

---

[18]   Several critics have explored the relations between Unamuno's insistence on the importance of recognition and Hegel's theory of how man acquires consciousness through the master-slave dialectic; Wyers' account (1976: 70–76) is particularly incisive and helpful for the reader unfamiliar with Hegel, but see also Regalado García (1968) and Cerezo Galán (1996: 571–629). What is distinctive in Unamuno's account is the religio-ontological weight the struggle for recognition bears: it is visible also in the confrontation between Augusto and Unamuno the author-figure in Chapter XXXI of *Niebla*.

most needs is passionate *attention* (i.e. recognition), precisely from the person he feels is standing in the way of his receiving it from others, even if this attention comes in the form of hatred. Indeed, when he imagines Abel's hating him, he feels 'un gozo como de derretimiento, un gozo que le hizo temblar hasta los tuétanos del alma' [a pleasure that was meltingly sweet, a pleasure that made him tremble in the very depths of his soul] (OCE II, 727; OCA II, 1069). It is clearly significant that Joaquín struggles painfully with religious belief. He is not able fully to place his faith in a God he thinks has condemned him irredeemably to be bad (OCE II, 719; OCA II, 1055–6); at another point he misdirects his religious desire praying before a painting Abel has made of the Virgin Mary, modelled on the woman that Abel had married and Joaquín coveted (OCE II, 719–720; OCA II, 1056).

As is consonant with Unamuno's reading of herostratism in *Del sentimiento trágico de la vida*, Joaquín never achieves the ultimate object of his longing. But his grandson (who, because Joaquín and Abel's children have married, is also Abel's grandson), seems to offer him some vital consolation at the end of the text, not just because he might offer a form of immortality (however inadequate), but also, more importantly, because in the absence both of Abel and a God with whom Joaquín can reconcile himself – both potential sources of recognition – the child can offer pure forgiveness (also a form of recognition). Joaquín claims to his grandson: 'only from you, you who don't yet have the use of reason, you who are innocent, do I need forgiveness' (OCE II, 758; OCA II, 1118). Just before his death, he also comes to realise that love (an alternative form of recognition) might have saved him. Amongst his last words to his wife are: 'If I had loved you, I would have been cured. I did not love you, and now it pains me not to have loved you. If we could only start again!' (OCE II, 758; OCA II, 1118–9). Joaquín's final unrealised desire is a fundamental part of the tragedy of the text; it also returns us to *Del sentimiento trágico de la vida*, in which Unamuno asserts 'The thirst of eternity is what is called love amongst men, and whosoever loves another wishes to eternalise himself in him' (Unamuno 1954: 39; OCE VII, 132; OCA XVI, 166). The most fundamental quality of Joaquín Monegro's character is not actually envy, then, but the hunger for immortality.

Despite the ugliness of some of Joaquín's actions and intentions – he claims, for example, to have had a child in order that she might serve as an instrument of revenge (OCE II, 713; OCA II, 1045) – it is this dimension of Joaquín's plight that to a large extent explains the sympathetic representation of him in *Abel Sánchez*: In a 1928 prologue to the second edition of text, Unamuno noted that he had tried to demonstrate that Joaquín's envy was 'a tragic envy, an envy that is a form of defence, an envy that might be called angelic' and refers to the 'grandeza de su pasión' [the greatness of his passion], distinguishing it from the more wretched envy that he regarded as the Spanish vice, an envy that was hypocritical, sly, and abject (OCE II, 686; OCA II, 1005). It is because he struggles so hard to find an elusive ontological security (although he is unable to articulate his search in such terms) that he is a tragic figure for Unamuno, and a figure far greater than the unquestioning, complacent Abel. Nicholas Round argues that Joaquín is represented sympathetically because he is 'actively striving to become fully human' (1974: 51). This is correct as long as we bear in mind that for Unamuno the very essence of the human is, ultimately, a religious hunger for immortality. It is only by reading *Abel Sánchez* in the light of *Del sentimiento trágico de la vida*'s arguments that we can appreciate its full 'sombre passion'.

Redefining Realism: *Tres novelas ejemplares y un prólogo*

At around the same time that Unamuno was writing *Abel Sánchez*, he also published a novella, *Nada menos que todo un hombre* in *La novela corta* (a mass-market weekly) in 1916; another novella, *El marqués de Lumbría*, appeared in the same periodical four years later. Both texts were then collected, along with another, previously unpublished novella, *Dos madres*, and published, along with a substantial preface, as *Tres novelas ejemplares y un prólogo*, in 1920. The prologue is an important document in its own right, illuminating the thinking behind the structure and style of Unamuno's fiction after *Paz en la guerra*. An at times slightly prickly essay, it is an explanation and defence of what Unamuno understands as realism in literature, and, particularly, in characterisation. It begins with a riposte to what Unamuno saw as lazily obtuse critical responses to the *nivola*, the term that Víctor Goti coined to describe the novel he was writing in *Niebla* (OCE II, 971; OCA IX, 413) in order to distinguish it from the conventional *novela*. As a new, invented genre, Víctor explains, it cannot be accused of overthrowing any laws governing the novel (OCE II, 616; OCA II, 896). Unamuno felt that the concept of the *nivola*, and the characters that peopled it, had subsequently been applied to his novels more widely, and they had been misread as 'thesis novels or philosophical novels, symbols, personified concepts, essays in the form of dialogue' (OCE II, 974; OCA IX, 419). Unamuno seemed particularly concerned that critics – and readers – confused realistic characterisation with the accumulation of exterior detail and 'catchphrases, tics and gestures' (OCE II, 975; OCA IX, 420).

For Unamuno, the reality of both real and fictional figures was defined by their plural and conflictive nature: all men contain the seven virtues and the seven deadly sins, and from their variable and shifting internal conflicts are created 'agonistas' [agonists] (OCE II, 972; OCA IX, 415). All men have not one but several identities: here Unamuno cites the popular US essayist Oliver Wendell Holmes, who argued that when two men – he dubbed his examples

John and Thomas – are in dialogue, there are actually six, not two, figures conversing – the real John and Thomas (known only to their Maker); the ideal John and Thomas (who they each believe themselves to be), and the John as seen by Thomas and *vice versa* (OCE II, 973; OCA IX, 416). The claim that realistic fictional characters are defined by their agonistic and multi-faceted nature is conventional enough, and the belief that a character's plural selves are revealed when he is in conversation explains the primordial importance of dialogue in the *nivola* – this was a feature that Víctor Goti had emphasised in *Niebla*. Where Unamuno's definition of reality and realism becomes distinctive, and where he departs from the model of self proposed by Wendell Holmes (whom he refers to disparagingly as an 'intelectualista yanqui') (OCE II, 973; OCA IX, 416) is in his discussion of the importance of will.

What a character might want to be – his will, or 'querer ser'– is, in contradistinction to Wendell Holmes's assertion, not his *ideal* self for Unamuno; it is instead the very source of his reality/realism (OCE II, 973; OCA IX, 416).[19] But it may not be immediately or easily knowable to him or others: this most intimate reality may only be revealed in a moment, through a phrase, a cry or a single action (OCA IX, 420; OCE II, 975). For Unamuno, creativity lies at the heart of the reality of man, who creates himself through his acts of will and desire; it also lies at the heart of the reading process: the reader (re)creates the work of art for himself with careful, questioning attention to characters whose reality may not be immediately visible. And the novelist can assist by not over-explaining characters and thereby, for Unamuno, stripping them of will so that they are reduced to being 'clothed mannequins', completely controlled by a puppet master author (OCE II, 972; OCA IX, 415); instead, he might follow the technique described by Víctor Goti in *Niebla*:

> My novel doesn't have a plot, or rather, its plot will gradually emerge [...] My characters will create themselves according to how they might act and, above all, speak; their character will take shape gradually [...] I'll let myself be carried along
>
> (OCE II, 615; OCA II, 894–5).

Thus the characters might acquire some of the vital, wilful dynamism which constituted both reality and realism for Unamuno.

The prologue gives us a clear understanding of the significance of Unamuno's distinction between what he called the oviparous [*ovíparo*] *Paz en la guerra* (a

---

19 Unamuno does not make a consistent distinction between extra-literary reality and literary realism. This is in keeping with the tendency of his novels to analogise life and literature—see the discussion above of Don Fulgencio's comments about the *morcilla*, and the metalepsis in *Niebla*.

novel that was largely conventionally realist in its characterisation and its representation of place and time), and the viviparous [*vivíparo*] *Amor y pedagogía* and *Niebla*, novels characterised by a heterogeneous structure, disparate elements and anecdotes, with plot and characters apparently written 'without knowing in advance what will come to them'.[20] The viviparous novel does not reflect a disregard for realism or a dislike of careful planning on Unamuno's part; instead it attempts purposely to recreate the contingency, and the will/desire that was the very core of the human/fictional subject's reality/realism for Unamuno.[21] The prologue also gives us a context to understand why a certain opacity of character, divided or plural self and lack of self-knowledge are so important in novels such as *Abel Sánchez*, and, later, *La tía Tula*: again, for Unamuno, these are realities of the human subject and should be reproduced in fiction that purported to be realist.

It clearly irritated Unamuno that his fiction was seen as disdaining realism or leaning towards abstraction when what he was attempting to do was fundamentally revise the understanding of literary realism. The prologue contains repeated criticism of realism predicated on the accretion of 'external' detail, not just because of its superficiality, but also because, for Unamuno, it encouraged passivity in those reading: Unamuno wanted his readers to be as voluntaristic and actively desiring as his characters.[22] It is in this sense that the novellas, Unamuno tells us, were designed to be exemplary (OCE II, 972; OCA IX, 414–5);[23] those who read novels just to pass the time or as a distraction from more fundamental vital questions were themselves less than fully real, mere 'sombra[s] de un sueño' [shadows of a dream] (OCE II, 977; OCA IX, 422) as Unamuno refers to them.

---

[20]   This is the phrase that Víctor Goti uses to describe his own *nivola* (OCE II, 895; OCA II, 615). Unamuno first wrote about the distinction between oviparous and viviparous work in his 1904 essay 'A lo que salga' (OCE I, 1194–1204; OCA III, 789–795).

[21]   It is Augusto Pérez who best exemplifies the kind of wilful character Unamuno holds up as real(ist). When he and Víctor are discussing Víctor's *nivola*, Augusto claims that 'in the beginning you might think that [your characters] are under your control; soon enough you'll become convinced that it is they who are taking *you* in hand. Very often the author becomes the plaything of his characters' (OCE II, 616; OCA II, 896). And of course Augusto goes on to challenge Unamuno the author-figure in Chapter XXXI, a challenge that Unamuno represents as unexpected to Unamuno the author-figure.

[22]   Will is the cornerstone of Unamuno's understanding of living being. The opening pages of *Del sentimiento trágico de la vida* cite Spinoza's argument that the essence of the living thing is the *conatus*, which Unamuno glosses in relation to human being in the following terms: the essence of man [...] is nothing but the endeavour, the effort, which he makes to continue to be a man, not to die' (Unamuno 1954: 4, 7; OCE VII, 111, 112; OCA XVI, 130, 133). It is this endeavour which produces the hunger for immortality. See also the discussion above of this hunger in relation to *Niebla*.

[23]   Unamuno invokes the resonances between his text and Cervantes's *Novelas ejemplares*, but really, the only correspondence is that in both texts, the label 'exemplary' was applied to the stories after they were written; they were not intended to be morally instructive writings.

The prologue, then, was the fullest explanation that Unamuno had hitherto provided of the rationale for his fictional practice, and is essential reading for the student of his longer narrative of this period. It also goes some way towards explaining the three novellas it accompanies: their protagonists are certainly realist in Unamuno's understanding of the term, because they exhibit a very strong – indeed ruthless – 'querer ser' [will/desire to be]. *Nada menos que todo un hombre* concerns a man unwilling to admit the strength of his feelings, and his dependence, on the woman he makes his wife (whom he mistreats dreadfully); *El marqués de Lumbría* tells the story of a woman prepared to withstand scandal and deep family division in order that she and her son be given what she feels is their due; *Dos madres* concerns a widow who plots to buy a baby by underhand means in order to satisfy her craving to be a mother, destroying the lives of those around her in the process. All involve an initial withholding of information about the protagonists, so that they are not immediately decipherable; all contain only the sketchiest outlines of place and time, and all involve deeply immoral behaviour that is not explicitly judged by the narrator of the tales. Given the points made in the prologue, it seems fair to assume that the stories are written in such a way as to resist the easy consumption of conventionally realist literature, and to oblige the reader to reflect on the motivation of the main characters. But even bearing in mind Unamuno's own criteria for realism, and perhaps partly because of their brevity[24], the tales are without nuance or depth, the characters are thinly one-dimensional and tend, as Shaw has noted towards melodrama (1975: 58). Indeed, as Olson has labelled them, the protagonists are 'monsters of will' (2003: 100). The novellas themselves do not add to an understanding of Unamuno's characterisation in post-1914 narrative that is not better obtained from, say, *Abel Sánchez* or *La tía Tula*, and it is difficult not to conclude that the real worth of the collection lies in its prologue.

* * *

Another novella from 1920, *Tulio Montalbán y Julio Macedo*, is more interesting, its melodramatic elements aside. As a young man, Tulio Montalbán becomes a national hero fighting for the liberation of his country from colonial rule. Having succeeded, he fears turning into just the kind of tyrannical ruler he struggled to overthrow, so feigns his death and attempts to invent himself anew as Julio Macedo on a remote island. But a lonely, bookish young woman

---

[24] It is not clear whether *Nada menos que todo un hombre* and *El marqués de Lumbría* were written specially for *La Novela Corta*, but if so, their melodrama and lack of complexity might also partly reflect Unamuno's assumptions about a slightly more popular readership than he was used to writing for (even though *La Novela Corta* published a wide range of fiction and authors).

there has read Tulio Montalbán's biography, and is in love with the heroic figure. She guesses the newcomer's identity. Despairing of ever escaping his heroic literary persona, Tulio/Julio kills himself. His attempt to explain his actions in a final letter, and to correct the record of his life is thwarted when the letter is destroyed, and the lonely young woman is left on her island with her books. The novella speaks to the wrenching inadequacy and inaccuracy of the historical or biographical record in capturing life, while suggesting that it might be the only, or most enduring form of any posthumous survival. In this sense, the novella may be read as a return to a preoccupation and uncertainty that Unamuno had previously discussed in *Del sentimiento trágico de la vida* (Unamuno 1954: 55; OCE VII, 141–2; OCA XVI, 182).[25]

The ideas examined in *Del sentimiento trágico de la vida* are also present in Unamuno's final narrative of this period, *La tía Tula*, published in 1921. Although Unamuno had characterised procreation as one way in which mankind strove for immortality, he also argued that for some, chastity could serve the same need: 'some [...] preserve their virginity in order the better to perpetuate themselves, and in order to perpetuate something more human than the flesh (Unamuno 1954: 134; OCE VII, 188–189; OCA XVI, 262). *La tía Tula*'s protagonist, whose desire for autonomy is as strong as her maternal instinct, perpetuates herself and her values both through virginity and through procreation by proxy. Urging motherhood first on her sister and on a family maid (for both of whom motherhood proves fatal) Tula helps raise their children while the two woman are alive, assuming the role of mother upon their death.

Like Joaquín Monegro, Tula is a complex, not entirely transparent figure. She is also a fully realist character in Unamuno's terms: her 'querer ser' is implacable. Indeed in some ways she is a 'monster of will', in Olson's formulation, in her hunger for motherhood by proxy; at the same time, she cleaves to the ethical ideal laid out by Unamuno in the penultimate chapter of *Del sentimiento trágico de la vida*, zealously fulfilling a lay vocation and making herself irreplaceable to those around her: this aspect of her characterisation is examined more fully in the chapter on gender and sexuality in Unamuno's work in this volume. *La tía Tula* is an important landmark in Unamuno's fiction of the time, being the first complex, fully realised female protagonist he had created. In addition to its exploration of concerns laid out in *Del sentimiento trágico de la vida*, and its rich characterisation of the wilful protagonist, *La tía Tula* is of interest because it may be read in part as a response to the very significant shifts in women's personal, educational and professional possibilities in the first two decades of the twentieth century.

---

[25] See also Stephen Roberts's chapter in this volume for discussion of *Sombras de sueño* (the dramatisation of *Tulio Montalbán y Julio Macedo*)

* * *

The period under examination in this chapter was the most fertile and innovative in Unamuno's literary career. A carefully emplaced, conventionally realist text such as *Paz en la guerra* representing a range of characters living through an identifiable national episode could not offer an adequate vehicle for his new and lasting preoccupations after 1897. Unamuno's crisis of values initially entailed putting fictional convention into crisis with the metaleptical play, self-ironising structures and schematic characterisation of *Amor y pedagogía* and *Niebla*, before he established a more austere, nuanced exploration of character and will in *Abel Sánchez* and *La tía Tula*. Although Unamuno wrote less fiction after 1921, these two modes remained the vehicles for his fictional enquiry for the rest of his career: the crisis of exile in 1924 produced a return to the structures of *Amor y pedagogía* and *Niebla* – though in a bleaker register than their tragi-comedy could allow –, and shorter fiction such as *San Manuel Bueno, mártir*, and *La novela de Don Sandalio, jugador de ajedrez* revisit the ambivalence and opacity/ambiguity of *Abel Sánchez* and *La tía Tula*. It is a testament to Unamuno's skill and imagination as a writer that, although all his fiction after the turn of the twentieth century is insistently informed by one insistent existential preoccupation, his texts are far from monotonous or repetitive; they are striking in their variety and originality of characterisation. And although inflected by an idiosyncratic, ultimately religious set of concerns, his exploration of ontological uncertainty (and the representational challenges it posed) place him firmly within the varied constellation of European modernism.

Further Reading

General:
Cerezo Galán (1996), Marías (1966), Olson (2003), Roberts (2007), Shaw (1975), Wyers (1976). *Amor y pedagogía*: Gullón (1964), Ribbans (1971), Unamuno (2002). *Niebla:* Blanco Aguinaga (1964a), House Webber (1964), Johnson (1993), Livingstone (1967), Macklin (1993), Morón-Arroyo (1966), Olson (1984), Ribbans (1971), Round (1992), Sinclair (1987), Spires (1988), Weber (1973), Weber (1990). *Abel Sánchez*: Gullón (1964), Round (1974). *La tía Tula*: Bretz (1993), Longhurst (1989), Ribbans (1987), Unamuno (2013). *Tres novelas ejemplares y un prólogo*: Batchelor (1972), Blanco Aguinaga (1964b), Cerezo Galán (1996), Ribbans (1989), Turner (1974).

3

Exile 1924–1930: Essays, Narrative and Drama

Stephen G.H. Roberts

Miguel de Unamuno's exile from the Dictatorship of General Primo de Rivera forms a self-contained period made up of three distinct moments and places: his deportation to Fuerteventura (February-July 1924) and then his voluntary exile in Paris (July 1924-August 1925) and Hendaye (August 1925-February 1930).[1] These six years, during which he would experience the privations and anxieties characteristic of exile, would place considerable strain not only on the man himself but also on the whole philosophical and intellectual worldview that he had built up over the previous decades. The resulting crisis starts to surface in his Fuerteventura and early Paris writings, including the 31 essays that make up the series entitled *Alrededor del estilo* (published between April and November 1924) and the chapters of *La agonía del cristianismo* (written between September and December 1924), and finally comes to a head in the original nucleus of *Cómo se hace una novela*, which was written in December 1924 and July 1925. The aftermath of the crisis can be seen in the Hendaye writings, including the three exile plays *El Otro* (written 1926), *Sombras de sueño* (written 1926) and *El hermano Juan* (written 1927–1929) and the poetic collection *Cancionero* (started in March 1928), but especially in the 'Prólogo', 'Comentario', 'Continuación' and other material that he added to the original nucleus of *Cómo se hace una novela* between May and July 1927. The aim of this chapter is to consider the nature of Unamuno's exile crisis as it is reflected above all in the three essayistic texts *Alrededor del estilo*, *La agonía del cristianismo* and *Cómo se hace una novela*. To do this, we first need briefly to consider the reasons for Unamuno's exile.

---

[1]   For biographical details concerning Unamuno's stay in exile, see Salcedo (1998: 277–351), Rabaté and Rabaté (2009: 451–553), Unamuno (2012: 13–40) and Juaristi (2012: 353–85).

The intellectual banished: Unamuno's politics and philosophy before 1924

According to General Primo de Rivera, Unamuno was deported to Fuerteventura in February 1924 because of his insulting and incendiary attacks on the King, the Royal Family and the Dictator himself.[2] In reality, the root cause of Unamuno's deportation lay in his long-term criticism of the virulently traditionalist strain of nationalism that he felt was coming to dominate the Restoration political regime. He had first identified this extreme traditionalism in his earliest major work, *En torno al casticismo* (1895), where he claimed that the traditionalists, or *casticistas*, despised the modern world and preferred to live in a past of supposed imperial grandeur and Catholic unity. Many of their opponents amongst the progressives, meanwhile, located their own ideal nation in a utopian future where their dreams of political and social justice had at long last been fulfilled. Both extremes, according to Unamuno, overlooked the present moment of their nation, that deep, *intrahistorical* moment where the past was constantly flowing into the future and tradition was continuously being transformed into progress.[3] Unamuno would become the champion of this national present and would mine it in search of the values of his nation, endeavouring in works such as *Vida de Don Quijote y Sancho* (1905) to define his own, more liberal and quixotic, form of cultural nationalism that could provide an antidote to the traditionalist and increasingly militaristic form of patriotism that he feared was gradually reasserting its hold.[4] Over the following years, especially those of the Great War (1914–1918), during which Spain remained officially neutral, Unamuno came to believe that King Alfonso XIII, certain high-ranking Army officers, and some of the leading politicians and businessmen of the age were starting to undermine the democratic foundations of the system in the hope of setting up a more authoritarian regime akin to that overseen by the Kaiser in Germany. When Primo de Rivera finally carried out his *coup d'état* in September 1923, Unamuno would believe it represented the victory of these militaristic and traditionalist figures and forces.

Unamuno's brave criticism of the injustices and increasing authoritarianism of the Restoration regime led to his removal, in August 1914, from the Rectorship of Salamanca University. He had recently published his most important philosophical work, *Del sentimiento trágico de la vida* (1912), in which, amongst

---

[2]   On the reasons for Unamuno's exile, see Ouimette (1976, 1977 and 1998: 71–188); Roberts (1986) and Urrutia (1997: 169–234).
[3]   See the first chapter of *En torno al casticismo*, 'La tradición eterna' (OCE I, 784–98; OCA III, 169–194).
[4]   See, for example, the essays 'La crisis actual del patriotismo español' and 'La Patria y el Ejército', published in *Nuestro Tiempo*, Madrid, on 25 December 1905 and 5 February 1906, respectively; in OCE I, 1286–98 and III, 843–53; OCA III, 937–956 and 975–991.

other things, he had given renewed expression to what he called his national, quixotic philosophy. This philosophy grew out of a new understanding of interpersonal relationships that was based on the concepts of irreplaceability and mutual imposition: individuals should endeavour to turn their lives into *obras* through which they can express and create themselves and also impose themselves on those around them and become irreplaceable for them; in that way, they can invade other people spiritually and also, hopefully, live on inside them (see Unamuno 1954 260–296; OCE VII, 421–425; OCA XVI, 384–419). As the Conclusion to that work made clear, Unamuno's own way of living out his new ethical imperative was to use his written works as a way of giving himself to his readers, awakening them in the process to the realities of their own lives and those of the world around them (Unamuno 1954 297–330; OCA XVI 420–451). With the loss of the Rectorship, which loosened Unamuno's ties to the Restoration even further, Unamuno turned more than ever to the daily press as his chosen vehicle for carrying out his mission of reaching out to and influencing others. He transformed his quixotic understanding of mutual imposition into a strikingly new philosophy of history that could guide him in his role as a politically committed intellectual. He would use his articles to root himself in the present moment of his nation and, from there, to engage in as radical and immediate a way as possible in the nation's everyday events, or *actualidad*, to show his readers how they too should take responsibility for their lives and for the larger context in which they lived those lives. They, then, would also in this way help to create the *historia* of their own nation (see, for example, Unamuno 1966: OCE VII, 998–1003 and III, 771–74; OCA XI, 953–962 and IV, 1154–1159).[5] It was this very personal and intellectual way of doing politics, so dependent as it was on the principle of free speech and on a free press, that brought Unamuno into direct conflict with what he saw as the militaristic and stultifying form of politics introduced by the new Dictator from September 1923 and led to him being deported to Fuerteventura the following February. It was also this way of doing politics, and the philosophy of history that underpinned it, that would enter into crisis during Unamuno's long years in exile.

Unamuno's Politics of Exile: Legend and Symbol

Legendary, mythical or symbolic politics is what Unamuno indulged in to the full during his time in exile. He started building his legend as an exile from the very moment that he was escorted from Salamanca on 21 February 1924, when,

---

5   For more details concerning Unamuno's quixotic philosophy, as expressed in *Del sentimiento trágico de la vida*, and his philosophy of history, as formulated in his press articles between 1914 and 1923, see Roberts (2007: 123–42 and 163–92).

as Salcedo (1998: 276) reminds us, he told the crowds that accompanied him to the railway station that 'I shall return, not with my liberty, which is worth nothing, but with yours'. With these words, Unamuno was signalling the fact that his case was more than just an individual one, that he was setting himself up as a representative of the best qualities of the Spanish people, a symbol of their precious but threatened freedoms. Unamuno was already functioning, therefore, on a higher, more symbolic level, that is, as an intellectual with a mythical presence on the national stage and in the national psyche. He knew full well that this was the best strategy for his time in exile. Primo de Rivera's obvious purpose in sending him into internal exile on Fuerteventura was to banish him to the margins of national life. But Unamuno would make a virtue of necessity and would focus instead on cultivating his legendary status and on ensuring his symbolic presence on the national scene. He would work hard, both in the essays that he continued to send to the Spanish press during the first seven or eight months of exile and in the poems that would eventually make up the collection *De Fuerteventura a París* (1925), to turn Fuerteventura itself into a mythical setting, a place where he could immerse himself in true *actualidad*, that is, in the deep present of his nation. He celebrated his literal isolation, the late arrival of news and the possibility of being in contact with *hechos* rather than *sucesos*, that is, with the underlying values of Spain (OCE VIII, 573–74 and 602–04; OCA X, 646–648 and 683–686). And it would be in this mythical, timeless setting that he would re-encounter Don Quixote and renew his profound identification with this emblem of the Spanish philosophy of life. As Unamuno's exile writings, not least the notes that make up the *Manual de quijotismo* (Unamuno 2005a: 79–134), reveal, Don Quixote would become his constant companion throughout these years, helping Unamuno to respond to all sorts of issues, political, ontological and religious. But, more importantly, Unamuno would use his essays and poems, above all those written in Fuerteventura, to present himself yet again to his public as a modern-day Don Quixote, forcibly absent now from a corrupt and decadent Spain.

There is no doubt that Unamuno's identification with Don Quixote played an important part in what Ana Urrutia Jordana (2003) has called the poeticisation of Unamuno's politics during his exile, but above all it allowed him to establish the terms of his political struggle. He would in fact fully indulge in a form of politics that he had started to cultivate in the early 1920s, that is, personality politics. Back in September 1920, he had reacted to the news that he had been sentenced to prison for insulting Alfonso XIII by announcing that the event had brought about a change of direction in his political activity and marked the start of a duel between the Monarch and himself: 'So a duel is being set up as a result? Let it be fought not on my behalf but that of Spain' (OCE VIII, 446;

OCA X, 463). A few years later, he would also turn his opposition to Primo de Rivera into a conflict between himself as a representative of the intellect, and the General as a representative of what he characterised as the brutal stupidity of the military and traditionalist mindset. Now, in exile in Fuerteventura, he would intensify this clash of personalities, transforming it into a mythical conflict between two symbols, Unamuno-Don Quixote and Primo de Rivera-Don Juan, who were engaged in a desperate struggle for the soul of Spain.[6] In this mythical schema, Primo de Rivera-Don Juan came to represent all that Unamuno took to be most reprehensible about the Spanish character and people, especially their espousal of a purely instinctual response to life (*gana*) and their consequent resistance to the message of ontological and spiritual openness and longing (*voluntad*) symbolised by Don Quixote.[7] Unamuno thereby reduced the whole of Spanish politics to a Manichaean conflict between himself and Primo de Rivera, that is, between two myths and two contrasting ways of understanding Spain and Spanishness, thereby cleverly signalling that all his many attacks on stupidity or on Spain's incapacity to espouse her quixotic heritage should also be read as political attacks on the Dictator and his Dictatorship itself. Moreover, he left his readers in no doubt that he had a higher power on his side in this struggle, presenting himself in the poems of *De Fuerteventura a París* as the disciple of Don Quixote whose job it was to save the soul of Spain or even as a modern-day Ezekiel directly receiving his orders from God.[8] Although he could no longer comment immediately in his articles on the political developments of his nation, therefore, he could at least use his poems and essays to keep alive his own personal legend and to point to its continuing significance in the moral drama being played out in Spain.

But Unamuno was not content to be the symbol of quixotic Spain solely within Spain herself. As his melodramatic escape from Fuerteventura to Paris in July 1924 reveals, he glimpsed in the idea of voluntary exile in a major European capital the possibility of both widening out his cause and calling international attention to it. On the one hand, he saw a move to Paris as an opportunity to become a Don Quixote with an influential role to play in the 'tragicomedia europea contemporánea', an opportunity exploited in *La agonía del cristianismo*. On the other, by accepting the plan for his escape drawn up and financed by Henri Dumay, proprietor of the left-leaning Parisian newspaper *Le Quotidien*, and openly rejecting Primo de Rivera's public pardon, Unamuno

---

6   See, for example, OCE VIII, 577–78 and 587–89; OCE X, 651–53 and 665–668, as well as Poem I of *De Fuerteventura a París* (OCE VI, 675; OCA XIV, 477)

7   See, for example, Poem CIII of *De Fuerteventura a París* and its accompanying note (OCE VI, 737; OCA XIV, 598–599).

8   See Poems XVII and XX (OCE VI, 683 and 685; OCA XIV, 493 and 496).

was deliberately choosing to continue to cultivate his role as an exile and also, as he would later admit, as a 'victim in the service of Spain' (OCE IX, 459; OCA VII, 1098–1103). He at first put the media attention that attended his arrival in France to good use and took advantage of the pages of *Le Quotidien* to play out his duel with Primo de Rivera and Alfonso XIII on a foreign and an international stage (for example, Unamuno 1996c: III, 280–94). But the internationalisation of his name and his cause came at a price, and Unamuno became wary of *Le Quotidien*'s use of his figure and also of the linguistic and ideological changes that were introduced into his articles by his translator; mutual mistrust soon brought his collaboration to an end.

Unamuno thereafter became more guarded about allowing his name and his cause to be used in foreign or international campaigns. His main objective in exile was clearly to aid in the overthrow of Primo de Rivera, and he would use his presence in a foreign land as a way of gaining prestige, cultivating his own personal legend, and thereby strengthening even further his idiosyncratic brand of personality politics. He would make these matters clear in the articles that he wrote for the clandestine broadsheets that became the main outlet for his political views once he decided, in late 1924, to stop writing for Spanish newspapers and journals. In 'No cabe elevar el tono' [Raising the Tone is not Fitting], one of the articles that he wrote for *España con Honra*, the weekly broadsheet that Blasco Ibáñez, Eduardo Ortega y Gasset and he founded in Paris in December 1924, Unamuno resisted the pressure to provide a doctrinaire reading of events in Spain and defiantly displayed once again his more personal and adversarial form of resistance to the Dictatorship (Ouimette 1976: 320–21). He would continue in the same vein in the twenty-three articles that he wrote for *Hojas Libres*, a monthly broadsheet that he ran with Eduardo Ortega y Gasset from Hendaye between April 1927 and January 1929.[9] Indeed, one of these articles, 'Mi pleito personal' [My Personal Plaint], offers a justification of his political tactics in exile. He reiterates first of all that his opposition to Primo de Rivera is not an individual but rather a personal affair, in the sense that he has deliberately transformed his individual case into a representative and a symbolic one. Then he explains that his duty as an intellectual is to increase his reputation and renown and to use it 'to free my country and to brand the tyrants permanently with the mark of the reprobates of history'. Finally, he goes out of his way to justify the personal and often violent invective that he employs against his enemies by claiming that the intellectual's main weapon is 'santo desdén' [blessed disdain]; in this, he adds, he is simply following the tradition of 'the great scornful figures of our religion', Moses, John the Baptist, St Paul, Dante,

---

[9]   Seventeen of these articles are reproduced in Comín Colomer 1968: 93–167; the remaining six are found in Unamuno 1996b: 57–88.

even Jesus Christ himself, all of whom had known how to use anger, disdain and insults in their various struggles against injustice (Comín Colomer 1968: 119–23). Unamuno's personalised political campaign led him, then, to adopt a tone of moral outrage and also to offer an increasingly inflated self-image as an oppressed outcast, suggesting perhaps that a growing sense of isolation was leading him to feel the need to shout ever louder in order to be heard in Spain. In the 1927 additions to *Cómo se hace una novela*, he once again likened himself to the great 'proscribed and scornful figures' Moses, St Paul, Dante, Mazzini and Victor Hugo (OCE VIII, 739: OCA X, 873), but also compared his position on the border in Hendaye to that of an usher guarding the doorway to his nation (OCE VIII, 769; OCA X, 923). Standing on the very threshold of Spain, he strove to transform himself into a symbol of what the Spanish people were lacking, and a scourge of their moral and spiritual incompleteness. He constantly reminded his Spanish readers that he was in possession of Spain's true personality and also of her conscience, and that he was, moreover, the moral judge who would not rest until he had silenced the tyrants and ensured that justice had been done (see, for example, Comín Colomer 1968: 120). In short, Unamuno's personality politics led him throughout exile to play the roles of victim, avenger, judge, jury, preacher and prophet, and even, at times, that of a jealous Old Testament God who was adamant that his people should rediscover the path to the Promised Land.

A return to the philosophy of history

As Unamuno played these symbolic or legendary roles in exile he also felt the need yet again to explore and explain the philosophy of history that underpinned his very notion of personality or legendary politics. This he did in the three main essayistic works that he produced in exile, *Alrededor del estilo* (1924), *La agonía del cristianismo* (1924) and *Cómo se hace una novela* (1924/27). Despite the fact that each of these works has a specific function of its own, they all end up also examining different aspects of this philosophy of history, the stylistic-ontological aspect in *Alrededor del estilo*, the religious-ethical aspect in *La agonía del cristianismo*, and the literary-political aspect in *Cómo se hace una novela*. I now intend to look at each of these works in turn, although I shall consider *Cómo se hace una novela* in greater detail, not only because it offers a more comprehensive examination of the contents and implications of Unamuno's philosophy of history but also because it reveals how that philosophy gradually comes apart under the pressure of the crisis that Unamuno started to experience in Paris in late 1924.

The main theme of *Alrededor del estilo*, a series of 31 short essays that Unamuno published in *Los Lunes de El Imparcial* (Madrid) in 1924, is literary style and, more specifically, the relationship between style and personality. But, as Unamuno explores how the writer expresses his personality in his work, he quickly and inevitably returns to the question of how he plays his own role as an intellectual and also to the philosophy of history that gives shape and meaning to that role. What ultimately comes to the fore, though, both here and in his other exile works, is the central importance that the activity of writing has for that role and that philosophy.

Alrededor del estilo offers a clear restatement of Unamuno's philosophy of history, itself based, of course, on the quixotic philosophy of selfhood first fully set out in *Del sentimiento trágico de la vida*. He starts by emphasising that meaningful human life can only take place within history (Unamuno 1998: 50 and 58–59): any individual who refuses to live in history is to be seen as someone who has not managed to become a full and self-aware human being with a role to play in civil society (42–43). Unamuno therefore provides a definition of the human subject that obviously has its origins in his own experience as an intellectual who lives his life on the public stage: 'el hombre', he tells us in the third essay, 'es la persona', a term that originally referred to the mask worn by Ancient Greek actors, later signified the role or the character that the actor played, and has now come to designate 'the role one plays in the tragicomedy of history, the character one plays' (42). It is by playing this role that one can come to know oneself, that one can discover one's personality and thereby become a fully historical being (42 and 45). Now, to know oneself is to know not what one is but rather what one wants to be (50). Unamuno equates the discovery of one's self with the discovery of one's *obra*, that is, one's life project, and makes clear that each person's duty is to create their individual *obra* through living and acting in history (101). And yet, despite Unamuno's exhortation that we should aim to complete our *obra* by the end of our lives, that is, that we should spend our lives fashioning a soul that can live on after our deaths, he is also at pains to point out that our *obra* reveals itself as it is, and is therefore finished and perfect, at each and every moment (125). This is where he re-introduces and re-establishes the temporal dimension of his philosophy of history. We must all root ourselves and our *obras* in the present moment, in the knowledge that 'what is specific to one time and place also belongs to all time and all places: it is eternal and infinite' (82).

Alrededor del estilo thus provides a reformulation of the general principles underlying Unamuno's philosophy of history. And yet what becomes very apparent over the course of the essays is the fact that this philosophy, although of relevance to all human beings who are willing to live in and through history, is at its core a writer's philosophy. As in *Del sentimiento trágico de la vida*, Unamuno clearly reveals that he creates his own *obra*, his own self, through the activity of writing. From this perspective, *Alrededor del estilo* offers an exploration of what it means to be an intellectual in the sense of someone who writes in order to create himself and influence others; it acts in effect as the poetics of the intellectual, the Unamunian intellectual.

Towards the end of the essays, Unamuno affirms that writing is his duty and obligation and that, like all those who write for their community, for their society, he must have style (137). By this, Unamuno means that he must express his personality, his own personal way of thinking, in his work (153–55). He who writes with style is in fact expressing and describing his own life in his writings (69–70). But writing is also and at the same time a creative or poetic activity (47), since the true creator, he tells us, creates himself by creating (66). What this means is that, for Unamuno, the self is not just a created entity but an entity that is created in and through the very act of writing itself. It is literally an *obra* that one writes moment by moment, and it is this historical *obra*, this written version of the self, that is finished and perfect at every moment (125). Unamuno believes therefore that art represents what he calls the 'eternalisation of the momentary' (126): by writing himself into the present moment, he hopes to achieve a literary form of lastingness (82), and the written self thus created will forever be rewritten and recreated by future generations of readers (127).

Unamuno puts forward a similar view of life in *La agonía del cristianismo*, a work in which he grounds his philosophy of history in his idiosyncratic and quixotic Christian beliefs. The overall intention of this work, which first appeared in French translation in late 1925, was to reveal to an international audience how Christianity should be seen as an agonic faith (OCE VII, 310–313; OCA XVI, 467–471), that is, as a faith that gains strength from the very contradictions that lie at its heart – contradictions which he had originally highlighted in *Del sentimiento trágico de la vida* –[10] although it becomes clear by the final chapter that Unamuno's growing sense of despair in exile has led him to a very negative reading of the present state of Christianity and of the civilisation that it has brought into existence (OCE VII, 359–364; OCA XVI, 552–559). Over the first chapters, however, he provides a confident reaffirmation of his philosophy of history. The historical man is the one who lives and will continue to live in others, in history (OCE VII, 317; OCA XVI, 478), and he can achieve this form of permanence by leaving his personality to history, that is, by bequeathing a verbal or written version of himself, a legend.

This is an idea that Unamuno develops further in *La agonía del cristianismo* through reference to Jesus Christ and St Paul, the very founders of the faith in

---

[10] In *Del sentimiento trágico de la vida*, of course, Unamuno focuses mainly on the contradiction between reason and faith, while in *La agonía del cristianismo* he also looks at the contradictions between active and passive faith, the Word and the letter, the resurrection of the flesh and the immortality of the soul.

which Unamuno is rooting his philosophy of history. For Unamuno, following Christian doctrine, Christ was God's Word made flesh, his whole life represented the direct and unmediated communication of the divine message (OCE VII, 315; OCA XVI, 475). But, once Christ died on the Cross, that message had to be conveyed in a different and less immediate way: the real, living Christ of flesh and blood had to be transformed into the historical Christ of legend. And this is what St Paul managed skilfully to do. He translated the ineffable Word into the written letter of his epistles and converted the living message into doctrine and dogma (OCE VII, 316; OCA XVI, 477 and 480); each of us can choose to submit to that doctrine and thereby transform the letter, the written legend, back into the living Word within us through an act of faith. Unamuno wishes to act as his own St Paul, converting his life, his message, his very self into a verbal, written form that he can then hand over to his present and future readers in the hope that they will learn from it and have both the desire and the capacity to bring it back to life within them (OCE VII, 309; OCA XVI, 464). At the same time, however, he is bitterly aware of two threatening facts that will come back to haunt him in *Cómo se hace una novela*: first, that the letter kills the Word (OCE VII, 318–320; OCA XVI, 480–484), that is, that the written version of the self will always be a debased and lifeless reflection of the lived experience of the self; and, second, that the writer's need to have his written self brought back to life makes him inescapably dependent upon his readers.

And so we reach *Cómo se hace una novela*, Unamuno's most important work of exile and one that is made up of two distinct parts: the original nucleus, which was written in December 1924 and July 1925 in Paris and published, in French translation, in *Le Mercure de France* in June 1926, and the 'Prólogo', 'Comentario', 'Continuación' and sundry bracketed commentaries that Unamuno added to the original nucleus in Hendaye between May and July 1927 as he translated it back into Spanish in readiness for its publication in Buenos Aires. The final result is an extraordinary and unclassifiable work that is part autobiography, part political commentary, part short story, part literary criticism and part philosophy. It also incorporates most of the genres that Unamuno cultivated as a writer and intellectual: a diary that captures the daily movements of his spirit; short articles that offer a chronicle of *actualidad*; essays that deal with questions relating to style, literary creation, role-playing, selfhood and the activities of reading and writing; fiction in the shape of a short story that is assembled in front of our eyes; and even a poem that captures Unamuno's state of mind as he gazes across the border into Spain. *Cómo se hace una novela* is, in short, a highly self-reflexive text that asks pointed questions about its own status, about the activity of writing, and also, more widely, about what it means to be an intellectual. More than any other of his texts, it reveals the full nature and significance of Unamuno's role as an intellectual, a role that he has been building and perfecting since the later 1890s. First, we shall see how Unamuno plays his role as an intellectual and attempts to reaffirm his philosophy of history in the original nucleus. Secondly, we shall consider how Unamuno's intellectual worldview gradually enters into crisis over the course of that original nucleus, with the result that he is forced to ask penetrating questions about the role that he is playing, his philosophy of history and his whole intellectual enterprise. Finally, we shall see how he manages to reassemble and reaffirm his philosophy of history in the 1927 Hendaye additions, and does so in a way that sheds new light on certain key aspects of his role as an intellectual.

The original nucleus of *Cómo se hace una novela* starts off like an article that reveals its workings to the reader and, in the process, gives voice to the very philosophy of history that animates it. Instead of providing us with a chronicle of *actualidad*, it reveals the chronicler preparing himself to write such a chronicle and thinking about what motivates him to do so. The chronicler, the intellectual, Unamuno sits in front of the blank page trying to pour his life into the written word in order thus to give it a lasting form (OCE VIII, 729; OCE X, 857). He wishes to use words in order to root himself in what he once referred to as 'la actualidad [...] perdurable' [the lasting present moment] (Unamuno 1996c: I, 270–73). And yet Unamuno is acutely aware that what he has so far written in exile has failed, in a sense, to live up to his philosophy of history, that is, that he has not managed to create a lasting version of his self, his *obra*, his soul in his daily writings, and he decides that the best way of remedying this situation is to show that philosophy in action, to reveal exactly how it works.

To that end, he undertakes to write a short story, the tale of a young man, Jugo de la Raza, who discovers a book that seems to awaken him both to the possibility of a richer life of self-creation and self-realisation and to the threat of death and annihilation. Unamuno's initial intention is to project himself into this autobiographical character or construct, which he can then create in front of our eyes. He stresses that all fiction is autobiographical and that all fictional characters form part of their author (OCE VIII, 731; OCA X, 860): by creating Jugo, therefore, he aims to reveal to us how he goes about creating his own personal legend in exile (OCE VIII, 734; OCA X, 865). And yet, before he starts telling the story, Unamuno changes tack and decides to tell us instead how he would go about telling it (OCE VIII, 734; OCA X, 865). Just as he started the original nucleus by revealing the workings of the press article, so he will now reveal the workings and inner significance of his short story. In this way, he will be able to show how he transforms it into an exemplary tale that uses the idea of reading a novel as a metaphor for living itself. In short, Jugo's tale becomes for Unamuno a means of expounding and explaining his philosophy of history, and it is perhaps for this reason that he chooses to call his autobiographical character 'Jugo de la Raza' (which may be translated as 'the essence of the race'):

Jugo's story does indeed convey the philosophy of history that has emerged from the specifically Spanish and quixotic philosophy of selfhood that Unamuno first set out in *Del sentimiento trágico de la vida*.

What Jugo de la Raza's tale illustrates first of all is the need to live in history. Before he finds the book that will change his life, we are told, Jugo lives 'in the impoverished self who has not yet reached history, in the sad man who has not made a novel of himself' (OCE VIII, 734; OCA X, 866). Before history there is nothing, no mirror for us to see and know ourselves in, no consciousness, no self-awareness (185). Jugo needs therefore to enter history, and his tale shows us how he attempts to do so by seeking out novels that can reflect his image back to him (OCE VIII, 735; OCA X, 866). Eventually he discovers a novel in a bookstall on the banks of the Seine that captures his attention and causes him to identify with the central character, who informs him that he, Jugo, will die along with him at the end of the story (OCE VIII, 735; OCA X, 867). What the opening of Jugo's tale neatly shows, therefore, is the very process by which we enter history and become fully historical beings. In *Alrededor del estilo*, Unamuno had stressed that the artist or writer can only find his own personal style by imitating that of those he admires just as, more radically and following the ideas on selfhood laid out in *Del sentimiento trágico de la vida*, the individual can only find and know himself as a human being through others (Unamuno 1998: 46 and 101). Jugo's experience captures this process perfectly: he discovers that the novel he is reading 'takes him out of himself [i.e., out of the impoverished self not living in history], inserts him into the protagonist of the novel, identifies him with that other and, in sum, gives him a history/story' (OCE VIII, 735; OCA X, 866). Jugo's task is therefore to make this 'history/story' his own, that is, to come to see his own life as a 'history/story' or a novel that he can forge and shape himself by acting and interacting with others. As the rest of the tale goes on to illustrate, this task is not an easy one, not least because it is both overshadowed and motivated by the threat and the fear of death. But, as Unamuno makes clear in his commentaries on the tale, it has to be done. The legendary, historical self (OCE VIII, 734; OCA X, 864) is the only one we can see and know, and the only one who may finally 'live in enduring and permanent history and not die' (OCE VIII, 747; OCA X, 885). And not only that, adds Unamuno, but, by making our novel-selves, we will also be able to contribute, like him, to the creation of the community, the *patria* to which we belong (OCE VIII, 733; OCA X, 863).

In Jugo's tale and the commentaries that accompany it, therefore, Unamuno not only justifies the fact that he has transformed himself into a legend that can act and live on in history but also skilfully exploits the metaphor of life-as-a-novel in order to encourage others to follow his own example. But he in fact goes much further than this, making clear that, for him at least, life is literally a novel, that is, a verbal and word-bound experience. Before starting Jugo's story, he claims that he is a biblical being, a man of books, a person who lives principally from and in reading (OCE VIII, 732; OCA X, 862). It is only by becoming a man of the Book, by living in and through words, that he can achieve self-awareness and self-knowledge and thereby become a historical being; he exists only in the novel or *historia* that he creates by writing. This is truly an intellectual's or a writer's view of the world and proves once again that Unamuno's philosophy of history is intimately wrapped up with the activity of writing. It also has some extremely important implications for Unamuno the intellectual, such as his belief that he is able to influence invents and create history in and through his articles and books (OCE VIII, 732–4; OCA X, 862–4).

As Unamuno sets about illustrating and communicating his intellectual worldview in *Cómo se hace una novela*, however, it gradually comes apart in front of his very eyes. He is then forced for the first time fully to confront the consequences of being an intellectual and the implications of his philosophy of history. This is not to say, of course, that he had never before entertained any doubts or misgivings about playing a public role. Frances Wyers (1976) has shown how the existential and religious crisis he suffered in 1897 left Unamuno with lasting concerns about the relationship between public activity and private identity. And it is quite clear that those concerns became more pronounced after 1914 as Unamuno became increasingly involved in political life and devoted more and more time to cultivating his public legend.[11] An awareness of the threat of insincerity that attended his particular form of legendary politics was also accompanied at times, as in the 1920 article 'Proletariado de la pluma' [Proletariat of the Pen], by a fear of the insubstantial nature of the self that lives in and through the publicity machine (OCE VIII, 441; OCA X, 457). And, in exile itself, it is clear that Unamuno gestured to the problem of living in words as he discussed the vexed relationship between *Verbo* [living word] and *letra* [written word] in the fourth chapter of *La agonía del cristianismo*.

And yet the doubts about his role that we find in the original nucleus of *Cómo se hace una novela* are of a different order and ultimately lead to the unravelling of Unamuno's entire philosophy of history. Why should this be so? The simple answer to this question lies in the fact that, by December 1924, Unamuno was at last feeling the full effects of exile. He considered Paris, unlike Fuerteventura, to be a truly foreign place, an alien landscape full of *sucesos* rather than *hechos*, as he put it in *La agonía del cristianismo* (Unamuno 1996a: 78). Exile there represented a huge physical and cultural displacement for him, but, much more

---

[11]   See, for example, the 1914 article '¡Que piensen! ¡Que piensen!' (OCE VIII, 337–339; OCA X, 299–303)

importantly, it also represented what could be called a temporal displacement.[12]
We have repeatedly seen how Unamuno's philosophy of history entailed him
inhabiting what he characterised as the deep or eternal present of his nation, a
space from which he could speak out as an intellectual, participate in the events
that were shaping Spain's history, and encourage his readers to do the same.
His voluntary exile in France served to remove him from this national, eternal
present and caused Unamuno to lose his temporal centre and coordinates. It is
for this reason that, as he eloquently reveals in the original nucleus of *Cómo se
hace una novela*, he comes to experience time in Paris in terms of a constant
and anguishing slippage either towards a future of hopes and expectations or
towards a past of memories and nostalgia (OCE VIII, 729–30, 736–737, 741–742;
OCA X, 857–859, 868–869, 877–878). In short, exile revealed to Unamuno just
how closely his role as an intellectual had served to bind him to the body of his
nation, to his readers, to his community. Through the national press, he had
created a space for himself at the very heart of Spanish public life that had also
placed him, in his own mind at least, at the very heart of Spain's present, her
actualidad, her history. He had lost all of that now, and, like many other exiles
before and since, came to feel that the only trace of his nation left to him was
to be found in his native language. He would turn to the Spanish language, as
we see at the very start of *Cómo se hace una novela*, in a desperate attempt to
stop time and rediscover the eternal – and national – present that he has lost.
But such a search is doomed to failure, since he is in fact writing and playing
his role in a vacuum, cut off both from the national present itself and from the
readers to whom his writings are addressed. Unamuno seems to be trapped
within his own written and verbal world and even, on occasions, strikes a frankly
delusional note, such as when he wonders not only whether Primo de Rivera
and his like exist as he describes them but whether they actually exist at all
outside his own mind (OCE VIII, 745; OCA X, 882).

Unsurprisingly, such conditions placed an enormous strain on Unamuno's
philosophy of history and on his whole project as a writer and an intellectual.
What we find in the original nucleus of *Cómo se hace una novela*, therefore,
is the expression of a true writer's or intellectual's crisis that asks some deeply
unsettling questions about Unamuno's notion of legendary politics and, more
specifically, about the self that is created through playing a role, and the activity
of writing through which that role is played. Unamuno desperately tries to
defend his personal strain of legendary politics throughout this text, especially
against those within Spain who advise him to leave politics altogether. The
latter, he states, in an indirect attack on those Spanish intellectuals who are

---

[12] On this point, see Roberts (2000b).

not bothering to oppose the Dictatorship, do not realise that his writings, even his literary and poetic writings, have a political function and that he is duty-bound to make his life into a poem that can help to bring about political change (OCE VIII, 736, 751; OCA X, 868, 892). In fact, Unamuno makes clear that he is existentially as well as politically compelled to turn his life into a poem or a legend, since, if he did not do so, he would in fact die (OCE VIII, 745; OCA X, 882). And yet, at the same time, he tells us, that poem or legend not only gives him life but also threatens the very core of his being: 'it creates and destroys me, it sustains me and it chokes me. It is my final suffering' (OCE VIII, 734; OCA X, 865).

Why should Unamuno come to see his legend as something that destroys him? The first reason lies in the very fact that it involves him playing a public role. As we saw in *Alrededor del estilo*, Unamuno believed that it was only by playing a role that the individual can become a historical *persona*. But, Unamuno is now forced to ask, how can he ever be sure that the role he is playing, and therefore the legend he is creating, is authentic? On three separate occasions during the course of the original nucleus of *Cómo se hace una novela*, Unamuno comes to question the authenticity of his role in exile: the first is when he claims that he cannot return to Spain because, if he were to lose his liberty or his life as a result, no-one would do anything or be able to take his place (OCE VIII, 745; OCA X, 882); the second is when he expresses the conviction that his political enemies must be feeling remorse for what they have done to him (OCE VIII, 745; OCA X, 882); and the third is when he admits that he may even be playing the role of an exile for his own family, especially by not looking after himself and cultivating a slovenly self-image (OCE VIII, 746; OCA X, 884). Unamuno is therefore becoming highly conscious of the fact that his role is causing him to strike poses, make grand statements and even become self-righteous. He tries to counteract the self-accusations of inauthenticity or hypocrisy each time by claiming that 'my role is my truth and I must live my truth, which is my life' (OCE VIII, 746; OCA X, 884), but the doubts remain, so much so in fact that he admits at one point that he has been avoiding writing and acting altogether 'for fear of being devoured by my actions' (OCE VIII, 736; OCA X, 868).

The second reason for Unamuno's doubts lies in his claim that his legend is not created by him alone but rather in conjunction with others, both friends and enemies (OCE VIII, 734; OCA X, 865). This idea is rooted, of course, in the concept of selfhood put forward in *Del sentimiento trágico de la vida*, where Unamuno had shown how the self needs others in the process of self-knowledge, self-creation and self-perpetuation. But what *Del sentimiento trágico de la vida* never considered were the implications of this view of selfhood and interpersonal relationships, especially the fact that it makes the self totally dependent on

others. In the original nucleus of *Cómo se hace una novela*, by contrast, Unamuno
becomes very conscious of the fact that, despite his best efforts, his legend floats
free of him and places itself at the mercy of those around him, both his supporters
and his detractors. He notices the effects that his words and writings have on
others and asks himself at one point whether what he thinks he says is what
they actually hear him say (OCA VIII, 874; OCE VIII, 740). At another point,
his concerns about the reception of the legend that he is creating of himself lead
him even to doubt whether his real self lies in the legend as he presents it to
others or in the legend as it is then used and abused by them: 'Am I the self I
believe myself to be or the self that others believe me to be?' (OCE VIII, 734;
OCA X, 865). And, underlying all these doubts about the authenticity of the
legendary self is the realisation that that self is in reality no more than a verbal
construct, the Word made letter, an insubstantial entity indeed that is completely
vulnerable to the manipulations of friendly or hostile readers.

So, legendary politics, Unamuno comes fully to realise in the original nucleus
of *Cómo se hace una novela*, involves the creation and projection of a legendary
self that may exercise political influence and may last in words but is also always
open to the charge of inauthenticity and insubstantiality. Such a realisation
becomes so overwhelming at one point that Unamuno talks as if he should like
to withdraw from historical activity altogether and take refuge in what he calls
his divine or intimate self: 'Am I not perhaps on the verge of sacrificing my
intimate, divine self, the self I am in God, the self I should be, to the other,
historical self, the self that moves in and along with its history?' (OCE VIII,
745; OCA X, 882). This question, so unexpected in a text that has hitherto
associated what lies outside history with nothingness, serves in reality to place
Unamuno's whole philosophy of history in jeopardy,[13] and, over the rest of the
original nucleus, Unamuno tries his best to cover up or deny the existence of
this gap that he himself has opened up in his notion of selfhood. He does this
by making a series of equivalences (between his role and his truth, phenomena
and noumena, form and substance, surfaces and depths [OCE VIII, 746, 753;
OCA X, 884, 895–6]) that seem increasingly contrived and unconvincing. In
the end, he decides to conclude by avoiding the issue altogether and by deflecting
all his doubts and concerns back onto the reader. In a clever but not completely
persuasive restatement of the main message of the work, he therefore says of
the imaginary reader who yet again accuses him of insincere role-playing that

[13]   As Zubizarreta (1960: 262–81) and Turner (1974: 111–12) both show, this momentary
longing for a God-given, unchanging inner self is reminiscent of the 1897 crisis, when Unamuno
gave expression to a dual notion of selfhood (the *eterno yo* and the *yo social*). After the crisis,
as Wyers (1976: 3–18) affirms, Unamuno tended to associate the idea of an inner self with the
self that one wants to be, that is, the self that can be realised through historical activity.

'this indignant reader is angered by my showing him that he, in turn, is also a comic, novelistic character, and, no less, a character that I want to place right in the middle of the dream of his life. If he can make this dream, his dream, a life, he will have saved himself' (OCE VIII, 753; OCA X, 895).

The original nucleus of *Cómo se hace una novela* is a powerful expression of an intellectual crisis that has almost led to intellectual paralysis. Like Jugo de la Raza, Unamuno has contemplated the idea of rejecting historical action altogether, fearing that a life in history not only undermines his very sense of self but also provides no substantial answer to the threat of death. He is held back from such a course of action, however, by the realisation that a life outside history would not be a real life and would end in death too, an even more definitive death, perhaps (OCE VIII, 748; OCA X, 887). And yet he can find no answer to the questions that have confronted him during his crisis in Paris, and will not in fact be able to do so until he leaves the French capital for Hendaye. There, on the French-Spanish border, as he makes clear in the 1927 additions to *Cómo se hace una novela*, his immersion in the Basque culture of his youth places him in renewed contact with his childhood, an experience that provides his self with a sense of the past, with depth and roots (OCE VIII, 757–8; OCA X, 905–6). But the proximity to Spain also enables him to rediscover the national and eternal present that he had so sorely missed in Paris, and this rediscovery leads him to produce a supremely confident restatement of his philosophy of history. He equates the eternal present with what he calls true *actualidad*, explaining that the here and the now represent for him the foci of infinity and eternity (OCE VIII, 765; OCA X, 846, 918). 'History, the only living force' he tells us, 'is the eternal present, the fleeting moment which remains as it passes and that passes as it remains' (OCE VIII, 711; OCA X, 830), and he strives to inhabit this present moment and to create and eternalise himself in and through it (OCE 765; OCA X, 918). By living in this way, he can become a truly historical person, someone who creates his spirit as an *obra* moment by moment (OCE VIII, 760; OCA X, 909). Leading such an existence lies at the very heart not only of his personal but also of his political project; his aim is to 'save, defend my person, to assert it, make it enter into history for ever' (OCE VIII, 723; OCA X, 846), and, by doing so, to encourage others to follow his example and do the same (OCE VIII, 725; OCA X, 849). He once again defends the 'mundo novelesco' or world of words in which verbal and written self-creation takes place (OCE VIII, 760–1; OCA X, 910), and adds that this world can never in fact end, since the life of those who have transformed themselves into novels, *historias* or legends lives on in those of their readers (OCE VIII, 763–4; OCA X, 913–915). His confident conclusion, which acts as a justification both of his attitude to life and of his activity as a politically committed intellectual, is thus that 'Every man, every true man, is son of a legend, whether written or oral. And there is nothing more than legend, or rather novel' (OCE VIII, 764; OCA X, 916).

Unamuno's time in Hendaye enabled him, therefore, to reassemble and reassert his philosophy of history. It also allowed him to clear up his doubts about inauthenticity and insubstantiality – and to do so in ways that shed new light on his whole project as an intellectual. Unamuno's re-encounter with childhood memories in his native Basque Country put him in renewed contact, as he made clear through the medium of Jugo de la Raza's tale, with the child that he had been before becoming a reader and an 'hombre de libro' [bookish man], that is, with what Unamuno calls his 'hombre interior [inner man], el *eso anthropos*' (OCE VIII, 758; OCA X, 906). But, unlike the original nucleus, where he had associated innerness with some sort of divine self cut off from the historical one, Unamuno sees the inner man in the 1927 additions simply as one dimension of a deep self that is fully committed to historical activity. Building on Wordsworth's idea that the child is father of the man, Unamuno develops the notion that the inner self can become the father – the author or creator – of the outer, historical self (OCE VIII, 758–761; OCA X, 906–911). He had already been finding his way towards such a notion at the end of the original nucleus, where he had told his reader to see himself as both the 'actor and author of your self' (OCE VIII, 754; OCA X, 896–7), but he now has the confidence fully to transform the mutually exclusive inner and outer selves that had appeared in that original nucleus into different aspects of the same historical self. According to this view, he explains, 'when he becomes a reader, contemplator, the inner man, the intra-man—if he is alive—must make himself a reader, a contemplator of the character he is reading, and, at the same time, making—a contemplator of his own work' (OCE VIII, 760; OCA X, 909). The truly historical man, in other words, must act in history and thereby create his *obra*, that is, his novel or legend, but he must also continually observe and revise that *obra* in order to ensure that it remains alive and retains its authenticity. He must also realise that the process of self-creation is a never-ending one and follow Unamuno's example when he says of himself towards the end of the 1927 additions that 'I have made myself a problem, a question, a project. How is this resolved? By making the problem into a trajectory, by making the problem into a "metablem"; by struggling' (OCE VIII, 766; OCA X, 918).

Self-revision seems therefore to be Unamuno's guarantor of authenticity. But he is very aware of the fact that authentic – and substantial – selfhood also depends on others. The individual acts and writes, creates a written version of himself, transforms his self into a written legend, precisely in order to be able to give himself to others, to his readers and fellow human beings. And yet he can only be confident that they will accept him if he ensures that his written self is of significance to them, that is, to quote *Del sentimiento trágico de la vida*, if that self is perceived to be 'irreplaceable'. This is why Unamuno goes out of his way to prove that he is not writing for purely selfish reasons but rather that he is defending others by defending himself (OCE VIII, 726; OCA X, 852) and shedding light on his own experiences (*alumbrarse*) in the hope that those experiences can in turn illuminate (*alumbrar*) those of his readers (OCE VIII, 768–9; OCA X, 922–3). It is more than clear, however, that the whole process of verbal self-creation is in fact a deeply problematic one. As we saw in *La agonía del cristianismo*, it involves turning the Word of lived experience into the letter of written experience. Writing kills, he informs us in the 1927 Prólogo to *Cómo se hace una novela*, and literature is death – although it is a form of death from which others can take life (OCE VIII, 711; OCA X, 830). But others can only take life from a text if they know how to read, that is, if they know how to transform the *letra* back into the *Verbo*. If they can do this, if they can bring the text and the self it expresses back to life within them, then they can both receive its message and afford it new life on every reading.

Unamuno therefore needs good readers, and this is why the greater part of the 1927 additions to *Cómo se hace una novela* is devoted to the task of teaching his readers how to read, a task that lies at the very heart of Unamuno's lifelong role and project as an intellectual: his aim ever since the late 1890s had been to create his readership and to educate and form his readers. In *Cómo se hace una novela*, Unamuno makes this role and project more explicit than ever. He urges his readers to eat his books, to live and relive them, to create and revive them (OCE VIII, 711, 720; OCA X, 830, 841). He exhorts them to write the books they read, that is, to turn them into a means of knowing and creating themselves (OCE 760–761; OCA X, 910–911). He also bitterly criticises those unable to eat and assimilate what they read, singling out the present leaders of Spain as sufferers from the resultant narrow-mindedness and stupidity (OCE VIII, 720, 769; OCA X, 841, 923). In short, Unamuno's main aim as an intellectual is to turn his readers into writers and intellectuals like himself, that is, into quixotic individuals who are able to join in the process of mutual and verbal self-creation and self-perpetuation. What the 1927 additions to *Cómo se hace una novela* confirm once and for all is that it is the activities of writing and reading that allow individuals to give the best of themselves, to meet and to fuse (OCE VIII, 761; OCA X, 911–12).

And here, finally, also lies the secret of Unamuno's notion of community. The activity of writing for the Unamunian intellectual is not solely or even principally about the self but rather has a deeply ethical and political aim: 'Why, or rather, to what end is a novel made? In order that the novelist be made. And to what end is a novelist made? To make the reader, make the novelist one with the reader' (OCE VIII, 768; OCA X, 922). Only in this way can the writer and the reader overcome their radical solitude and actualise and eternalise themselves and each other (OCE VIII, 768; OCA X, 922), so also creating a *patria*, a *patria* that is a community of intellectually and spiritually aware writers and readers, a community, that is, of true intellectuals. These intellectuals create their *patria* by coming together to write and create their own novels, their own lives; that *patria* is thus like a collective text that is constantly being written and rewritten, created and recreated, which is why Unamuno ends *Cómo se hace una novela* by claiming that 'I am here, in exile, to make our novel, our history, that of our Spain' (OCE VIII, 769; OCA X, 923). Unamuno's ideal Spain is not, therefore, a fixed entity but rather something that is forever being made through its inhabitants' constant search to find permanence in and through each other. It is a *camino* (pathway) rather than a destination or an arrival point, he concludes, echoing the ideas on community implicitly contained in the pages of *Del sentimiento trágico de la vida*, where he had claimed that the ideal community represents the eternal coming of God's Kingdom on Earth (OCE VIII, 768; OCA X, 921–2).

Other exile works

Cómo se hace una novela is undoubtedly the most important work that Unamuno wrote about the role of the intellectual. It both expresses the doubts and anxieties that he felt about intellectual activity and provides the most detailed and eloquent defence of his role and his aims as an intellectual. It also confirms once and for all that the fact of being an intellectual lies at the very heart of his worldview, informing his views on selfhood, otherness, role-playing, writing and community, and gathering these disparate elements up into a complex and coherent philosophy of life. And yet, despite the confident nature of its 1927 additions, *Cómo se hace una novela* remains a work of crisis that is built out of a number of tensions and conflicts, such as those between commitment and withdrawal, the drive to act and write and the fear of inauthenticity and insubstantiality, tensions and conflicts that continued to surface in the other works he wrote in Hendaye, especially the three plays of the time. He had in fact written two of these plays, *El otro* and *Sombras de sueño*, shortly after his arrival in Hendaye, that is, between the original nucleus of *Cómo se hace una novela* and the 1927 additions. Not surprisingly, these plays had dealt with the issues of selfhood, role-playing and authenticity that had dogged Unamuno during the crisis of 1924–1925. While *El otro* explored the question of envy and the fragility of personal identity in terms directly borrowed from *Del sentimiento trágico de la vida*, *Sombras de sueño* took on what was an even more topical theme for Unamuno by considering how the central character, Julio Macedo, attempts to escape public activity and take up a life outside history, only to find that his exploits as the famous revolutionary Tulio Montalbán have gone before him and that he will never in fact be able to slough off his legendary self. Through Julio, Unamuno expressed all his frustration with the weight of his public role and with the fact that his sense of self was totally dependent on the way in which the legend he was creating was perceived by others, and yet he still had his protagonist say towards the climax of the play that 'those of us who tread the stage of the theatre of history are the truest beings, the enduring beings' (OCE V, 641; OCA XII, 789). In the play that he wrote shortly after the 1927 additions to *Cómo se hace una novela*, *El hermano Juan*, Unamuno considers the same theme through the character of Don Juan, the Spanish literary archetype who had hitherto featured heavily in Unamuno's anti-Primo de Rivera propaganda. This play represents something of a reconciliation with Don Juan, an attempt by Unamuno to understand the deeper significance of the figure and the myth.[14] In the 1934 Prologue to the work, he would explain that 'the entire ideal grandeur, the entire universal and eternal reality—that is, the historical reality—of Don Juan Tenorio lies in his being the most eminently theatrical, representative, historical character, in that he is always being represented, that is to say, always representing himself' (OCE V, 714; OCA XII, 866). Unamuno's Hermano Juan is in fact no more than a role or a character that is constantly being played for the benefit of others; he is literally a legend whose entire existence depends on the response and receptiveness of other people. Through him, therefore, Unamuno gives voice to the anxieties that he feels about the nature and status of the legendary self that is created through public activity. Even when Juan convinces himself that the only possible existence takes place in the theatre of the world (OCE V, 814; OCE XII, 983), he still has to face up to the fact that his legendary self is insubstantial and does not actually belong to him: 'Juan, Juan, Juan, can you see yourself? Can you hear yourself? Can you hear yourself? Can you feel? Are you your own being? Are you the creature of Inés and Elvira? Of Matilde? Are you the creature of Antonio and Benito? Are you the creature of the audience?' (OCE V, 785; OCA XII, 951). There is in fact something almost posthumous about this play, as if Unamuno, resigned as he is to having to create his legend, is desperately trying to come to terms not only with how that legend is being perceived by those around him but also with the question of how it will be treated once he is dead.

El hermano Juan, and also the 1,445 poems of the *Cancionero* that Unamuno wrote before his return to Spain on 9 February 1930, reveal the ebb and flow of his spirit as he waited for the Dictatorship to end. Whatever the misgivings that he may have felt about legendary politics and the insubstantiality of the self created through writing, there can be no doubt that the legend he had forged of himself had haunted and hunted Primo de Rivera over the years and would play an important part in his downfall in late January 1930. It is clear that

---

14   On this point, see Roberts (2011) and Biggane (2013).

Unamuno himself felt as much, as is witnessed in a talk that he gave in Valladolid on 12 February, where he claimed that it was the students who, as his spiritual children and under his tutelage and guidance, had done more than any other group in society to bring about the Dictator's fall.[15] The fervent and multitudinous welcome that Unamuno received upon his return to Spain represented both a vindication of his legendary politics and the apotheosis of the intellectual. Never since the generals of the nineteenth century had a public figure been so feted and lionised, and this was an intellectual, not a general, who was being touted by some as the possible Head of State of a future Republic.[16] The final six years of his life, however, which saw him espouse and reject both the Second Republic and the military rising against the Republic in July 1936, continued to be marked by the attraction and fear of public activity that had come so painfully to the surface during Unamuno's exile in France.

Further Reading

Biggane (2009, 2013), Cerezo Galán (1996), Juaristi (2012), Ouimette (1998), Rabaté & Rabaté (2009), Roberts (2007, 2013), Sinclair (2001) Unamuno (2005a), Urrutia Jordana (2003), Urrutia León (1997), Zubizarreta (1960).

---

[15] Pascal Mezquita (2003: 111). See also Unamuno's talk in the Madrid Ateneo of 2 May 1930; in Unamuno (1986: 83).

[16] On this point, see Pascal Mezquita (2003: 26–27).

4

Return from Exile: Politics and Poetics 1930–1936

PEDRO RIBAS RIBAS

During the years of his exile in France (1924–1930), Unamuno suffered greatly as a victim of the Primo de Rivera military dictatorship, but he took on the struggle against the regime as a moral and political duty. This period was painful, then, but at the same time, exile became the best platform for the international dissemination and resonance of his work: he received many offers to translate his writings from a variety of countries. Unamuno was sixty-six years old when he returned to Spain, and the remaining seven years of his life were not tranquil or easy: he took on a formal political role as a member of parliament in the new Republic; his beloved wife, Concepción Lizárraga died in 1934; he became increasingly alienated from the Republic, and lent initial support to the military coup against it in 1936—a coup that triggered the Spanish Civil War. He continued to produce literary work only in the first part of this period; after 1931, his output was mostly journalistic, and social or political in content. This chapter will examine his final literary texts, and will explore his political activities and thought during the Second Republic. It will seek, in particular, to elucidate his actions and evolving position vis-a-vis the Civil War, which have been the subject of much debate, controversy and at times misrepresentation. Certainly his actions during the war have shaped his reputation in some quarters, so careful, objective analysis of his changing political position over this period is crucial.

Shortly after his return from exile, Unamuno completed three novellas—*La novela de Don Sandalio, jugador de ajedrez*, *Un pobre hombre rico, o el sentimiento cómico de la vida*, and *San Manuel Bueno, mártir*—that would turn out to be his last fictional works. This late literary production is partly characterised by a return to earlier preoccupations and themes: *San Manuel Bueno, mártir* reprises elements of the rural, intrahistorical existence represented in *Paz en la guerra* and *En torno al casticismo*; *Un pobre hombre rico*'s subtitle – *el sentimiento cómico de la vida* – playfully evokes the title of the 1912 essay *El sentimiento trágico de la vida*, and both *San Manuel Bueno, mártir* and *La novela de Don Sandalio* explore the oppressive discontinuities between one's public persona and one's interior self—a focus of earlier texts such as *Tulio Montalbán y Julio Macedo* (1920). This last preoccupation seems to have been intensified by Unamuno's experience of exile: it is a notable theme of *Cómo se hace una novela*, and features prominently particularly in Unamuno's drama of the period: *Sombras de sueño* (1926 – an adaptation of his 1920 short story *Tulio Montalbán y Julio Macedo*), *El otro* (1926) and *El hermano Juan, o el mundo es teatro*, which was written in 1929, all address the determined, painful attempts of protagonists to throw off an erroneous public or exterior image. All discover, though, that there is no straightforwardly knowable or communicable personality lying intact beneath the outward persona. Furthermore, unlike public reputation, which can long outlast mortal life, personality is, in the words of M. Gordon, 'condemned to insubstantiality' after death (1986: 157). The protagonists' struggle with these problems ends tragically in *Sombras de sueño* and *El otro*; it is more redemptive in the tragicomedy *El hermano Juan*, but all protagonists are irrevocably divided and remain mysterious figures—both to themselves and to others. Given the international attention thrust on Unamuno by his banishment in 1924, together with the hostile scrutiny he was subjected to by the Primo de Rivera regime and its sympathisers thereafter, it is unsurprising that this already-present theme in his work should be heightened by exile and persist after Unamuno's return to Spain in 1930, which, for all its triumphs, created an unwelcome burden of public expectation.

Unamuno's late fictional work, then, readdresses previous philosophical preoccupations, for all that it may also be marked by Unamuno's experience of exile. But it also departs from earlier work in notable ways. *Un pobre hombre rico* is one of the very few Unamuno texts that apparently ends on a note of happiness. An ageing, wealthy, cautious protagonist, Emeterio, lonely but single partly because he is afraid of being loved only for his money, finally marries, acquiring a step-family and then an heir. As Robert Nozick notes, the tale ends with Emeterio's paean to the 'satisfactions of even a belated marriage, the indispensable comic sense of life (despite what Unamuno says, declares Emeterio) which is the enjoyment of creaturely pleasures [...] anything is preferable to solitude, even being taken in' (1971: 159). *La novela de Don Sandalio*, too, represents a structural, if not thematic departure from previous work in that it is the only epistolary text that Unamuno ever wrote. In the novella, an unnamed letter-writer, who has left his hometown and has largely withdrawn from social life for reasons unknown to the reader, becomes briefly and barely acquainted with the enigmatic Don Sandalio in a gentleman's club in the remote coastal town: the two men play near-wordless games of chess with each other. The reader is presented with only one side of the correspondence between the letter-writer and a friend called Felipe, and this structure is a particularly effective formal device for the thematic substance of the text: the enigma of personality, and the poverty of our knowledge of others and ourselves. Although the letter-writer knows only a taciturn and reclusive chess-player, he learns of another Don Sandalio—a talkative family man and a convict gaoled for an unspecified crime. The letter-writer rejects opportunities to investigate or learn more about Don Sandalio, and also withholds information about himself: both figures remain elusive. At the end of the text, Unamuno raises the possibility that the letter-writer might be Don Sandalio himself, and that the letters represent an attempted autobiography at one remove, but the exact provenance and purpose of the letters remains unresolved. The novella is an interesting demonstration of how little one can ever know the other—be that an acquaintance, friend or fictional creation, and how little one can ever know of the self too. Its epistemological scepticism, and the metafictional possibilities debated in the epilogue also demonstrate that Unamuno's writing retained important modernist elements to the end.[1]

At around the same time, Unamuno wrote *San Manuel Bueno, mártir*, a novella that has overshadowed *La novela de Don Sandalio*, and is, without a doubt, the most famous work of Unamuno's final years. It is an ostensibly simple story in which we are shown the dual life of a rural parish priest. On the one hand, we are shown the painful personal drama of his own conscience, and on the other the persona of the priest as he is seen by the villagers—that is, as a self-assured man of unshakeable Catholic faith. The villagers have no inkling that he does not believe what he preaches. Much to his anguish, the priest has no faith in the doctrine of the resurrection of the dead, but he is very careful not to reveal this to his parishioners, whom he tries to console with the hope of an afterlife. This double life is magisterially presented in a brief story full of biblical allusions and poetic evocations of a beautiful Castilian village by the Sanabria lake, a site shrouded in historical legend and myth. It is narrated some time after Don Manuel's death by Angela Carballino, one of his most devoted parishioners. She is writing her account as the local bishop begins to investigate the life of Don Manuel with a view to his possible beatification. The tale is striking for its great emotional intensity and pathos—both because of Angela's deep attachment to the priest and her sympathy for his private suffering, and because her own life is shattered by the discovery of his unbelief.

Clearly, *San Manuel Bueno, mártir* shares important thematic similarities with *La novela de Don Sandalio*: the split between public persona and private feelings lies at its heart, and both texts are recounted by a notably non-omniscient narrator-character: Angela's knowledge of Don Manuel and his unbelief is

---

[1] For further discussion of *La novela de Don Sandalio*, see Chapter 6 in this volume. Additional readings are offered by Turner (1974: 129–138) and Olson (2003: 199–211).

partial and is not always first-hand – it is instead recounted to her by her brother Lázaro, whom the priest wins over to his 'piadoso fraude' [devout fraud], as Angela ambivalently refers to it (OCE II, 1152; OCA XVI, 625). Part of Don Manuel's anguish, which Julián Marías describes as 'wanting to believe in everlasting life without being able to do so' (1966: 113), also evokes the central human dilemma posited in *El sentimiento trágico de la vida*. But in that text, Unamuno cites from the French essayist Senancour's early nineteenth-century novel *Obermann* to advocate an appropriate ethical response to the possibility of the absence of an afterlife: 'Man may very well be perishable. But let us resist such a possibility, and, if nothingness is what really awaits us, let us make it an injustice' (Unamuno 1954: 263; OCE VII, 263–64; OCA XVI, 387).[2] Don Manuel's tireless work for his rural parishioners, and his kindness to them, might well be his way of resisting or protesting against a possible nothingness, but he denies them the same chance. Believing that they would be unable to live with such uncertainty, he keeps them in a state of unquestioning simplicity and ignorance, telling Angela's rationalist brother Lázaro that 'la protesta mata el contento' [protest destroys contentment] (OCE II, 1145; OCA XVI, 611). For Don Manuel this principle applied also to the secular social realm: he is keen that his parishioners should not become politicised. Lázaro initially opposes Don Manuel's hegemony over the village, wanting to free its inhabitants from the feudal 'oscura teocracia' [theocratic darkness] (OCE II, 1138; OCA XVI, 599) into which Spain has sunk. But Don Manuel manages to persuade Lázaro that in a society where material needs were fully met, *taedium vitae* would emerge to destroy the inhabitants' contentment. Alluding to Marx's famous saying that 'religion is the opiate of the people', the priest says 'Opio, sí. Démosle opio, y que duerma y que sueñe' (OCE II, 1146; OCA XVI, 613) [Opiate indeed. Let us give them opium, so that they sleep and dream]. Later, Lázaro explains to Angela that '[Don Manuel] me curó de mi progresismo' (OCE II, 1150; OCA XVI, 620) [Don Manuel cured me of my progressivism].

It is easy to read Don Manuel's struggle with belief and resulting existential anguish as voicing Unamuno's own well-known preoccupations. Much early criticism saw the text as at least partly autobiographical and a return to the themes that Unamuno had worked through in texts such as *Del sentimiento trágico de la vida* (Marías 1966: 113–119; Blanco Aguinaga 1974: 273–296, Gullón 1964: 331–355; Barea 1952: 50–55). A significant strand of – again mostly earlier – criticism assumed that Don Manuel's scepticism about the value of political progress was also Unamuno's, and so concluded that the text was reactionary

---

2   'L'homme est périssable. Il se peut; mais périssons en resistant, et si la néant nous est reservé, ne faisons pas que ce soit une justice.' Etienne Pivert de Senancour, *Obermann*, (Paris: Ledoux, 1833), Lettre XC.

(Díaz 1968; Regalado García 1968; Blanco Aguinaga 1981). Díaz, for example, saw *San Manuel Bueno, mártir* as spelling out the implications of Unamuno's conception of religion, and argued that 'Unamuno's religious disposition—an overwhelming, anguished and tragic religious disposition—leads to his spiritualism ultimately taking on a genuinely conservative and almost immobilist political valence/meaning/sense: religion is the consolation for the irremediable ills of this world, and the struggle or the efforts of mankind for his liberation constitute nothing more than a way of passing the time...' (1968: 25).

The difficulty with both these strands of interpretation is that they conflate Unamuno with Don Manuel too readily, ignoring other aspects of the text. Later criticism has moved away from a reading of *San Manuel Bueno, mártir* as autobiography or confession, concentrating instead on the literary specificity of the text, and particularly on the way that the figure of Angela mediates all that the reader learns about Don Manuel (Longhurst 1981; Gordon 1986; Bacarisse 1991; Butt 1981; Summerhill 1985). C.A. Longhurst argues that we should regard Angela as an unreliable witness: 'her recreation of Don Manuel is an equivocal and contradictory one, governed by her ambiguous (and ambivalent) relationship with Don Manuel' (1981: 591–2). Noting Angela's explicit uncertainty about the veracity of her own account at the end of the novel, Longhurst contends that *San Manuel Bueno, mártir* raises the question of narrative authority, a plausible argument if we consider the prominent exploration of this question in Unamuno's previous work, most famously in *Niebla*. At the very least, as Pedro Cerezo Galán notes, the use of Angela as narrator suggests a certain authorial distancing from Don Manuel (1996: 716). Overall, then, criticism has moved from seeing the text as a transparent document of Unamuno's political and religious preoccupations to viewing it as amongst his most intractably ambiguous texts (see, for example, Butt 1981: 80–81).

* * *

We shall pass, now, to the subject of Unamuno's late politics, insofar as existing sources allow us to examine them accurately. It hardly needs saying that in studying Unamuno's final seven years, we are dealing with a period that has become vastly complicated. His great intellectual authority and prestige as a public figure were used, both at the time and posthumously, for opposing purposes: both Republicans and enemies of the Republic sought the support of the venerable and highly esteemed intellectual for their own political ends. It is an understatement to say that even today, there is no critical consensus on the matter of Unamuno's political stance during this time. Now that a great part of his uncollected work has been recovered (including correspondence, journalism and unpublished writings), it is possible to reconstruct Unamuno's political trajectory during the Republic and the initial stages of the Civil War more accurately. But we should not forget that the war remains to this day a very divisive issue in Spain because of the trauma it entailed and the polarised political positions which came into conflict. Although such positions are now viewed with a certain amount of distance, they represent orientations which attract sympathy or aversion according to the optic through which they are viewed. The fate of Judge Baltasar Garzón, who was suspended from judicial activity for his investigations into Francoist crimes, is living proof of how sensitive an issue the Civil War still is in contemporary Spain. This chapter will attempt to trace Unamuno's trajectory during his final years, placing his work in historical context, while also recognising that the context itself is immensely complex, not just in the Spanish arena but internationally too, given that Nazi Germany, fascist Italy and the USSR all intervened in the war; at the same time, there were volunteers fighting for the Republican cause (in the International Brigades) from many countries of the world. The governments of neighbouring countries such as France and Great Britain, which the Republic erroneously thought would support its cause against fascist intervention, manoeuvred in favour of non-intervention for fear that a Communist or Anarchist Republic would emerge in Spain (Casanova & Preston 2008; Tuñon de Lara 1985).

When he returned from exile, the illustrious professor of ancient Greek was acclaimed the length and breadth of Spain. He refused to write for the press while censorship remained in place (Pascal Mezquita 2003: 140) – it lasted until October of 1930 – and extolled a strong civic-mindedness and spirit, alongside a fraternal liberalism. After having been given a rapturous hearing in his native Bilbao, he spoke in Valladolid to a student audience, telling them that 'on my return I see what I predicted a good while back: that if a healthy civil society and liberty were to be restored, as is now gradually happening in part, it would be driven by the young' (Pascal Mezquita 2003: 111, 113). At the Casa del Pueblo in Salamanca, he declared himself a 'liberal, a republican and a socialist'. Again he emphasised the faith he was placing in the young, whom he referred to as 'the most vigorous element in Spain' (Pascal Mezquita 2003: 158). The expression of this hope in the young was sometimes accompanied by a certain amount of criticism of their parents for not having demonstrated sufficient belligerence in the face of the Primo de Rivera dictatorship. For Unamuno, they had failed to fulfil their civic duty (Pascal Mezquita 2003: 167). But Unamuno's valuing of the young would soon change as the Republic progressed.

In the 1931 elections he campaigned with the Republican-Socialist alliance. With the coming of the Republic, Unamuno declared that Spain was free of praetorianism, which he regarded as the country's worst enemy (Pascal Mezquita 2003: 177). He believed—wrongly, as he would soon find out—that the military putsches typical of the nineteenth century would not return: 'compulsory military service has made our youth so anti-military that I think the era of military uprisings is over, and with that, also the possibility of Russian-style *soviets* and Italian-style *fasci*', adding 'so I think there is no danger either from communism or fascism in Spain' (Unamuno 1979: 78–79). The Constitution of the Second Republic was ratified in December 1931. It was not long before Unamuno, who represented Salamanca as a member of the new parliament, began to express reservations about it. From November 1932, he clearly disapproved of the so-called Law for the Defence of the Republic (an exceptional public order instrument), was increasingly uneasy about the statutes of autonomy for Cataluña, the Basque Country and Galicia, and rejected the Republican-Socialist government policy on religious matters (the separation of church and state, the legalisation of divorce, the secularisation of education, limitations to the status and powers of religious orders, etc.). On the issue of the statutes of autonomy, Unamuno's attitude was one of apprehension or suspicion – he saw in them a danger of the division or break-up of Spain. As far as the question of language was concerned, he was quick to reject Basque and Catalan as languages of civilisation or learning. His 1884 doctoral thesis had tackled the question of the Basque language, and had been very critical about the arguments of its defenders, who, he felt, lacked intellectual rigour and mythologised the Basque tongue. Subsequently, his position was that Basque was too impoverished to be a language of civilisation, so that Basques should venerate it as a symbol of their ancestors; if they wanted to be part of the great universal civilisations, they should be so via Castilian Spanish, although they could incorporate distinctive Basque linguistic components.[3] His position on Catalan was broadly similar. But in this case, Unamuno was dealing with a language different from Basque in two important respects: it had long enjoyed a great literary, philosophical and poetic tradition, and, in contrast to the Basque Country, contained a large number of people who spoke the language fluently. Unamuno argued that the Catalans should conquer Spain, but using Castilian Spanish. For Unamuno, who could appreciate the richness of the Catalan language, and who numbered Catalans amongst his close friends (the poet and journalist Joan Maragall, for example), Catalan was a regional language rather than a universal one; Castilian Spanish was the language through which all Spanish, and Hispano-Americans, gained access to universal culture and learning.[4]

---

[3] This argument is clearly expressed in his speech of 26 August 1901 in the Juegos Florales de Bilbao (OCE IV, 237–250; OCA VI, 326–343). See also Unamuno 1997 and Rivero Gómez 2010.

[4] Hispano-America was used by Unamuno to illustrate his point. There are too many examples to be listed here, but the idea is found in the 1901 speech in Bilbao referred to above.

On several occasions, Unamuno accused scholars of the Basque language of turning what he saw as an academic matter into a political question. But was *he* not the first to do this? Is it coherent to assert, as he did, that language is a living organism, that is born, develops and has a capacity for enrichment while at the same time proclaiming that Basque, Catalan and Galician are incapable of developing and incorporating whatever they might need in order to be languages of civilisation and learning? Taken to its logical conclusion, Unamuno's argument would favour the whole of mankind's speaking one single language, which would be universal by definition. Of course Unamuno would never have accepted this conclusion; I am simply pointing out the logic implied in his argument, leaving aside questions about whether language entails a way of seeing or thinking ('language thinks in us', as he puts it), such that there is a man-made cultural world or wealth that is lost when a language is lost. Unamuno tends to shy away from questions such as these, training his gaze instead on the majority language, which he would have liked to have been, in effect, a 'super Castilian', a Castilian that was not just the language of Spain but that of Spanish America as well.

He also failed to deal with the question of bilingualism. Or rather, he rejected bilingualism (which was recognised in the Republican statutes of autonomy) because he held it to be incompatible with national unity: 'Pay no mind to this matter of bilingualism: we should be trying to kill off one of the languages, not letting both live' (Pascal Mezquita 2003: 195 [1931]). During the Republic he remained so belligerent on the matter that he became a representative of old Castilian. 'Su Majestad la lengua española'[5] [Her Majesty the Spanish Language] could not share space with Catalan, Basque or Galician in the classrooms or official institutions of Cataluña, the Basque Country and Galicia. He accepted these languages only as a colloquial, domestic vernaculars. In short, he denied them any serious cultural status.

Unamuno was equally uneasy about the way the first Republican government dealt with the question of religion. Although he usually had little interest in philosophy in the technical or academic sense, Unamuno argued that philosophy was sustained by religion, which gave life to the philosophical disposition 'because one does not think only with one's head; one thinks with the whole of one's body' (Pascal Mezquita 2003: 318 [1934]). Religion, then, played a fundamental role in the concepts that oriented human thought. During the Republic, the question of religion, which lay at the core of Unamuno's philosophical thinking, became for him a political issue, because he opposed the Republican government's treatment of religious orders (the Jesuits were expelled) and the

---

5   This was the title of a 1908 article of his: (OCA VI, 534–542; OCE IV, 374–379.)

separation of church and state. Unamuno, who had so often before criticised religious dogmatism, advocating instead an intimate, tragic religion, distanced from ceremony and external manifestations, did not accept that crucifixes should disappear from classroom walls, nor that divorce should be legalised.[6] Like the Castilian language, the Christian religion was, for Unamuno, a basic element of Spanish culture (Pascal Mezquita 2003: 247–248 [1932]). Just as for Bergson, whose work Unamuno knew well, religion was a binding agent uniting humanity. Unamuno tended to neglect the historical anthropological aspects of religion which have so often shown it to be a source of discord and confrontation between peoples, communities and individuals.

Unamuno was clearly overwhelmed by the problems that emerged over the course of the Republic. The protests, demonstrations and strikes, the presence of the masses on the streets, the growing political tension across a Europe in turmoil because of the economic crisis and the fascist governments in Italy and Germany were in Spain translated into political upheaval on a grand scale. The forces that had been dominant in the nineteenth century – the landowners, protected by a Church as conservative in the countryside as it was in the city – resisted the loss of the privileges that they had hitherto enjoyed. And there is one circumstance that I deem very important in relation to Unamuno's attitude to the policies of Azaña (the President of the Republic), and to the Republic more generally. Salamanca, the city which the Basque Unamuno had adopted as his own, was an urban centre unlike any other: this Castilian city was home to the great religious houses of all orders—male and female. Its episcopacy was deeply conservative, and its clergy a perfect incarnation of what in Spain is called the union of sword and altar. This alliance was apparent in the belligerent anti-Republicanism exhibited by the landowners' associations, members of the clergy, religious orders and military authorities. As Ricardo Robledo has indicated, in terms of discrediting the Republic, justifying violence and turning the Civil War into a religious crusade, 'Salamanca made the most important contribution, with chapter, episcopate, Dominicans and the university vying to outdo each other (Robledo 2007: 84). We should not forget that Bishop Pla y Daniel, author of the Pastoral Letter *Las dos ciudades* [The Two Cities] (September 1936), had occupied the city's episcopal palace since 1935, and the military leaders of the coup that triggered the Civil War initially established their headquarters at Salamanca. No other city was as well equipped to offer the rebel generals the ideological cover – a new Catholic Spain – they needed to establish their nascent regime. Apart from his years in exile (1924–1931),

---

6   See, for example, his speech from 1931 reproduced in Pascal Mezquita (2003: 209). The issue of crucifixes and other religious symbols remains a live and contentious issue in Spain to this day. Doyaga (1967) highlights the conservatism of Unamuno's views on marriage and divorce.

Unamuno had lived in this environment since 1891, and he spent the final seven years of his life there too. This is not to suggest that atmosphere in Salamanca entirely explained the position he came to adopt, but the evolution in Unamuno's position from the enthusiasm of his triumphant return from France, through his increasing hostility to Republican policies to, finally, his inconceivable support for the military coup of the 18 July 1936, does not otherwise seem fully comprehensible. Without aiming to explain away something that history simply cannot explain – because the human soul is too complex to be dismantled and analysed as if it were a watch – I will limit myself to some brief considerations about his political trajectory over this period.

Unamuno, out of place in the Republic

In 1931 Unamuno did not appreciate that the Spain he had known previously was being transformed on a massive scale. The family, education, the political centralism of the Restoration government and the Primo de Rivera dictatorship, the role of youth, the workers' organisations, women's roles and rights were all undergoing major change, as the Republic faced up to the difficult task of modernising the country in all respects. As Elías Díaz has argued, in 1931 Unamuno simply failed to understand the problems that the Republic was facing in areas such as agrarian and military reform, the separation of church and state, decentralisation, education and mass politics (1968: 175).

Unamuno's position on the agrarian question changed during the Republic. He had frequently concerned himself with the agrarian problem in the past, particularly in his Socialist period (1894–1897), during which time he even reproached the Spanish socialists—quite rightly—for not paying attention to the peasants who constituted the vast majority of Spanish workers.[7] Between 1912 and 1914, he had played an active part (now as a Liberal, rather than a Socialist) in the agrarian campaigns waged by intellectuals within Castile. For that reason, the language that Unamuno uses to refer to the issue during the Republic is surprising. The Russian writer Ilya Ehrenburg wrote in 1935:

> when speaking of the hunger of land-workers, or of strikes or fascist conspiracies, Unamuno is more concerned with the beauty of the Spanish countryside, and invokes the testimony of the all the poets and philosophers. Unamuno understands perfectly well the significance of the Agrarian Reform legislation and the struggle against the clergy; but in his heart of

---

[7]   For many historians, the great problem of Spain, and the most important for explaining the Civil War, is agrarian landownership and its unjust distribution. See Edward Malefakis's now old, but not superseded study (1970).

hearts he misses the moving wretchedness, the abnegation, the disinterest of the old Spain

                                                    (in Bazán 1935: 18 21).

Ehrenburg was here surely thinking of what Unamuno had said in Almería in September 1931:

> I have never felt a son's love for my poor Spain as much as when I have encountered these sun-beaten lands, with this divine poverty of its fields; this is the poor mother. This is the mother who is all the more motherly because she is poor, all the more a mother for being poor. And it is because of that that we, her children, should indeed make a contribution towards her richness, but above all we should embrace her because she is poor, because of what she has suffered'
>
>   (in Pascal Mezquita 2003: 209, 210).

In 1933, he stated that the difficulty of the situation for Spain's agricultural workers had been exaggerated, and added that in some regions of France, workers on the land earned less than those in Spain. He did not approve of reform, arguing that the agrarian reforms that the Communists and Socialists would have liked to have seen carried out in Castile went against its natural economy, and that such poor land did not lend itself to the reform schemes (Pascal Mezquita 2003: 369 [1936]). What is certain is that this topic, of such central importance during the social crisis of the Republican years, features very little in what Unamuno writes during this period.

His liberalism led him to sympathise with the left, but as he saw workers claiming greater rights, the Church opposing the separation of church and state, those regions with their own language demanding autonomy and the military rejecting the modernisation imposed by Azaña, Unamuno increasingly declared himself against Azaña's policies. Marxism, which thrived during the Republican years thanks to the publication of writings by Marx, Lenin and other, mostly Russian theorists and political figures, was dismissed by Unamuno as vulgar materialist theory and extremist politics, equivalent in its extremism to fascism.[8] One originally Marxist ideology which had taken root amongst the working classes, particularly in Cataluña and Andalucía, was anarchism, whose culture had a popular base, opposing the state as a repressive apparatus and the Church as an instrument of legitimation for that repressive apparatus. Unamuno did not make the connection between this aspect of the Church and popular anticlericalism.

---

[8]   Unamuno repeatedly equated communism with fascism. See, for example Pascal Mezquita (2003: 177 [1931]), where he referred to communism and fascism as 'twins' ('hermanos gemelos').

As noted above, from November 1932, Unamuno was at loggerheads with Republican policy. Increasingly, he began to use psychological or pathological terms and concepts to describe the Republic, associating it with unhealthy passion, madness, envy, Cainism[9], desperation, dementia, infantilism, destructive or bellicose instinct, spiritual leprosy, a psychiatric epidemic, poisoning, epilepsy and many other psychical or physical defects. From praising the young people who overthrew the Primo de Rivera dictatorship and who aspired to a new, democratic, studious, liberal country, he gradually began to criticise them as puerile (Pascal Mezquita 2003: 309 [1933]). A year later, he claimed that 'a surly, narrow-minded, bitter, dim, dogmatic and biased younger generation is forming' (Pascal Mezquita 2003: 320 [1934]); later still, amongst the young who had joined political parties, he perceived a 'total absence of intellectual activity' (Pascal Mezquita 2003: 369 [1936]).

In the speech to the Ateneo de Madrid on 28 November 1932, he asserted that 'we are sinking increasingly into a boggy field of passions', a phrase he repeated in March 1933, elsewhere referring to a 'hurricane of toxic public passions' (Pascal Mezquita 2003: 288, 303). Semantic niceties, in which he had always revelled, proliferated more than ever in relation to terms such as 'revolution', 'the right(-wing) left', and 'civil war'. But the main stress was on the psychological, and what pertained to passions or states of mind. In this sense one might argue that Unamuno represented a weathervane of the atmosphere of Republican Spain during this time. The bitter debates in parliament, the constant presence of the masses claiming their rights, the confrontations between land-workers and the Guardia Civil (the paramilitary rural police force), the bullying tactics that landowners and business-owners used to impede the loss of their privileges, the destruction of religious buildings, when combined with a politicisation of youth and organised labour, together triggered a growing social instability which some military leaders were able to use as the pretext to mount a coup against the Republic. Unamuno's writings reflected the state of tension that Spain was experiencing in the final years of the Republic, but he tended to see it only as a psychological phenomenon, or as a scenario in which passions, confrontations and discord were expressed; there was no dissection of the causes of these passions or confrontations. In other words, Unamuno abandoned all social analysis and limited himself to the description of hatred and rancour in the language of an old bourgeois liberal fearfully witnessing the explosive social situation

---

9   In this respect, Unamuno's position is close to Bishop Pla y Deniel's: in the aforementioned pastoral letter *Las dos ciudades*, the Bishop not only sees representatives of the City of God as crusaders 'for Christ and Spain', but brands the Communists and Anarchists (representatives of the earthly city) as 'sons of Cain…who revel in murder, in sacking, destruction and firesetting'.

of the 1930s. He resorted more than once to the language of biological 'defects' in his analyses, such as allusions to 'gypsy blood' or a 'certain pathological-corporeal substrate'.

Towards the end of his life, Unamuno saw himself as being surrounded by what he called 'resentment' or *ressentiment*, a term he used in the title of a work he never managed to complete, and which was eventually published posthumously.[10] He often used the hammer and sickle as symbols of insane passions (Pascual Mezquita 2003: 311 [1934]), and drew attention to the feelings of hatred penetrating the political atmosphere of Spain (Pascal Mezquita 2003: 325 [1934]). The following year he agreed to a meeting with José Antonio, son of the recent dictator Miguel Primo de Rivera and founder of the Falange, a fascist party emulating Mussolini's movement.[11]

Support for the military coup

Unamuno's support for the uprising led by a cabal of generals in July 1936 – an uprising that triggered the Civil War – is very surprising, given that he had fought all his life against praetorianism, and had stood up to the military dictatorship with admirable courage and directness. It proves very difficult to understand how a man like him, who had criticised courts martial, could make common cause with a military uprising against the Republic. But there is incontrovertible documentary proof of his support for it. Above all, there is the speech he made as a city councillor at Salamanca's city hall on 26 July 1936. This speech alone shows that Unamuno accepted the function that the military assigned the town halls, something he is very clear about, given that it was a military man (Francisco Valle) occupying the office of mayor, while the elected mayor, the Republican Casto Prieto Carrasco, a friend of Unamuno, was arrested, and then assassinated.[12] In this speech of 26 July, Unamuno presented himself as a figure of 'continuity' in an unconvincing attempt to demonstrate that nothing had changed in his position. He recalled that he had been elected a councillor, and before that a member of parliament by the people, and that in both posts:

10   *El resentimiento trágico de la vida*, a play on the title of his famous 1912 essay *Del sentimiento trágico de la vida*. See Unamuno 1991.
   11   This fact seems to have been decisive in Unamuno's being considered undeserving of the Nobel Prize for Literature. It is more than likely that Unamuno, who was clear about his rejection of fascism, agreed to meet José Antonio, and attended the Falangist rally in order to show the dictator's son that he was able to maintain a dialogue with those whose views he did not agree with.
   12   The speech is reproduced in Rabaté & Rabaté (2009: 671–672); see also Borzoni (2009: 184). I am grateful to Dr Borzoni for allowing me to read his thesis.

I came to serve Spain in the regime that it conferred on itself [i.e.the Republic]. [...] And now that the remaining healthy elements of the country, the people lawfully armed [el pueblo regularmente armado] have called on me, I am here to continue serving Spain

(Rabaté & Rabaté 2009: 671–672).

It seems incredible that Unamuno could have written phrase such as 'the remaining healthy elements of the country, the people lawfully armed' (that is, the military – and here Unamuno is referring to the rebels, not to those in the armed forces who remained loyal to the Republic). It seems, then, that the continuity is not a continuity with the Republican regime, but with the new order that is being established by the military. What other meaning could this expression have? Of course on 26 July, the date of the speech, neither Unamuno nor the majority of Spaniards knew exactly what the intentions of Franco or the other generals were: they were still proclaiming fidelity to the Republic, and the Republican flag could still be seen flying from official buildings for several weeks afterwards.

Don Miguel's name's next to the sum of 5000 pesetas on a list of donors to the military cause is usually adduced as further evidence of Unamuno's support for the military uprising.[13] I have very serious doubts about this donation, which represents almost half his annual professorial salary—a very considerable sum for Unamuno, particularly at that moment, when he had already retired, and still had five children living under his roof.[14] It is likely that this was a falsehood circulated for propaganda purposes, appropriating his national and international prestige for the Nationalist cause.[15]

In September 1936, Unamuno put his signature as rector to the statement that the University of Salamanca put out to the 'Universities and Academies of the world on the subject of the Spanish Civil War'. The statement mentions the 'enormous impact of the Spanish defence of our Western Christian civilisation, which built Europe, from a destructive Oriental ideology and from a 'collective dementia''.[16] That Unamuno signed this document does not mean that he composed or wrote it, but it does mean that he took responsibility for it. Some expressions are surprisingly close to those characteristic of his own writing: a 'Western Christian civilisation', set against 'a destructive Oriental ideology' are staple terms in his articles from this period, as is 'collective dementia'. Eight

---

[13] *La Gaceta Regional*, Salamanca, 11 de Agosto 1936.

[14] It was the equivalent of two years' worth of a worker's wages at the time.

[15] Reig Tapia also questions whether such a donation was made (1999: 296). Prado Herrera (Robledo 2007: 208) argues that donations could not be considered separately from the climate of terror that, in addition to masking reality, 'made what was compulsory merely seem voluntary'.

[16] The text is reproduced in Salcedo (1964: 410–411).

days after signing this endorsement of the coup, and in his capacity as rector, Unamuno attended the solemn act of the proclamation of Franco as Head of the Government in the Plaza Mayor of Salamanca. From that point on, Unamuno could no longer have any doubt that he was the functionary of an undemocratic regime, and that the post he occupied in no way represented 'continuity' with the Republican regime.

The rectorship he now occupied was a military appointment. Perhaps such formalities were of little concern to him; perhaps he was far more focused on the whirlwind of tragic events that the war brought with it on a daily basis. But what is beyond doubt is that to place one's trust, as Unamuno assuredly and repeatedly did, in a leader such as Franco,[17] is the sign of an ingenuousness hard to reconcile with the political acuity that Unamuno had demonstrated on other occasions.

The draft of the impromptu speech that Unamuno made in the University of Salamanca's great hall on the occasion of Columbus Day (12 October) 1936 has also been preserved. As rector of the University, Unamuno was representing no less a figure than General Franco, who was unable to attend the solemn ceremony. Emilio Salcedo, one of Unamuno's biographers, intimates that Unamuno had not intended to speak at the ceremony for fear that he might say something rash (1964: 413); he was expected simply to introduce the speakers at the event. However, after having listened to the discrediting of Basques and Catalans and other nonsensical assertions, Unamuno took to the floor in order to respond. I am reproducing here Salcedo's version[18] of Unamuno's words:

> 'I said that I did not want to make a speech today, but I feel obliged to speak out. Mention has been made here of an international war in defence of Christian civilization; I myself have described the war in similar terms on previous occasions. But that is not correct: ours is simply an uncivil war. I am someone for whom Civil War was a cradle-song, so I know what I am talking about. To win over physically is not the same as to win over intellectually or morally,[19] and one must seek to convince and persuade before all else. Hatred that cannot find room for compassion will never convince; nor will hatred for intelligence that is critical and differentiating, inquisitive but not inquisitorial. Reference has also been made of the Basques and the Catalans as representing the anti-Spain, but they could say the same of those who

[17]   It seems that Unamuno never lost his trust in Franco, seeing him as an honest military man rather than the bloodthirsty dictator that he actually was. As late as December 1936, he was blaming General Mola, rather than Franco, for the savage repression in the Nationalist rearguard (Unamuno 1991b: II, 353)

[18]   For another reconstruction of the ceremony, see Azaola 1996: 153–172.

[19]   Translator's note: Unamuno's now famous formulation in Spanish is much neater, a play on words: 'vencer no es convencer' (literally, 'to win/defeat is not to win over/convince').

criticise them. With us today is his grace the Bishop, a Catalan, to teach
you Christian doctrine that you do not want to know. And I, a Basque, have
spent my whole life teaching you the Spanish language, which you also do
not know. Now *that* is empire—the empire of the Spanish language, and
not...]

(Salcedo 1964: 407–11)

At this point Unamuno was interrupted by General Millán Astray, who, like
Unamuno, was sitting on the platform presided over by the rector. He made some
angry remarks, justifying military uprising and shouting out the Foreign Legion's
motto '¡Viva la muerte!' ['Long Live Death!']. Unamuno answered back the
General, and it seems that uproar ensued in the great hall. Unamuno also made
reference to José Rizal, the hero of the fight for independence in the Philippines
who was executed by the Spanish armed forces. Unamuno's praise for Rizal
infuriated the military men (Millán Astray had fought in the Philippines) and the
Falangists present. The following day, Unamuno was stripped of his post as
councillor by the municipal authorities in Salamanca; two days later, he was
removed as rector by the University Senate—that is, by his own peers and
colleagues. On 22 October, Franco signed the decree which removed him from
the rectorship. Unamuno was utterly alone: already despised by the Republican
press, who had branded him a traitor, he was now also shunned by the rebels.

Friends such as Casto Prieto could not understand his support for the rebels
(Robledo 2007: 296); other friends, such as the politician and writer Luis
Araquistáin, the poet José Bergamín, and indeed the majority of his socialist or
Republican friends were equally baffled. As he had done throughout his life, he
followed his own independent path, claiming the right to do so as a free man. In
this sense he was consistent: he did not accept the Falangists' methods of savage
repression, but he did not want a secular Republic either, and still less a Soviet or
anarchist revolution. In any case, it is surprising that he agreed to accept a rectorship
which would involve political purging. That he made use of the post to intervene
in favour of specific people does not exempt him from such a responsibility. If
there was on Unamuno's part an attempt to save the Protestant pastor Atilano
Coco, it proved futile, given that he was shot on 8 December 1936.

When Unamuno saw the crimes that were committed against friends of his,
and the brutal methods employed by the military in Extremadura, Andalucía
and the Basque Country, he realised that the civil war he had recalled often in
laudatory terms as a preparation for the final embrace of the combatants, had
nothing to do with the conflict unleashed in 1936. This new Civil War was not
civil – that is to say, civilised – but instead was uncivil, brutal, cruel and inhuman.
Throughout his life, as Azaola astutely notes in his study *Unamuno y sus guerras
civiles* [Unamuno and his Civil Wars], Unamuno propagated an overly rosy

image of the nineteenth-century civil wars, tending to fuse them with his own childhood memory of the bombs that fell on Bilbao. His positive view of civil war glossed over the terrible destruction, pillaging, human tragedy and cruelty which accompanied all the Spanish wars, starting with the war that he remembered from his childhood—the Carlist war to which his first published novel *Paz en la guerra* is devoted. There are countless texts in his oeuvre in which civil war appears as a sort of catharsis, a purification of hatreds or passing/fleeting conflict, and as a necessary prelude to authentic and lasting accord. In 1936, when he experienced at close quarters the terrible nature of the war that had broken out amongst Spaniards, he realised that he had to correct the naive vision of war that he had defended so often. In April 1935, for example, on the occasion of the opening of the Colegio de España in Paris, he made a speech in which he spoke of 'the necessity of civil war, the most noble and fruitful of wars, the only worthy type of war—I was brought up in the middle of war—because it is not a material or corporeal conflict between peoples but an intimate, spiritual struggle, the struggle between Esau and Jacob, the twin brothers whose struggle began in their mother's womb' (Pascal Mezquita 2003: 335–336).

In contrast, in *El resentimiento trágico de la vida*, he wrote: 'the experience of this war presents me with two problems: that of understanding, and rethinking my own work, beginning with *Peace in War*, and that of understanding and rethinking Spain' (Unamuno 1991a: 33). There is no doubt that one of the things that he felt obliged to rethink was the meaning of civil war, a task that meant reconsidering many aspects of Spanish life. The phrase 'understanding and rethinking Spain' indicates a subject that had been for Unamuno lifelong object of attention and study. Normally Unamuno spoke of Spain in the context of the question of language, which for him was a guiding thread in his vision of the country. In this vision, religion played a fundamental part, but not in the same way as it did for Menéndez Pelayo and other Catholic traditionalists. Menéndez Pelayo considered Catholicism and Spain to be two indissoluble realities: Spaniards who were not Catholic were necessarily bad Spaniards, or were the 'anti-Spain'. Francoism exploited Menéndez Pelayo's defence of Spanish Catholicism to the hilt, but did so by simplifying it, and emptying his work of other, valuable elements. From the establishment of the military dictatorship, this erudite native of Santander, who died in 1912, became the great ideologue whose principles would guide the re-Catholicisation of the new Spain. Taking an opposing line, Unamuno spoke of the need to reform Spain's Catholicism, to 'Christianise' it, to give it life by 'dis-ecclesialising' it, making it part of lay or civil life.[20] It was to be transformed into an option for the individual –

---

[20] 'Civil' can mean civil or lay, a coincidence which Unamuno often plays on in this context.

something to be assumed autonomously, along the lines of Kant's position (although of course the cordialism and vitalism of Unamuno's stance was quite some way from the rationalism of Kant).

If Unamuno treated civil war too lightly, his treatment of fascism also failed in some ways to take it seriously enough. Unreservedly condemning fascism for its brutality and incompatibility with liberty, Unamuno had noticed the dangerous drift of groups of young people to allow themselves to be seduced by barbarous, unthinking slogans – indeed this was something he specifically raised with José Antonio Primo de Rivera, leader of the Falange movement (Pascal Mezquita 2003: 330–333). As far as I am aware, Unamuno never published an in-depth analysis of fascism. In March 1929, he sent the International Antifascist Congress a letter of support, but rather than being a criticism of fascism, it speaks out against military dictatorship.[21] Perhaps where he came closest to a firm stance and a clear rejection of fascism was in the letter he wrote to Umberto Zanotti-Bianco (Unamuno 1991b II: 154) and in his correspondence with Ernesto Giménez Caballero (Unamuno 1991b II: 212–214; 215–218; 222–223), but it is undeniably the case that he tended to trivialise the movement, writing in 1933, for example, that: 'its manifestos, its demonstrations, the leaflets it hands out, its liturgical exercises, would be laughable if it were not for the pity one feels at the mental debasement they reveal' (248). Although he condemned fascism without reservation, he tended to believe it was a foreign movement from Italy and Germany that could not take root in Spain. It is true that fascism was not a mass movement before the Civil War, but the fascist militia played a prominent role in the repression of intellectuals, trade unionists and Republicans across the board. Borzoni (2009) has traced the correspondence between Unamuno and Giménez Caballero, and the repugnance that from the 1920s onwards Unamuno felt towards fascism is very clearly discernible. His position does not change in the 1930s. If anything, his disgust hardened, as can be seen, for example, in letters he wrote in 1936 to Esteban Madruga, Francisco de Cossío and to Quintín de Torre.[22] The Falangists' posthumous appropriation of Unamuno (right up to supplying coffin-bearers on the day of his funeral) was a farce as opportunistic as it was unjustifiable. It did immense damage to Unamuno's reputation.

Other documents indicating Unamuno's collaboration with the wartime military regime have been preserved. Interviews provide the main evidence, but, often used in an uncritical way, they must be treated with the utmost caution unless verifiable, as is the case of the interview published by Jérôme

---

[21] Reproduced in Urrutia (2007: 215–217).
[22] 'I would never have believed that the filthy Falangery—daughter to such an extent of the servile fear of the afflicted or weak—could sink to such an abject level'. Unamuno 1991b: 349.

Tharaud,[23] a much-discussed encounter, and one that Pascal dates as having taken place at the end of 1936. Interviewers often distorted Unamuno's words, whether intentionally – in order to support the cause of the military rebels by making use of his intellectual authority and prestige – or unintentionally because they mistranslated what he said (or did both things at once).

The idea of saving a 'Christian western civilisation' in peril, which Unamuno had made reference to in the 26 July speech, is repeated several times in interviews which were published widely in Spain and across the world: Tharaud's is but one example. This idea is not new in Unamuno's work. Spain did not take part in the First World War, but the War was an object of intense debate in the press between those supporting the Allies, and those supporting the Central Powers. Like the majority of intellectuals, Unamuno supported the Allies, and one of the central pillars of his support lay in the thesis that the Allies were defending Christian civilisation against the paganism of military discipline.[24] Don Miguel takes the side of civilisation—in the sense of the civic, of citizenship, with its requisite morality and law—over *Kultur* (technical and professional efficiency). As well as arguing in 1915 that 'a chemist, a mathematician or a doctor, who may be very learned as such, may be a reprehensible citizen' (OCE, IX, 1296–1302 [1296]), Unamuno linked civilisation specifically to democracy, in for example, 'Las indias occidentales y la Europa asiática' (1918), OCE IX, 1539–1543 [1540]). Finally, he goes on to link European civilisation with Christianity, as, we might note, Kant, Herder, Hegel and so many other German writers had also done--something that Unamuno omitted to mention during this First-World-War period when he was supporting the Allied forces. In other words, this defence of Christian civilisation is nothing new. The novelty in his very late thought—and what comes as a shock to any serious reader of Unamuno—lies in his attributing such a defence to the rebel generals. During what he lived through of the Civil War, Unamuno continued to link civilisation and Christianity, but he barely mentioned democracy. In the notes that he entitled *El resentimiento trágico de la vida*, I have not come across a single reference to the word.[25] The linkage between civilisation and democracy, so prominent in the period of the Great War and during Unamuno's exile in the 1920s, does not appear to be compatible with his support for the military putsch. The Second Republic was the fruit of the most democratic elections ever held in Spain; the generals' coup shattered that democracy, substituting violence for the popular will as the way to effect regime change.

It is surely in this context that we should understand Unamuno's actions on 12 October 1936, in the infamous celebration of 'Columbus Day' in the

---

23 Reproduced in Pascal Mezquita 2003: 404–408 [1936]
24 Unamuno to Jacques Chevalier, 15–03–1915, in García Blanco 1964: 43.
25 See footnote 10.

University's Great Hall, and undoubtedly the most famous day of Unamuno's life. It has been much commented on and much debated. There are wildly differing accounts of it, as Unamuno's words were unscripted, and there remains no reliable textual account.[26] What is beyond doubt is that by October 1936, Unamuno knew what shape the conflict was taking. And it is important to note that his behaviour on that occasion makes it very clear that he is not on the side of the military rebels; he is openly against them. As President of the Republic, Manuel Azaña had stripped Unamuno of his rectorship of the University of Salamanca for having supported the uprising against the Republic; the military had restored him, but Franco now definitively removed him from the post.The obvious question about Unamuno's behaviour at the outbreak of the Civil War is this: why the sudden confidence in the military as saviours of Christian civilisation in the west when he had never previously considered them in such a light? A sensible explanation will be found by analysing the increasing sense of alienation that Unamuno felt in relation to the course followed by the Republic, and what the 1936 Popular Front represented. This man of order was disconcerted and overwhelmed by the unruly appearance of decidedly unbourgeois forms of social protest. Anticlericalism, widespread amongst the Spanish proletariat, was one way of expressing a rejection not of religion, but of the Church's support for the most privileged sectors of society; it was a phenomenon akin to the rejection of the paramilitary rural police force the Guardia Civil as a guardian of the property and privileges of the bourgeoisie. But Unamuno seems to have seen it solely in terms of resentment and savagery. Like many other Spanish intellectuals, he was ill-disposed to totalitarianism of any stripe; he tried to be 'alterutral'—not to be neutral, but to remain unaligned with either side, and to mediate between them (without seeking facile reconciliation). But he soon discovered that the war unleashed by the rebel generals was not an arena in which the mediating activities of naive intellectuals was permitted.

The Civil War has often been simplified as just one chapter in the struggle between fascism and Stalinism, but this characterisation forgets that, although it was indeed a chapter in this struggle, the tragic events that Spain lived through arose also from conflicts proper to Spanish society itself. In the latter stages of his life and career, Unamuno lacked the theoretical tools which would have helped him if not to understand, then at least to explain the several aspects of the intense social conflict unleashed by the Civil War, and his 'psychologisation' of the Spanish situation is a symptom of this lack. In a letter to Lorenzo Giusso, he wrote in November 1936:[27]

---

[26] The ceremony has given rise to the most wildly disparate accounts. I believe that Azaola (1996) and Salcedo (1964) give the most credible versions.

[27] Letter from Unamuno to Lorenzo Giusso 21.11.1936. Reproduced in Azaola 1996: 139.

[w]hat is happening in Spain is a collective mental illness, a phrenopathic epidemic [...] There has been an outbreak of Catholic *and* anti-Catholic leprosy. Both sides howl and bay for blood. The mental deficiencies of our totalitarian youth – *giovinezza*—is terrifying.

Confining himself to the world of passions prevented him from valuing, in the midst of the turmoil of war, the dream (a dream shared by many of his compatriots) of a Spain that contained greater social justice, and more democracy, equality and fraternity. By the time he died, he had come to understand that the liberalism he defended was fiercely combated by the rebels, and that the western Christian civilisation that he wanted for Spain and for Europe was not what the victors of the Civil War were going to bring. In a letter that Unamuno wrote in December 1936, he wrote on the reverse: 'I'm afraid that under the Franco dictatorship, what will least be permitted is frankness. What will prevail is the grinding down of the population'.[28] On this occasion, at least, his judgement was highly accurate.

Further Reading

Azaola (1996), Blanco Aguinaga (1974), Longhurst (1981), Pascal Mezquita (2003), Salcedo (1964).

---

[28]   Letter to Quintín de Torre, in Unamuno 1991b II, 355

II

Themes

5

Faith and Existence

SANDRO BORZONI

> A tragic combat that of truth and reason! And truth is
> something that is felt and lived, not something to be
> understood. Nevertheless, we need logic, that terrible
> power, in order to transmit thoughts, and even to think
> them, because we think with words.
>
> (Unamuno 2005b: 577)

Introduction

If we survey the path of all the alternatives to reason, because we discern that
logic is too distant from concrete man, and if, at the same time, we do not
completely lose faith in it, because a logic of the heart based on simple feeling
is pure irrationalism, then we are at the crossroads where Miguel de Unamuno's
philosophy has its origin. It is a crossroads between the nineteenth and twentieth
century, between the paths of metaphysical rationalism and the currents of
positivism which made a rather late entry to Spain – precisely during Unamuno's
formative years. His alert gaze, and his restless riffling of books and notes were
accompanied by a growing anguish, because lack of certainty was not easily
compatible with the peace and serenity of certain Castilian bucolic scenes that
he had described so magisterially in his literary work; rather, it was wedded to
pain, distress and desperation.[1]

Arriving at this crossroads from the pathway of positivism were new political

---

[1]   In some of his works, Unamuno abandons the dramatic tension between faith and
reason, and finds refuge in the contemplation of the countryside, in open spaces where one's
gaze can extend toward infinity. In his study *El Unamuno contemplativo* (1959) Carlos Blanco
Aguinaga offsets this contemplative and lyrical aspect of Unamuno's work against the other
agonic and tragic aspect, contending that there are 'two' Unamunos. Blanco Aguinaga
emphasises that the agonic Unamuno, author of works such as *Del sentimiento trágico de la
vida*, has, however, been the more influential of 'two' figures in the history of Spanish thought.

and social doctrines; these were joined by new spiritual currents such as Liberal Protestantism or Catholic Modernism. Following this path appeared not to require much effort, rather as it is easy to walk through the avenues of big cities such as Madrid or Paris, for example, with their wide pavements, and benches on which one can sit and rest. But a secret inner voice which had been whispering to Unamuno since his childhood invited him up a rocky, unpaved track, which climbed towards mountains whose peaks Unamuno could not discern. What if Something were there? And what good were all the books in the world if none of them could answer that question definitively?

Human beings live within a paradox: faith and hope in everlasting life are incompatible with reason. There is struggle between them: 'life is tragedy, and the tragedy is perpetual struggle, without victory or the hope of contradiction, life is contradiction' (Unamuno 1954: 14; OCE VII, 117; OCA XVI, 140). I prefer the term 'dichotomy' over Unamuno's 'contradiction' to refer to these two actors in the human tragedy, as reason and faith are equal in force or strength. One cannot be subordinated to the other, as Unamuno explicitly points out:

> Faith in immortality is irrational. And, notwithstanding, faith, life and reason have mutual need of one another. This vital longing is not properly a problem, cannot assume a logical status, cannot be formulated in propositions susceptible of rational discussion; but it announces itself in us as hunger announces itself.
>
> (Unamuno 1954: 111; OCE VII, 175; OCA XVI, 239).

It is the old problem of *ratio* and *auctoritas* that, according to historians of philosophy, goes back to John Scottus Eriugena. The ancient father of the church argued that the reasons and the teachings of Christian doctrine cannot be in contradiction with themselves: 'Vera enim auctoritas rectae rationi non obsistit, neque recta ratio verae auctoritati. Ambo siquidem ex una fonte, divina videlicet sapientia, manare, dubium non est' ['True authority does not stand in the way of right reason; nor does right reason stand in the way of true authority. Since there is no doubt that both have sprung from one source—divine wisdom, clearly'] (*De divisione naturae*, I, 66).

The voice of *auctoritas*, the voice of the doctrine that Unamuno had studied since he was a child, taught him about the immortality of the soul, about paradise and hell, and Unamuno was unable to reconcile these teachings with the philosophies of his time, which were reductionist and materialist. As Unamuno put it: 'The vital longing for human immortality finds no consolation in reason and that reason leaves us without incentive or consolation in life and life itself without real finality' (Unamuno 1954: 106; OCE VII, 172; OCA XVI, 234). Catholic thought offered no clear solution to this manifest contradiction. Medieval scholasticism, a philosophy dating back to the thirteenth and fourteenth centuries, was the official doctrine of Catholic theologians after the First Vatican Council (1869–1870); Unamuno characterised scholasticism as a marvellous cathedral in which all the problems of its architectonic mechanics had been solved, but which was also made of adobe, a material that could not endure in the real world (Unamuno 1954: 75; OCE VII, 153; OCA XVI, 202).

Salamanca Cathedral, which Unamuno saw every day as it was behind his rectorial residence, bore a closer resemblance to his conception of human reality than the scholastics' ecclesiastical construction: the original medieval construction is combined with the high walls of the 'new' cathedral dating from the seventeenth century. The cracks that appeared in the belltower (which dominates the whole city) were repaired with stones of the same colour in order to hide the damage of the terrible Lisbon earthquake in 1755. It was a contingent, somewhat irrational, but immanent element in the architect's vertiginous dreams. And, for Unamuno, such was life, where at times genus and species do not function, where there is non-being, where reality and human reason are not reconciled, and where reality manifests itself at times in a tragic way.

From Madrid to Valverde de Lucerna

We might say – if only for for simple reasons of concision – that the career of this singular Spanish philosopher begins and ends with two novels which, more than any essay or treatise, address problematics that remained constant over the entire development of his intellectual personality. *Nuevo mundo* (c. 1895) and *San Manuel Bueno, mártir* (1931), may serve as the starting and end points for our reading of his work. *Nuevo mundo* is the culmination of Unamuno's rejection of academic philosophy and religiosity as defined by the Catholic Church. Unfortunately, it was never published during Unamuno's lifetime (it would have been his first novel in print, given that *Paz en la guerra* appeared in 1897), and the same fate befell another manuscript, *Diario íntimo*, which is so interesting for readers seeking hermeneutic clues to the crisis of religious faith he underwent in 1897.

Nuevo mundo tells the story of a young man who leaves his home town to study in a large city (Madrid), in which, surrounded by a world which he had been ignorant of in his childhood, he gradually loses the simple, ingenuous faith of his youth. He tries to stand on his own two feet when he completes his studies, but his plans fail, because the young man does not have sufficient guile to triumph in a world where honour or decency count for little. Gradually, he completely loses not just his religious faith, but also his faith in political and social ideals. And his decision to travel to Argentina (whence the title of the text) also proves unsuccessful. The 'new world' that Unamuno references, however, is not simply the Americas. Before his death, the unfortunate protagonist, Eugenio Rodero, leaves his unfinished writings with a friend. It is here that the protagonist's true thoughts come to light, and this 'new world' is outlined. In the fictional universe of the novel, Rodero's notes take up the second part of the text. They are fragments of differing lengths that address various questions, a little along the lines of Pascal's *Pensées* (Unamuno 2005: 184–203). And it is here possible to glimpse for the first time in Unamuno's work an existentialist conception of philosophy, which sets the human being, with all his feelings, against the coldness of logic. In one of Rodero's supposed fragments, it is argued that 'only for love are things a true reality: love is the only thing that saves us from transcendental phenomenism' (Unamuno 2005: 202). Implicit here is the criticism of Hegelian rationalism. The ambiguity of this system lies in its reconciliation of absolute philosophy, and a concrete philosophy considered in terms of its contingent conditions and particular setting. Unamuno removes the possibility of an objective philosophy, and, successively in his work, demonstrates the personal and historical character of philosophy, because the philosopher exists and shares his life with the world he is set on analysing; his object of analysis is not alien to him. The subject places himself under question because of his particular condition of being. He determines and is also determined by his own discourse on being. Everything is rational *a posteriori*, but what about tomorrow? It is not possible to know the future, and it is not possible to imagine our consciousness as 'not thinking', so that death remains an irrational and inexplicable phenomenon in terms of the categories of rationalism. Without being able to explain death, it is not possible to assign meaning to human existence either. If, for Kant, immortality was the second of the three postulates of practical reason, then for Unamuno, our immortality has the status of a fifth antinomy of pure reason, something that our wish for eternity cannot deny, but at the same time something that we cannot affirm within any category of thought.

If we do not address the philosophical dimensions of Unamuno's thought, we will not be able to understand his poetry, theatre or prose fiction, because all his characters embody, each in his or her own way, the tensions and possible contradictions of human life faced with the mystery of eternity. It is no exaggeration to say that the artistic production of Unamuno is a plural and distinct series of expressions of his metaphysical eschatology. Without doubt we are here dealing with a peculiar philosophy, influenced by the experiences [*Erlebnis*] of its author. It is grounded on an anthropology that considers man exclusively as a *person*, and that sees all philosophy as the thought of a man of *flesh and bone* addressing another man of *flesh and bone* (Unamuno 1954: 28; OCE VII, 126; OCA XVI, 155). Man exists as a being with the capacity to think, but thought is inescapably tied up with materiality, the physical and earthly dimensions of existence, and thus with life itself. The rupture here with Descartes and his abstract *res cogitans* could not be more explicit; indeed, referring to the *Discours de la méthode*, Unamuno asserts 'The primary reality is not that I think [and therefore I *am*], but that I live, because those also live who do not think' (Unamuno 1954: 35; OCE VII, 130; OCA XVI, 162), and animals are not machines, as Descartes had argued. The other element that is key to understanding Unamuno's thought, as mentioned above, is the yearning for immortality. Man, as a person, needs to find an answer to the problem of death, and the God of the philosophers has helped him not at all in his quest. Along with Pascal (1952: 186 [§ 77]), Unamuno would argue that the Cartesian God who gave a fillip to the world to set it in motion is of no use to him; Unamuno longs for a paternal God, who, in his infinite goodness, gathers us to his bosom after 'the harsh struggle' of life.[2] Nor did Unamuno accept the possibility of a rational demonstration of the divine, given that it was precisely here that the rupture between Unamuno and the neo-scholastic current of Christian philosophy occurred. The existence of God cannot be demonstrated; perhaps it might be demonstrated that the idea of God necessarily exists within us, but this would be just an idea, and would entail a God without qualities or attributes (Unamuno 1954: 150; OCE VII, 198; OCA XVI, 278).

After his arrival in Salamanca, where he took up the Chair of Greek in 1891, Unamuno suffered a profound religious crisis in 1897, the subject of much critical study. Without entering into the delicate question of its problematic authenticity (it seems that in a certain sense Unamuno may have dramatised his experiences), suffice it to say that Unamuno suffered at first hand the drama that Eugenio Rodero in *Nuevo mundo* went through: the loss of his childhood faith and his inability to succeed in rationalising his religious beliefs. It is after this crisis, which he relives in the *Diario íntimo* mentioned above, and in much of his private correspondence, that his most intense mature works appear. Unamuno was feverishly busy in the early years of the twentieth century, penning novels, essays, poetry and short stories. Given that his achievements as both poet and novelist are not in any doubt, it seems unlikely that he was wanting to put his narrative skills and techniques to the test. I believe that the plurality of styles and genres responded to a clear need to make his message available to a wide and diverse readership, and thus to many and varied interpretations, outside the terrain proper to philosophical research. For Unamuno, writing was a coherent and organic activity, and did not need a demarcating line between prose or verse, novel or essay; what was important was establishing a bridge, a dialogue with his readers.

---

2   'Salmo III' 'Méteme, Padre eterno, en tu pecho / misterioso hogar / dormiré allí, pues vengo deshecho / del duro bregar' [Gather me, Eternal Father, to your bosom/ mysterious dwelling/ where I shall sleep, since I come to you undone/ by the harsh struggle] (OCE VI, 224; OCA XIII, 291).

In 1900, Unamuno published a slim collection of three essays: '¡Adentro!', 'La ideocracia', 'La fe', the last bearing a telling epigraph by Ibsen ('Liv og skal smelte sammen' [Life and faith have to be merged]) (OCE I, 962–970; OCA XVI, 99). The first of the three essays comes close to being a manifesto for Unamuno's approach to philosophy. He rejects all labels, refusing to follow any type of dogma: 'la realidad [...] no cabe en dogmas' [Life cannot be contained in dogmas] (OCE I, 950; OCA III, 423) and declaring that, rather than reflection centred on abstract ideas, he prefers meditation centred on himself, in the first person: '¡Mi centro está en mí!' [my centre is within myself] (OCE I, 948; OCA III, 419). An implicit core existentialism lies within this statement, and Unamuno leaves no room for doubt when, a little further on, he says 'Cada cual es único e insustituíble; en serlo a conciencia, pon tu principal empeño' [Each person is unique and irreplaceable: make it your principal undertaking to be so conscientiously] (OCE I, 950; OCA III, 423–4). For Unamuno, the obsession of many philosophers to reduce reality to a sole principle is not well-grounded, because a mere principle reduces down to a simple idea, and the human being – the real starting point of any human reflection, is always individual and not subject to an abstraction. Life in general is not *my* life; existence in general is not *my* existence. This is the topic of the second essay, 'La ideocracia'—the tyranny of ideas, which are dead forms, currency between abstract concepts which aim to pigeonhole a content 'que goza, vive y sufre, y que, por fin, se desvanece con la muerte' [which enjoys, lives and suffers and who, finally, disappears with death] (OCE I, 955; OCA III, 429). Here a conception of the vertiginous truth finds expression: logical concordance is not enough for Unamuno; he wants an intimate union between his spirit and the Spirit of the universe. Truth is something that is lived, not something that is simply understood like Pythagoras's theorem (OCE I, 958; OCA III, 434). At the end of the essay Unamuno once again cherishes a utopia he had alluded to also in *Nuevo mundo* and in other writings: the arrival of a kingdom of the spirit in which creatures would communicate amongst themselves through *spiritual love* rather than through concepts (OCE I, 961; OCA III, 439).[3] The third and final essay addresses another major subject of Unamuno's thought: faith. Unamuno's position is close to the '*credo quia absurdum*' [I believe because it is absurd] attributed to Tertullian. Unamuno asks '¿Qué cosa es la fe? [...] Crear lo que no vemos' [What is faith? Creating what we cannot see' (OCE I, 961; OCA XVI, 99). Faith

---

[3]   See, for example, 'Sobre mí mismo' from De mi vida (OCE VIII, 300–303; OCA X, 243–248); 'Sueño' OCE II, 781–783; OCA IX, 142–145), and, in *Del sentimiento trágico de la vida*: 'Primitive man [...] feels himself to be in social communion, not only with beings like himself, his fellow-men, but with the Whole of nature, animate and inanimate, which simply means, in other words, that he personalizes everything' (Unamuno 1954: 157; OCE VII, 202; OCA XVI, 285)

for Unamuno is not just something that cannot be reached through reason; it is creative and vital. He returns to this theme in the ninth chapter of *Del sentimiento trágico de la vida*, where his position remains unchanged: 'The road that leads us back to the living God, the God of the heart, and that leads us back to Him when we have left Him for the lifeless God of logic, is the road of faith, not of rational or mathematical conviction' (Unamuno 1954: 186; OCE VII; OCA XVI, 313).

This brief volume, which we have only been able to touch upon, is but the first in a series collecting the prolific essay-writing of Unamuno during the earliest years of the twentieth century. Unamuno reserves his most serious spiritual and moral explorations for the Madrid journal *La España moderna*: it is here that the essays '¡Plenitud de plenitudes y todo plenitud!' [Plenitude of Plenitudes and All is Plenitude!] (1904) (OCE I, 1171–1182; OCA III, 753–770), 'Soledad' [Solitude] (1905) (OCE I, 1251–1263; OCA III, 881–901), 'El secreto de la vida' [The Secret of Life] (1906) (OCE III, 876–886; OCA III, 1027–1042), '¿Qué es verdad?' [What is Truth?] (1906) (OCE III, 854–864; OCA III, 992–1009), 'Ibsen y Kierkegaard' (1907) (OCE III, 289–293; OCA IV, 426–432) all first appeared.[4]

The brief essay, which is 'at liberty to digress' [*de libre divagación*] in Unamuno's wry formulation, is one of his most accomplished genres, and is, without doubt, the medium which best reflects his thought. During this time, so fertile for Unamuno, and, in my humble opinion, the period in which his most illuminating philosophical work was produced, we must take note of one particularly exceptional event. Unamuno began to read Kierkegaard's *Either/Or* in 1904, in the original Danish, and in short succession he produced his *Vida de Don Quijote y Sancho* and the draft of *Tratado del amor de Dios*, which, roughly five years later, would be entitled *Del Sentimiento trágico de la vida*: we are here dealing with Unamuno's two most accomplished, most important and most translated essays.[5]

During Unamuno's steep intellectual climb away from positivism, Kierkegaard would come to be one more amongst his travelling companions, because a

---

4   Almost all these pre-World War I essays were published successively between 1916 and 1919 in the seven volumes of his collected *Ensayos* [Essays]. Other uncollected essays had already been published in 1910 under the title *Mi religión y otros ensayos breves* (OCE III, 259–367; OCA IV, 1178).

5   The long essay is unusual within Unamuno's work. He only returned to this longer medium twenty years later, during his exile, when he published, in French, *Agonie du Christianisme*, subsequently translated into Castilian. In any case, in this later work, which is excessively polemical, we find neither the vigour nor polish of the earlier period, which also coincides with the culmination of his professional career. For further detail on the significance of Unamuno's encounter with *Either/Or*, see Teira 2008.

philosophy that begins and ends with the problem of immortality (*meditatio mortis*), a philosophy of existence like that of St Augustine's, Pascal's and Kierkegaard's, would also come to be Unamuno's who, like them, had imbibed the words of the Gospels as though from an authentic wellspring. Unamuno, though, did not enjoy the gift of sainthood, unlike Saint Augustine; neither was he willing to dwell on, let alone resign himself to, Montaigne's *skepsis*; nor did he ever attain the serenity of Pascal, who accepted faith and found solace in the monastery at Port Royal near his sister, who had taken the veil (as had one of Unamuno's sisters, Susana). 'But the truth is that my work – I was going to say my mission – is to shatter the faith of men here, there, and everywhere, faith in affirmation, faith in negation, and faith in abstention from faith, and all this for the sake of faith in faith itself; it is to wage war against all those who submit, whether it be to Catholicism, or to rationalism, or to agnosticism; it is to make all men live the life of inquietude and passionate desire' (Unamuno 1954: 322; OCE VII, 297–298; OCA XVI, 444).

Like Kierkegaard, Unamuno felt the call of Christ, but was never able to dedicate himself to the religious life. He embraced instead the ethical life, like Judge William in *Either/Or*: he was a family man, faithful to his wife, accustomed to the routine of university life and to walks in the countryside surrounding Salamanca. Reading widely was also an ingrained habit of his, and he liked to explore and then recreate in his own 'voice', the classics (Cervantes, Fray Luis de León), or figures from the Gospels or the Old Testament (Nicodemus or Abishag the Shunammite). He also based some of his literary protagonists – Abel Sánchez and 'el Otro' amongst them – on biblical figures.

The influence of Kierkegaard on the work of Unamuno was previously a contested question, principally because of the almost total ignorance of the Danish language and of *Either/Or* on the part of Unamuno's earliest critics— almost no-one had actually read Kierkegaard at the time. However, by the 1940s, José Ferrater Mora was arguing that Unamuno was more of an existentialist than Kierkegaard himself (Ferrater Mora 1985: 36–37), and, much later, Javier Teira demonstrated the almost verbatim correspondence between passages in Unamuno's 1904 and 1905 essays and passages in *Either/Or* (Teira 2008: 69–124). A long quotation from Kierkegaard also concludes the prologue to the second edition of *San Manuel Bueno, mártir,* written in the early 1930s, as Unamuno took up his reading of *Either/Or* again after his exile (OCE II, 1122–23; OCA XVI, 576).

For Unamuno, who had declared the impossibility of philosophy's attaining any absolute, existentialism opened up an escape route towards an a-philosophical way out. Man can pursue truth through action, through his own life, and this call to action, is most prominently and insistently voiced in his 'Quixotist' essays between 1901 and 1905 (when the two volumes of the *Vida de don Quijote y*

Sancho were published), has been defined, a little superficially, in terms of 'pragmatism'. In this long essay, there are indeed frequent calls to action, and Don Quixote, with his singular crusade for Spain, leaves behind empty words and books to make a mortal leap towards the world and towards contingency. The following paragraph from the *Vida* has often been cited as an example of supposed Unamunian pragmatism:

> Every belief that leads to works of life is a true belief; every belief that leads to works of death is an untrue belief. Life is the criterion of truth, not logical concordance, which is the criterion only of reason.
>
> (OCE III, 130; OCA IV, 189).

However, Unamuno's thought here has nothing in common with the premises of American pragmatism. Don Quixote is an action hero, triumphantly checkmating the man who does not know whether to climb the steep hill of faith or to resign himself to a reductionist and positivist reading of reality, because with his deeds, Don Quixote constructs a fantasy world that is in some sense even more real than the one that surrounds him. It is a realm where justice always triumphs, where evil is defeated by goodness, and where love is pure and eternal. The deeds of Don Quixote are above reason itself (they attain 'suprareason', as Don Miguel would have it). He acts in pursuit of ideals; he is not governed by mere concrete facts. What does it matter that windmills are not giants, when the ideals shining like the stars in the Manchegan gentleman's sky are goodness and immortality? The agonic tension that lacerated Unamuno's spirit, eternally suspended between two irreconcilable paths, is resolved in Don Quixote's madness, which listens only to reasons of the heart, because it understands no others, just like those in love, since, ultimately, to believe is to love. And in a dialectical turn, his madness becomes wisdom, a wisdom that is not, of course, *episteme*, but *phronesis*, and consists of not believing or accepting reality: 'and how did you come, oh wondrous Knight, to the depths of wisdom, which consist of taking as invisible and fantastic the things of this world, and, by virtue of doing so, not being vexed by them!' (OCE III, 106; OCA IV, 150).

The lines of Carducci that Unamuno cited so insistently—*meglio oprando oblïar, senza indagarlo, questo enorme mister de l'universo!* – 'it is better to work and forget, without enquiring into this enormous mystery of the universe'—are not to be interpreted through a pragmatic optic (resigning oneself to ignorance and ploughing an earthly furrow) (Carducci 1902: 666). Rather, Unamuno wanted to teach us, and he does so with the metaphor of the Knight of La Mancha, so that our conduct should be projected towards the ultimate ends of life, and not towards the singular and particular.

Mathematising and scientific reason, which are always and exclusively analytical, destructive and dissolvent, must be opposed by the heart, which can 'vivify' knowledge (in the Pauline and Augustinian sense). This, in my opinion, is the meaning of the pragmatism of Don Quixote, and for that reason I am more inclined to read the *Vida* through an existentialist optic than see it as an example of pragmatism.[6]

In those early years of the twentieth century, Unamuno was drawn towards the currents of Catholic Modernism and Protestant Liberalism. He was interested in the idea of revitalising the Church, explaining doctrine in the light of present-day conditions and the contemporaneous meaning it might have: to that end, Don Miguel read Adolf Von Harnack, George Tyrrell, Albrecht Ritschl and Ernest Renan, amongst others. It was the discussion of the Christ of faith and the historical Jesus which were of greatest interest to him, because Christianity depends entirely on resurrection. Unamuno no longer believed the dogmas; nor did he believe in the neo-scholastic doctrine of the First Vatican Council, or in the infallibility of the Pope *ex cathedra Petri*, for the reasons we have seen above. His vision of Christianity responded more to an interest in the evangelical way of life as developed by the person of Christ, whom he saw as a model for and master of life, and above all as a guarantor of personal resurrection. But at the same time, Unamuno was convinced that a new biblical hermeneutics would also perhaps have reduced the enormous distance between the exegesis of Catholics and Protestants, and would have the enormous advantage of returning the stultified Spanish clergy to the present day so that they might breathe some fresh intellectual air. The Modernist adventure was short-lived. In a severe 1907 Encyclical, the 'Pascendi', Pope Pius X excommunicated clergy and lay members of the Church who professed such doctrines. He declared that Modernism was the synthesis of all heresies, and that was an end to the matter. Unamuno's reaction to the Encyclical was highly polemical:

> The present Pope has condemned the doctrines of so-called Modernism simply because the Modernists – Loisy, Le Roy, el padre Tyrrell, Murri, etc. – are trying to breath the life of truths back into dead dogma, and the Pope, or rather his advisers — the poor old man himself is completely out of his depth in such matters—foresee, with astute wisdom, that vivifying such dogma actually leads to their dying off completely. They know that there are corpses that, when one tries to breathe new life into them, crumble into dust
>
> (OCE III, 268; OCA IV, 395–401).

---

6   For further discussion, see Borzoni (2012).

The image of the dogmas of faith as crumbling mummified skeletons is very powerful, but this rupture with the traditions of the Catholic Church did not dim Unamuno's interest in religious problems. In his *Del sentimiento trágico de la vida*, published just six years after the 'Pascendi' encyclical, the key concern continues to be the search for immortality. It is a search that is conducted, as always in Unamuno, in a very singular way, but the reader is forewarned:

> El que busque razones, lo que estrictamente llamamos tales, argumentos científicos, consideraciones técnicamente lógicas, puede renunciar a seguirme [He who looks for reasons, strictly so called, scientific arguments, technically logical reflections, may refuse to follow me further]
> (Unamuno 1954: 125; OCE VII, 183; OCA XVI, 252).

This long essay, which appeared in 1913, is the fruit of many years' work. It combines reflections from previous essays, and above all the notes that made up 1905 draft that Unamuno entitled *Tratado del amor de Dios*, and which he did not otherwise subsequently publish. Perhaps what sets this work apart from others is that it attempts to be organic, but the guiding thread of its twelve chapters is very thin. Darwin, Cicero and Clement of Alexandria can all appear on the same page without its seeming inappropriate to Unamuno. There is frequent use of quotation: a whole life's reading is compressed into three hundred pages, and there is an eclecticism here rarely seen in other authors. Chapters IV, V and VI deal with immortality, and they represent a synthesis of Unamuno's exegesis of the Bible. With the mediation of Von Harnack, Ritschl and other theologians, Unamuno, who loved conflict, reminds his reader of the intrinsic dualism of the Catholic religion, which springs from two very different sources: Judaism and the Greco-Roman thought of Hellenism. Each, in its own way, had a particular vision of the immortality of the soul. In the words of one ancient Greek adage: 'Much worse is he who says that it were good not to be born, but when once one is born to pass quickly through the gates of Hades'.[7] I do not know if Unamuno had read these lines in class with his students – since Greek thought is conspicuous by its absence from *Del sentimiento trágico de la vida* – but there is no doubt that Unamuno knew, and in other passages cited, the verses of Homer and his despairingly bleak vision of the dark and empty beyond (Odyssey, XI). Now, this idea of nothingness, is, in short, what Unamuno is attempting to exorcise over the entire three hundred pages of the *Del sentimiento trágico de la vida*, but he

---

[7]   Legend has it that these were the words pronounced by Silenus to Midas, after Midas had asked him what was the best and most desirable thing for man. The quotation reappears also in Epicurus' letter to Menoeceus (126).

does not succeed in convincing the reader, and above all, does not succeed in convincing himself. The strangest and most extreme part of the work lies in the way in which Unamuno conceptualises God, which is as a product of our consciousness. The act of eternalising our temporal self, and of expanding our spatial self to infinity, is what produces the idea of God:

> The divine, therefore, was not originally something objective, but was rather the subjectivity of consciousness projected externally, the personalisation of the world. [...] The clearer our consciousness of the distinction between the objective and the subjective, the more obscure is the feeling of divinity in us. Subsequently reason—that is, philosophy—took possession of this God who had arisen in the human consciousness as a consequence of the sense of divinity in man, and tended to define him and convert him into an idea
> (Unamuno 1954: 157–9; OCE VII, 202–203; OCA XVI, 285–287).

But in another passage, Unamuno seems to recant and admit that without love, it is not possible to reach God. Without sacrifice and revelation, there would be no Christianity:

> The attributes of the living God, of the Father of Christ, must be deduced from His historical revelation in the Gospel and the conscience of vey Christian believer, and not from metaphysical reasonings which lead only to the Nothing-God of Scotus Erigena, to the rational or pantheistic God, to the atheist God—in short to the de-personalised Divinity
> (Unamuno 1954: 167; OCE VII, 208; OCA XVI, 295).

One of Unamuno's most accomplished poems, 'El Cristo de Velázquez' is dedicated to the path of love and suffering. Christ, the anti-metaphysical hero par excellence, not the Aristotelian, mechanical, 'clockmaker' God, but instead the Son of man, who translates the father's message into flesh and bone, the *Logos* made man. Of all the many artists who depicted the Redeemer, it is the painter Velázquez's representation that caught Don Miguel's eye and gave the poem its title. Already in *Del sentimiento trágico de la vida*, Unamuno had explicitly said that in Velázquez's painting, 'that Christ who is for ever dying but who never finishes dying, in order that he may give us life', represented 'the highest artistic expression of Catholicism, or at least of Spanish Catholicism', just as Bach had given the mightiest artistic expression of Protestantism through his celestial music.

It was rare for Unamuno to be able to give himself up entirely to faith; he does not always breathe the serenity that is present in the *Cristo de Velázquez*, which concludes precisely with the poet abandoning himself to *spes*:

> ¡mis ojos fijos en tus ojos, Cristo,
> Mi mirada anegada en Ti, Señor
> [My eyes fastened on yours, Christ,
> My gaze subsumed by You, Lord!]
> (OCE VI, 493; OCA XIII, 801).

God is also a person for Unamuno, because there is no other way of guaranteeing the totality and the independence of the human person. In order that a person can recognise himself as such, not only must he be connected to a totality which surpasses him; he must also be recognised as a person by that superior entity. Otherwise, the afterlife would be a simple Nirvana, something very different from the personal immortality invoked loudly in his contemplation of the pale Christ painted by Velázquez:

> Blanco el cuerpo está como el espejo
> Del padre de la luz, del sol vivífico.
> [Your body is as white as the mirror
> Of the father of light, of the enlivening sun]
> (OCE VI, 420; OCA XIII, 655)

During his years of exile, the course of Unamuno's life was dramatically interrupted, and not just in terms of his career or family life. It seems as though the flame that fuelled his writing went out. Unamuno published very little during these years: apart from the essay *Agonie du Christianisme* [The Agony of Christianity] written in 1925, first published in French in Paris, his work was made up of travel writing and polemical articles criticising the military directory led by Primo de Rivera. Unamuno did publish one novel—*Cómo se hace una novela*—but nothing that bears comparison with the *Vida de Don Quijote y Sancho*, or the earlier essays published in *La España Moderna*. I know that many critics will disagree with this judgement, which is perhaps too personal, but his *Agonie du Christianisme* is a text in which the serenity of the writer is vitiated by the forced condition of exile:

> The agony of my fatherland, which is dying, has also stirred in my soul the agony of Christianity. I feel at once politics elevated to religion, and religion elevated to politics. I feel the agony of the Spanish Christ, Christ in his death throes. And I feel the agony of Europe, of the civilisation that we call Christian, Greco-Latin or Western civilisation. And the two agonies are one and the same
> (OCE VII, 359–360; OCA XVI, 552).

It was only on his return to Spain that Unamuno's pen took up once more the long monologue with God, and my rapid survey, which began in Madrid with

Eugenio Rodero, will end in a small northern Castilian fictional village, Valverde de Lucerna, which many critics have identified with a village on the shores of Lake Sanabria (north of Salamanca). It was here that we find a priest much loved by his parishioners, called Manuel 'el Bueno' ['the Good'] by some; 'Saint Manuel' by others, because no-one had seen a priest so absorbed at the moment of transubstantiation during the Eucharist:

> En el pueblo todos acudían a misa, aunque sólo fuese por oírle y por verle en el altar, donde parecía transfigurarse, encendiéndosele el rostro [Everyone in the village attended mass, even if it were just to hear him, and see him at the altar, where he appeared transfigured, his expression/face aflame]
>
> (OCE II, 1132; OCA XVI, 589).

Don Manuel suffered, genuinely suffered, when holding up the holy Host, and everyone believed that it was his faith in the sacred mystery that fuelled his contrition. But what his parishioners did not know was that, inside, 'Saint' Manuel had lost his faith. What kept his vocation alive was his love for his people, for the families of the peasants and cattle-farmers of Valverde, who believed in the only way they knew how, with the faith of innocents, and of the humble; they believed with the faith of those that were last, and so would be first in the Kingdom of Heaven. In a parish priest like St Manuel, they found a model to follow:

> Y para un pueblo como el de Valverde de Lucerna no hay más confesión que la conducta. Ni sabe el pueblo qué cosa es fe, ni acaso le importa mucho [and for a village like Valverde de Lucerna there is no other confession than conduct. The people don't know what faith is, and in any case don't much care about *what it is*]
>
> (OCE II, 1154; OCA XVI, 628).

St Manuel does not want to shake up people's minds; he does not want to destroy the beliefs that kept his villagers united during the slow passing of the centuries. But Unamuno *did* want to do these things, and the result is that his thought is almost unique within the history of philosophy, excepting the Spanish-speaking countries. Nevertheless, I think that although Unamuno may not enjoy the importance that the history of philosophy has granted to other pre-World-War-II writers, he remains an author of universal importance, required reading for all those who feel attracted by the mystery that dwells *in interiore hominis*. It is in this sense that the originality of his thinking should be valued, and we should not concern ourselves with long debates about whether he may be considered a member of this or that literary movement, or this or that philosophical current.

We should instead remember that Unamuno's thought can ultimately be understood as a form of moral writing that looks towards becoming and futurity:When you write, because writing is the form your action takes, think of a universal readership, not just a Spanish one, and still less of the contemporary Spanish readership. ('¡Adentro!', OCE I, 947–948; OCA III, 419)

Coda: a Heretic of Thought?

The avant-garde literary magazine *La Gaceta Literaria* published a special issue in homage to Unamuno on his return from exile in 1930.[8] It contained notable pen portraits by Ramón Pérez de Ayala, Gabriel Miró, Manuel García Blanco, Joan Estelrich, Keyserling, Enrique Diez Canedo and José Francisco Pastor. There are also two articles dedicated to the philosophical thought of Unamuno, and I want to highlight one of them, 'Unamuno y la filosofía' [Unamuno and Philosophy], by Ramiro Ledesma Ramos, who would go on to be founder of the fascist JONS movement. Here Ledesma Ramos debates a problem which has been the object of many controversies—and which remains polemical—since Unamuno is an intellectual whose strikingly compendious thought resists containment within stereotypes. In response to the question 'was Unamuno a philosopher?' Ledesma Ramos writes:

> There is no doubt that those who have some culture in this country (through their studies, reading or education) routinely ascribe Unamuno's work, and its significance, to that cluster of problems that is philosophy [...] If Unamuno's work may in any way be classified within the field of philosophy—and strictly speaking we think he may not—it is precisely as a dismantler of philosophies (6).

For Ramiro Ledesma, Unamuno is a master of the problematisation of philosophy—even though he may not have the analytical purchase of other problematisers such as Nietzsche—but these problems are not, by themselves, of any interest to him. Ledesma stresses that philosophy is the disinterested search for truth and the desire to know. If, Ledesma writes, Unamuno enters the terrain of philosophy, he does so because his search for personal immortality, his desire to find an answer to the ultimate question about death, leads him to the writings of the great medieval metaphysicians, the mystics and other modern philosophers. But what matters to him is not metaphysics, nor ontology. For Unamuno, Ledesma argues 'problems are exclusive to the individual life in itself':

8   15 de marzo 1930.

For Unamuno, the individual life is the central justification of being. He is interested not in philosophies, but in the beating hearts of the men behind them, men afflicted by panic-stricken agonies. But philosophising assumes the acceptance of questions that are not objectively given, whose validity lies precisely in the fact that they are thought by a subject, but which does not detract in any way from their objectivity (6).

I share some of Ledesma Ramos' views here, but what he fails to appreciate is that this is precisely what characterises philosophical existentialism, in which existence precedes essence, living precedes thinking, and therefore, also precedes the admissibility of certain questions. This is a crucially important problematic, because Ortega himself, Ledesma Ramos' teacher, judged existentialism and its followers very harshly, dismissing them as 'youths from Montmartre who merely strum the guitar of existentialism, playing by ear'.[9] Ortega also compared Unamuno's hyperbolic, gigantic 'self' with the bill of a duck-billed platypus,[10] and in a sense he was right, because if Unamuno had not been the way he was, for better or worse, there would not be as much critical literature about this author.

We cannot deny existentialism its rightful place in the history of philosophy, given that it has posed some important questions, although in a way that differs from the classical academic method. Existentialism was an expression of the philosophical crisis that became full-blown after the disintegration of the metaphysical rationalism running from Descartes to Hegel. The first existentialist in this sense was Kierkegaard, and Unamuno, despite living far from northern Europe and not initially being versed in Danish, nevertheless discovered him, immediately recognising a fellow traveller and soulmate. Secondly, existentialism, which interprets the problem of personhood, has developed the concept of singularity, that is, the notion of the self as unrepeatable and unmistakeable: Unamuno repeatedly used the effective and fortunate expression 'the man of flesh and bone'. Finally, existentialism eliminates the possibility of an objective philosophy, demonstrating the personal and historical nature of all knowledge, as the philosopher exists and shares his life with the world that he is determined to analyse, and so is not alien to his object of analysis. In his 1932 work *Philosophy*, Karl Jaspers radically stresses that existence escapes any philosophical discourse because it is unobjectifiable and irreducible. Without

---

9   In 'La idea del principio en Leibniz' (Ortega y Gasset 1983: VIII, 275).
10   'There was no room for dialogue with him [...]. There was no choice but to embrace a passive role and form part of the circle around Don Miguel, who had unleashed his 'self' on the room, as if it were a duck-billed platypus'. 'En la muerte de Unamuno' (Ortega y Gasset 1983: V, 265).

entering into an impossible comparison between Jaspers and Unamuno, we can note that the latter had been arguing something similar since the beginning of the twentieth century. A definition of philosophy offered by Luigi Pareyson is well suited to Unamuno: 'philosophy is, in reality, speculative, and discovers an absolute value of truth through the personal interpretation that the philosopher gives it from himself, and, with it, from reality' (1950: 97). Unamuno might further add:

> There are, in fact, people who appear to think only with the brain, or with whatever may be the specific thinking organ; while others think with all the body and all the soul, with the blood, with the marrow of the bones, with the heart, with the lungs, with the belly, with life
>   (Unamuno 1954: 14; OCE VII, 117; OCA XVI, 141).

Existentialism is by its very nature unstable and problematic, and so is Unamuno's own thought, which is unsystematic, marked by distress, despair and the tragic sense, and sunk within a sea of contradictions that at the same time offer a coherent and organic vision of being, if we are able to discern them in their totality. The anguish of Unamuno, considered alongside his criticisms of the Spanish clergy and religious dogmatism, entail a radical spiritual renewal, not an atheism or a nihilism, so Unamuno's philosophy is not reducible to a Nietzschean 'hammer' or its *pars destruens*.

The renewal of consciences opens up a new problem: if he was not a philosopher in the classical academic sense, was he a Christian? The Christianity of dogma and rite seems to Unamuno a fact resolved in exteriority, and there are ample sectors within modern culture who define themselves as Christian and provoke the same criticisms of dogmatic Catholicism and of certain baroque or showy manifestations of faith. But one could raise the criticism that, if we cede nothing but interiority to Christianity, it is easy to brush up against anti-Christianity, because non-believers also admit conscience and individual interiority. Indeed, in 1957, the Church judged that two of Unamuno's works, *Del sentimiento trágico de la vida* and *La agonía del cristianismo*, had to be placed on the *Index Librorum Prohibitorum*, because, amongst other things, they did not admit the possibility of a rational explanation of God's existence or the articles of faith. Thus, with the decree of 23 January 1957, both works, together with all their translations, were condemned posthumously, when their author's remains had been resting in the cemetery of Salamanca for two decades. Fortunately, the Church's position has changed, and the recent Biblioteca de Autores Cristianos publication dedicated to Unamuno is a sincere attempt at reconciliation. Father José Vicente Rodríguez recognises that there is nothing atheistic about Unamuno:

If this study, for all that it is risky and criticisable on several points (of which I am all too aware), has succeeded in rescuing him to some degree from the many affronts to which he has been subjected on the basis of his religious values and his authentic longing for eternity, we will be gratified (2005: 436).

In conclusion, this solitary sniper is not so alone after all. He follows in the footsteps of Augustine, Montaigne, Pascal and, above all, Kierkegaard; his approach towards philosophy is, in short, very close to Christian existentialism. The Church reversed its stance, forgiving him his 'sins' and his views on Pope Pius X—'the poor old Pope' as Unamuno had dismissed him. It remains to be seen whether philosophers will be able to forgive him his highly personal views on the great figures of Western thought, given that Unamuno did all – or almost all – he could to perpetrate this struggle against all the boughs of the Porphyrian tree.

Further Reading

Cerezo Galán (1996), Orringer (1985), Unamuno (2007b).

6

Wordgames: Unamuno and the Primacy of Language

C. ALEX LONGHURST

Unamuno's interest in linguistic matters can be traced back to at least age sixteen, when he was already making notes on the Basque language, a topic which was to figure prominently in his 1884 doctoral memoir on 'El origen y prehistoria de la raza vasca' [The origin and prehistory of the Basque people] and was to be the subject of many later articles. During his undergraduate studies at Madrid University he chose to attend the Spanish philology class even though this was not officially part of his degree. Early in his Salamanca career he put a great deal of effort into preparing a detailed philological study of the *Cantar de mío Cid*, and in 1900 he added the new Chair of Comparative Philology to his teaching responsibilities as Professor of Greek. He also became interested in the provincial lexicon of the *charros*, inhabitants of the Salamanca countryside and villages, and even of that of neighbouring provinces, collecting thousands of popular words and expressions. He was a prodigious learner of foreign languages, able to read easily in fourteen different ones, and for several years he supplemented his professorial salary by translating into Spanish, mainly from English and German (Spencer, Carlyle, Schopenhauer, Humboldt).

After the Real Academia Española rejected his *Mío Cid* study in favour of Menéndez Pidal's, Unamuno experienced a certain reaction against philological investigation, and in letters to his friend Pedro Múgica in 1894 and 1895 he several times expressed his loss of interest in philology. Yet by 1896 he had recovered his curiosity, if not his enthusiasm: 'No crea usted que tengo abandonada en absoluto la lingüística'[1] [Do not think that I have completely abandoned philology]. Unamuno's relationship with philology, then, had its ups and downs, but in any case what appears to have happened is that his early scientific training, which had included historical grammar, morphology, etymology and semiotics,

---

[1]   The letters to Pedro Múgica from 1890 to 1904, which contain many references to linguistic matters, can be consulted in Larraín.

gave way to a much broader interest in the phenomenon of language which was rather more psychological and cultural and rather less philological, or, as Unamuno himself put it, linguistic inquiry became for him 'campo fecundísimo de enseñanzas psicológicas' [a very fertile field of psychological lessons] (Larraín: 100), something he was to confirm in later letters when he mentions his reconciliation with linguistics. In this movement away from traditional philology and towards the emergent discipline of modern linguistics, his reading of some of the nineteenth-century masters of linguistic thought – Friedrich Schleiermacher, Wilhelm von Humboldt, Max Müller – played a crucial role.

Unamuno's linguistic philosophy is so all-pervasive that it needs to be better known, and the highly suggestive work of such scholars as Mario J. Valdés (1982), Paul Ilie (1987), Alison Sinclair (1987), Marsha S. Collins (2002), and Álvarez Castro (2005) should form the basis of further investigations into the linguistic dimension of Unamuno's versatile incursions into other areas of cultural activity. In his major philosophical and religious essays, in all his major novels, in his poetry, and in dozens of shorter essays and speeches on a wide variety of topics the subject of language makes an appearance, often in a quite central way, as is the case of *Niebla*. Language was at the very heart of his chosen profession of university teacher, and in his retirement speech delivered on his seventieth birthday, a speech devoted yet again to language, he insisted that 'este hombre, a quien se le ha supuesto tan versátil, ha seguido, en su profesión académica como en la popular, una línea seguida' [this man, regarded as so protean, has followed, both in his academic and in his extracurricular activities, an unwavering line], and immediately referred to himself as 'siempre el filólogo' [always a philologist] (OCA, IX, 1126; OCE IX, 451).

Language and the Community

Unamuno's nineteenth-century education brought him into contact with the ideas about collectivities typical of that period, and this is as true of language as it is of other disciplines such as history, sociology and anthropology. From Schleiermacher Unamuno learnt of the close relationship between language and thought, that language makes thought possible, or as Schleiermacher put it, that 'no-one can think without words'. From Humboldt he learnt that language reflects the mental life of the nation that speaks it, that is, the degree of sophistication achieved by the community that uses it as well as the particular way in which that community views the world. From Müller he learnt that the history of mankind begins with language, and that language is capable of expanding almost indefinitely as it generates ever more combinations of words and meanings and therefore of possible worlds that go far beyond our physical environment, so that even primitive myths and religions take us far beyond the mere perception of nature. Unamuno was to absorb and recycle these and related ideas to such an extent that language became for him the fundamental principle without which little pertaining to human existence and society can be explained. As he constantly repeated, echoing St John the Evangelist, 'en el principio fue la Palabra' [in the beginning was the Word]. The Word became the Book, and the book – that is, the written word – became the mirror of mankind. For Unamuno, then, our human universe was primarily a verbal one.

Unamuno held that language reveals much about ourselves, our identity, our cultural allegiance, and even our human condition, but it also beguiles us into a virtual world that lies outside nature. The human mind is not content to limit itself to empirical phenomena. Our experience may perhaps prompt our queries, but the answers we seek are often not to be found in the realm of experience. Where experience ends, intuition and imagination are only too ready to take over, and the realm where they wander is by and large a linguistic one. For Unamuno the starting point of our linguistic adventure is the communality of language. Language is something that we inherit and absorb, and when we learn a language as children we are also absorbing the cultural attitudes or ways of thinking associated with that language and the community that speaks it. Given that 'el pensamiento depende del lenguaje, puesto que con palabras se piensa, y el lenguaje es una cosa social' [thought depends on language, since we think with words, and language is a social artefact], it follows that 'pensar es una función social'[2] [thinking is a social function] (OCE III, 400; OCA IV, 590, 591) The way we think, then, reflects the language in which we think. Across time a language represents the accumulated experience of a people; it is the most reliable testimony, indeed the embodiment, of its collective identity: 'la lengua lleva, a presión de atmósferas seculares, el sedimento de los siglos, el más rico aluvión del espíritu colectivo' [language, under the atmospheric pressure of centuries, carries with it the sediments of time, the rich alluvial deposits of a collective spirit] (OCE, I, 963; OCA XVI, 101). This was written in 1900, but the idea of language as constituting our sediment and our vital outlook is so fundamental to Unamuno's thought that he was still enunciating it in 1934, two years before his death:

> Cada lengua lleva implícita, mejor encarnada en sí, una concepción de la vida universal, y con ella un sentimiento —se siente con palabras—, un consentimiento, una filosofía, y una religión.'

> [Implicit in each language, nay embodied in it, is a universal conception of life, and with it a sentiment —one feels with words— a co-sentiment, a philosophy, a religion.]

(OCE IX, 449; OCA VII, 1084).

---

2   *Alrededor del estilo* (see footnote 4).

Interestingly, this view of language as rooted in and arising from our collective circumstances coincides significantly with that of the later Wittgenstein. When the latter abandoned the scientific pretensions of the *Tractatus Logico-Philosophicus* and developed in his *Philosophical Investigations* a far more pragmatic and fluid concept of language as something based on usage and not on logic-derived rules, he introduced the key idea of 'form of life', the inextricable link between a language and the traditions, beliefs, attitudes and habits of the community to which it belongs. Language is a public enterprise, not a private one. To learn a language is to learn the assumptions of a linguistic community, which is of course what Unamuno said on numerous occasions. Not that Wittgenstein read Unamuno. The idea was already in Schleiermacher and especially in Humboldt; it could even be traced back to Herder. A case perhaps of, as Unamuno liked to say, 'nihil novum sub sole'.

It is tempting to discern in Unamuno a modern philosopher of language in the manner of his near-contemporaries Ferdinand de Saussure and Fritz Mauthner; and it is true that there are certain coincidences to be found. With Saussure he shares the idea that the language system of the community (*langue* or linguistic code) is imposed on the individual and his utterances (*parole* or speech events); and with Mauthner (whom Unamuno read much too late to have been influenced by him) he appears to share a radical scepticism about language, namely a disinclination to accept that language can lead us to the truth about anything. But these coincidences can be easily explained by the simple fact that all three had a common and strongly influential predecessor, Wilhelm von Humboldt, in whom the germ of most of the ideas found in these later thinkers can be found. One of Humboldt's central ideas was that language is a web of interconnected elements, so that, when we speak or write, what we are doing is plugging in to a network. This clearly means that we cannot function linguistically without the network, that language therefore has a hold over us because no individual can control an entire network, and that our input can be a creative but never a conclusive one. The question then arises as to whether we can ultimately express a stable, definitive and complete truth linguistically. This idea, later exploited by Derrida and other late twentieth-century post-structuralists, is already found in the linguistic philosophers of the Romantic period.

For Unamuno the virtual equivalence of language and thought, the idea that our thought is governed by our language, means that there is a particular world-view common to all the nations that have Spanish as their mother tongue. This forms the basis of his pan-Hispanism, his passionate belief that Spanish speakers across the world shared a common outlook. They did so because the language formed a bond and furnished a mental viewpoint or disposition towards the world. This did not necessarily bring about cultural homogeneity—which

Unamuno never advocated—since the same language could be used in infinitely varied ways. A modern language, rich in its evolutionary experience and range of expression, was perfectly capable of expressing a varied assortment of cultural and historical experiences and aspirations. Spanish provided a common grammar, a common syntax, and in large measure a common vocabulary, yet Castilians, Catalans, Basques, Galicians, Argentinians, Peruvians, Mexicans etc. had their own distinctive way of using the Spanish language. Indeed for Unamuno the richness of a specific linguistic culture depended more than anything else on the diversity of its manifestations. Unamuno applauded the local identity of each territory while emphasizing the common root. As Stephen Roberts has written, 'diferenciación e integración, divergencia y convergencia, por lo tanto, son las claves de la comprensión unamuniana de los vínculos culturales entre España e Hispanoamérica' [differentiation and integration, divergence and convergence, are thus the keys to Unamuno's understanding of the cultural links between Spain and Spanish America] (Roberts 2004: 73).

As far as Spain itself was concerned, Unamuno made a distinction between the Latin languages of the Iberian Peninsula and the pre-Roman language, Basque. He saw no future in Basque because it had not kept pace with modern developments and lacked the vocabulary and flexibility of the Latin languages. Although he had initially favoured research into the history of the Basque language, he later deplored the efforts of Basque nationalists to modernize Basque on the grounds that all they were doing was importing Castilian words and giving them a Basque-looking orthography, something which for Unamuno was as artificial as it was hypocritical. Much better, he argued, for Basques to use the Castilian they had all learnt as children than to use an adulterated tongue for purely political motives. The essential reason why Unamuno placed Castilian, Catalan and Galaico-Portuguese above Basque was that the latter lacked the literary tradition of the former, that is to say, it had shown itself to be culturally less productive and more backward since most of its literature was confined to popular folktales. In fact, since Unamuno's death, much Basque literature that had lain forgotten has been located in French archives, but this recent development is one that Unamuno could hardly have foreseen. His dismissive attitude towards Basque has earned him the odium of many Basque nationalists, but his standpoint is easily explained. Firstly, it is true that this ancient tongue had not developed as had the Germanic and Latin languages of Europe, and secondly, Unamuno had been very impressed by Wilhelm von Humboldt's thesis that a language reflects the degree of cultural development of the peoples who speak it. It follows from this that since the Basques had developed culturally every bit as much as the Castilians, many having indeed played an important role in Spain's history, *it must be because they were using the Spanish language, not the Basque language.* Today we may not agree with Unamuno just as we may not agree with Wilhelm von Humboldt's thesis, but there is nothing inconsistent or vengeful in Unamuno's position. Where he lays himself open to justified criticism is in condemning the attempt to bring Basque up to date. Since Basque had been from time immemorial the language of a rural people (in cosmopolitan Bilbao, Unamuno's native city, people spoke Castilian), its philosophical and scientific potential in the contemporary world was limited, unless it developed very rapidly, but this development could only be achieved by reference to other languages that had already developed this potential. This is what Basque reformers and nationalists were aiming to do, and what Unamuno deplored, seeing in it a politically motivated enterprise rather than a philological or cultural one. For him Basque remained the language of country folk and not of the sophisticated industrial society of his native Bilbao, and as such should be given a decent burial and not invoked to legitimate the spurious Basque nationalism invented by Sabino de Arana and his followers in their efforts to sustain their ambitions of political power.[3] By contrast Castilian, Catalan and Galaico-Portuguese all had a rich literary heritage stretching back to the Middle Ages and the potential to express a modern outlook. In the nineteenth century both Catalan and Portuguese literature had outstripped Castilian literature in depth and authenticity. It is clear that it is the richness of nineteenth-century Portuguese writing and of the Catalan Renaixença that made Unamuno more positively disposed towards those two Iberian languages than to that of his own native region. While he urged the Catalans and the Galicians to use the Spanish that, as he put it, they were perfectly capable of using (forgetting that some Galician peasants and some Catalan *payeses* were not fluent in Castilian) and to use it in their own manner and style, he did not, all the same, advocate the abandonment of their regional languages. Unamuno believed that nineteenth-century Castilian Spanish had become stagnant, that writers and politicians in Castile had adopted a rhetorical and clichéd style that had robbed the language of its capacity to engender new ideas. The remedy could only come from the periphery, from those who were capable of using the language in a fresh and stimulating way. It is for this reason that he more than once advocated the 'americanización del castellano' and urged Basques and Catalans to exert their influence on the centre by writing Spanish in a non-Castilian style, in precisely the way that he himself was doing (and indeed other contemporary writers of the Iberian periphery such as Ramón del Valle-Inclán, Pío Baroja, and *Azorín* [José Martínez Ruiz]). Such was the importance he attached to the manner of expression, that Unamuno clearly hoped that changing the style of writing would bring about the revitalization

---

[3]   For the invention of a Basque tradition with which to bolster the claims of Basque nationalism see Jon Juaristi, *El linaje de Aitor. La invención de la tradición vasca* (Taurus: Madrid, 1987).

of the stagnant culture, or *marasmo* as he called it, of Castilian Spain. In this his intuition was unerring, for the new literature that stretches from the late 1890s to the 1930s, the *Edad de Plata* as it came to be known, was above all a revolution of style, as Unamuno had preached.

Unamuno's defence of Castilian as the language of the Hispanic world is often mistaken (mostly by regional nationalists) for the expression of a hegemonic sentiment in favour of Castile and against the Iberian regions. In fact it was nothing of the kind. Far from wanting Castile to dominate the Iberian world, Unamuno admitted, indeed welcomed, cultural divergence. He several times repeated, not just for the benefit of separatists but just as much for the benefit of intransigent Castilian centralists, that Castile could not seek integration on its own terms: '¿Y es que [Castilla], pues que su lengua se extiende a dilatados países y se hace la lengua hispanoamericana, puede pretender monopolio de su casticidad o hegemonía en ella?' [And is it therefore the case that Castile, whose language has spread to numerous other countries and become the language of Spanish America, can thereby aspire to establish a monopoly of Castilianness or hegemony through that language?]. And Unamuno's answer to the question is categorical: '¡No!' (OCE, IX, 327; OCA VII, 900). Not only did Unamuno not advocate Castilian hegemony, but he was very clear that Spain's national identity, or her 'personalidad colectiva' as he called it, depended heavily on the regions and that regional consciousness was a force for good:

> Todo, pues, lo que sea dar vigor y fuerza a la vida regional, fomentar el regionalismo, es asentar las inconmovibles bases de la nacionalidad. Es un profundo error, error jacobino, el de creer que la nacionalidad es descendente, que se hace de arriba abajo, imponiéndola desde el centro directivo. Así se hará la nación tal vez, pero no el sentimiento de la nacionalidad, el cual, para ser robusto, ha de ser ascendente o más bien centrípeto, de la periferia al centro.

> [Anything that invigorates and strengthens regional life, that encourages regionalism, serves to lay down the unshakeable foundations of nationality. It is a profound error, a Jacobin error, to believe that nationality moves downwards, that it is created top-down and imposed by the controlling centre. A nation may be constructed in that way perhaps, but not the feeling of nationality, which, if it is to be robust, has to be created from below, or even be centripetal, moving from the periphery to the centre]
>
> (Unamuno 1993: 149).

For Unamuno, then, the perennial Spanish problem of reconciling centre and periphery would be resolved by the periphery taking over the centre, not vice versa. At the same time he held that this act of possession carried with it a recognition that the language of a common culture had to be the Spanish language, since this was the most widespread. But Unamuno did not stop here: his undoubted linguistic preference for the language of Castile went hand in hand with an avowed cultural pluralism. Every inhabitant of the Iberian Peninsula, he declared, had the responsibility to acquire a reasonable knowledge of the other Neo-Latin languages, and this was obviously directed much more at the Castilians than at the non-Castilians. Unamuno, who could read in thirteen foreign languages but struggled to speak any of them bar French, knew that to expect Castilians to acquire fluency in a language they had not heard as children was unrealistic. But this did not exempt them from acquiring a good knowledge of those other Iberian languages in their written form. On the contrary, Unamuno held that 'es un deber hoy de todo español culto llegar a leer catalán y portugués sin que se los traduzcan' (OCE, IX, 329; OCA VII, 904) [it is the duty of every educated Spaniard today to learn to read Catalan and Portuguese without the need for translation], as he declared in a public lecture given in Valladolid, the heartland of Old Castile. Those Basques and Catalans who today accuse Unamuno of being a turncoat and of advocating Castilian hegemony have forgotten or ignored the real basis behind his call for Iberian solidarity. France had built its nationhood on a strong, common language, as indeed had Britain and Germany. From this Unamuno drew the obvious lesson: that a common language, without detriment to other languages with a strong cultural heritage, was a pre-requisite for a resurgent Spain. His vision of Spain was thus of a multi-cultural state, with each culture as valid as any other, but one with a common language. That language could only be Spanish, because it was Spanish that gave the Hispanic world at large its family likeness.

Language and the Writer

Unamuno's fascination with language did not just affect his attempts to retain the allegiance of the historic regions by appealing to a shared outlook among Spanish-speaking peoples. It comes through powerfully in his view of the writer and the function of literature. The problem at the outset was how to reconcile language as a communal phenomenon and language as a tool of the individual writer.

Language arises in the community, but a community's writings have been the work of individuals. What, then, is the role of the writer and the function of literature? For Unamuno writing was a compromise between what belonged to others and what belonged to him. Given that any thought or sentiment we care to formulate must of necessity be clothed in worldly garb, in the lexicon, grammar, syntax, images and concepts which are our common heritage, it follows that what the writer can contribute is a mere reformulation, a personal form of expression, and this Unamuno calls the 'savia vivificante', the life-giving sap that rises from the roots of his being. It amounts to putting his own personal enduring stamp or 'sello eterno' on what he takes from the community, a two-way process that is the hallmark of human existence. The challenge for the serious writer is how to use an inherited tool in such a way as to make ideas come to life.

Unamuno believed that there are no new ideas, that everything is a perpetual recycling. He claimed no originality of thought: 'Casi todas las cosas que he dicho las han dicho cientos, miles, antes que yo' [Nearly everything I have said has been said before by hundreds, thousands, of other people] (OCE III, 393; OCA IV, 580). Ideas can only be re-freshed, re-clothed, and this requires a new expression, or as he called it 'tono' [tone]. Paradoxically the fact that 'ese tú de escritor es algo que es de todos' [that 'you' which is the writer belongs to everyone], the fact that as a writer 'estás en medio de la calle recibiendo las voces de todos y devolviéndolas' [you are standing in the middle of the street hearing everyone's words and returning them] (OCE III, 401; OCA, IV, 591), makes the writing enterprise both possible and worthwhile. This is where Unamuno's concept of style comes into its own. A writer may not be able to choose his own language, but he can choose his own style, in much the same way as each of the many Spanish-speaking territories of the world could speak with its own voice: 'Es el estilo, en efecto, más bien que no la lengua, lo que distingue entre sí a las literaturas y a sus pueblos. Cada uno de estos tiene su estilo propio' [It is in fact the style, rather than simply the language, which distinguishes one literature, and its nation, from another. Each one has its own style] (OCE IX, 328; OCA VII, 901). Such importance did Unamuno attach to the concept of style, that when exiled in the island of Fuerteventura in 1924 he conceived the idea of recycling his past comments on style and adding further thoughts on the subject with a view to publishing the material in a single volume under the title of *Alrededor del estilo* [On Style], although the project never saw the light of day in his lifetime.[4]

Unamuno establishes a crucial distinction between *estilismo* and *estilo*, just as he had earlier done between *literatismitis* (the disease of Restoration Spain that only produced shallow and clichéd writing) and *literatura* (the genuine article). There is nothing spontaneous about style; like personality, it comes from outside us in the first place and it has to be learnt. Recognizing a distinctive style in other writers will make us want to develop our very own. But one's

[4]   The closest we come to such a collection is Miguel de Unamuno, *Alrededor del estilo*, ed. Laureano Robles (Unamuno 1998b). Most (not all) of the articles in this collection were actually written in 1924 and published that same year in the Madrid newspaper *Los Lunes del Imparcial*, but they do incorporate earlier material going back many years. See also OCE VII, 885–947; OCA XI, 789–884.

own style is not a copy, it is rather a creative response to what we read. Indeed a copy is an absence of style, rather than a style. The writer who develops a personal style becomes, in Unamuno's parlance, a poet, irrespective of whether the writing is in prose or verse. *Estilismo* is the ready-made garb that allows us to show off while hiding our vacuity; but *estilo* is the re-fashioned garb we make to fit ourselves, not a material but a spiritual garb.

Essentially Unamuno is transferring the argument he had used earlier in his career for linguistic communities (that a language reflects its community's *weltanschauung* or life-view) to the realm of the individual. It is not the individual's language that contains his or her life-view, since the language is publicly owned; it is the use that he or she puts it to. Unamuno argues that style is biographical, by which he means that it is life-dependent, referring back to its creator and his life-moment.[5] Indeed Unamuno explicitly equates the two when, referring to Salvador de Madariaga's quotation of Buffon's 'le style c'est l'homme même' [the style is the man himself], he comments that 'lo mismo pudo haber dicho "el lenguaje es la nación"' (Unamuno 1998: 73) [he might just as well have said "language is the nation"]. A nation is made by its language and the way it uses it; a writer likewise is made by his personal usage of the language. The personality of the writer emerges from his style; 'el estilo nos hace; no hacemos el estilo' (Unamuno 1998: 102) [style makes us; we do not make style]. Style thus becomes an irreducible quality; it comes to belong to the psyche. To refer to the style of a great writer, explains Unamuno, is tantamount to uttering the name of that writer: name and style are synonymous. Style is the soul of the writer just as language is a country's soul, a term, *alma*, which Unamuno uses profusely. The idea is powerfully expressed in a poem from the *Romancero del destierro*, which Unamuno wrote some time after his return to Europe from Fuerteventura while in self-exile in France. In this poem, which relies on hyperbaton for its effect, Unamuno compares the power of writing with the power of the sling:

> La vibración de mi mano
> no sólo la espada lleva,
> la lleva al salir de mi honda
> temblando de ardor la piedra.
>
> Va en la palabra caliente
> alma de sangre de lengua
> y en el escrito acerado
> alma de sangre de diestra.

---

5   The argument is derived from Schleiermacher, according to whom a person is to be found in his or her way of expressing him or herself.

[It is not only the sword that
carries the vibration of my hand,
it is carried by the stone which pulsates
with passion as it leaves my sling.

From the heat of the word oozes
the bleeding soul of language
and from the steely writing
the bleeding soul of my right hand.]
                    (OCE, VI, 977; OCA XV, 91)

Here the soul makes itself felt through the power of words. The hand that writes is a sling projecting stones (i.e. words), stones that carry the blood of the soul (i.e. the sentiments of the poet). Language, then, is the only powerful tool at our disposal to reveal or project our intimate being; in Unamuno's words, it drips with the life-blood of the poet's existence. The role of a writer is to give back to his community what he took from it in the first place, language, but to give it back in a personalized, fresh and challenging way that will further the collective cultural enterprise of the nation. For Unamuno the literary corpus of a nation embodies the collective soul of that nation. 'No es el héroe otra cosa que el alma colectiva individualizada' [a hero is nothing but the individualization of the collective soul] (OCE I, 917; OCA III, 373), he said of Cervantes's famous literary hero. Cervantes's novel was to the Spanish nation what the Old Testament is to the Jews or the New Testament to the Christians. If Don Quixote is the distillation of a whole race, it follows that the writer's role is to penetrate, imbibe, embody and finally crystallize the spirit of his nation, a spirit which has to be found within himself, in other words within his style. Unamuno's own style was certainly idiosyncratic, characterized by short sentences, elisions, frequent appeals to etymology in order to adjust the meaning of words, often unconventional syntax, and perhaps above all by the use of chiasmus, the repetition of phrases in the reverse order of words. The latter habit, well studied by Thomas Mermall and Paul R. Olson, becomes something of an indulgence in his essays but has important repercussions in his fiction. In a revealing study, Olson has shown how the 'syntactic microstructures' of Unamuno's prose-style are reflected in the 'larger narrative structures' (Olson 2003, 223). Phrase reversal, then, is not simply a matter of grammar or diction but also of thought and structure. One of the clearest examples of this occurs in *Niebla*, where the character Unamuno, having declared that Augusto Pérez is but a fictional creation of his, has the tables neatly turned upon him when Augusto declares that Unamuno is simply the instrument of fictional characters, 'cosa de libros', a bookish entity. Unamuno's style is directed at exercising a powerful effect upon the reader, not only by his frequent playing with the meaning of words, but also by his emotional appeals through the liberal use of exclamation marks and, in his novels and stories, by the use of a sharp, tense, and often dramatic dialogue. Avoiding anything that might smack of nineteenth-century Castilian rhetoric, which he abhorred, he developed a very untraditional style that was terse, headstrong and not averse to creating paradoxes. The fretful style goes hand in glove with the restlessness of his mind. His self was in his writing, in 'el Unamuno de la leyenda', using the word in its original sense of reading. For him, a writer was but a reader of himself.

Two years before his death, in his retirement speech of 29 September 1934, which also happened to be his seventieth birthday, Unamuno declared that 'la historia, la tradición viva, queda y vive en la palabra, en el verbo, en el nombre, siempre presente. Historia no es letra, no es documento escrito, no es escritura, antes bien, lectura, lección, leyenda' [history, the living tradition, remains alive in its language, in its word, in its naming, always present. History is not simply the script, the written document, what has been written down, but rather the reading of it, the lesson drawn, the legend] (OCE IX, 447; OCA VII, 1080). In writing, a writer reads, i.e. re-creates, himself. His readers in turn re-create him and, in reading creatively, themselves, and therefore their culture, which, through the reading act, becomes endlessly transmissible from generation to generation. In his poem 'Para después de mi muerte' the poet addresses the reader and declares that the verses belong to him, a sentiment conveyed through the power of language, which recreates the mind of the poet in the mind of the reader:

> Oye tú que lees esto
> después de estar yo en tierra,
> cuando yo que lo he escrito
> no puedo ya al espejo contemplarme;
> ¡oye y medita!
> [...]
> tuyas serán estas palabras mías
> que sonarán acaso
> desde otra boca,
> sobre mi polvo
> sin que las oiga yo que soy su fuente.
> Cuando yo ya no sea,
> ¡serás tú, canto mío!
> Tú, voz atada a tinta,
> aire encarnado en tierra,
> doble milagro,
> portento sin igual de la palabra,
> portento de la letra,
> ¡tú nos abrumas!
> ¡Y que vivas tú más que yo, mi canto!

[Listen you who are reading this
after I have been consigned to earth,
when I who have written it
can no longer in my mirror see myself;
listen and consider!
[...]
yours will be these words of mine,
the sound of which perhaps
from another mouth may fall
upon my dust without being heard
by me who am their source.
When I no longer am,
you will be, oh my song!
You, a voice held in ink,
air in earth embodied,
a miracle twice over,
a peerless wonder of the word,
a wonderment of writing,
you overpower us!
To think that you will outlive me, oh my song!]
                    (OCE, VI, 172: OCA XIII, 206–7)

Writing, then, becomes detached from the writer and attaches itself to others, no longer faithful to its progenitor. But this, though in a way paradoxical or painful, is part and parcel of the writer's calling. For Unamuno also declared that writing, like teaching, was an *oficio*—a duty or obligation, from the Latin *officium*—and that this *oficio* entailed an obligation towards his community. We can easily observe how for Unamuno his writing was an extension of his teaching, of his sustained devotion to his students. In his valedictory address to those students in 1934, Unamuno chose to return to the theme that had obsessed him for most of his life: the role of language in human existence. His whole life had been a life of words, like Quevedo's, like Gracián's, like Calderón's, like the mystics'. In his writing he had set himself the task of making his readers aware of themselves in the mirror that is literature;[6] to discover their personalities, their traditions, their circumstance, their sentiments, their preoccupations, and even what for him were the dangers of ignoring their common roots. 'El hombre es hombre por la palabra' [man is man through the word] (OCE III, 857; OCA III, 997): to forget our culture, which is an essentially linguistic phenomenon, is to revert to an animal state. What keeps us human is our sense of community,

---

6   The word *espejo*, mirror, is one that was used repeatedly by Unamuno to refer to the self-reflective effect of books.

and what gives us our sense of community, what makes community possible, is our language. Unamuno's life-mission was thus to 'conocerme mejor para conocer mejor a mi pueblo — en el espejo sobre todo de su lengua' [know myself better to better know my people—above all in the mirror of its language] (OCE IX, 451 OCA VII, 1087). Did he ultimately achieve this higher knowledge of himself?

Language and the Self

For Unamuno literature had a cognitive function, both in discovering the nation and in exploring the self. This exploration is of course a linguistic one, but there is nothing unusual about it. On the contrary, it represents the fact that much of our life is fictional, mythical, that we create our own realities over and above our physiological existence. Our systems of social and political organization, our notions of truth, justice, liberty, friendship and so on have no physiological counterparts. Only physiological processes are phenomenologically real, as Unamuno explores in his novel *Niebla*. All else may be regarded as a linguistic fabrication in the sense that it depends overwhelmingly on language for its existence, but these linguistic entities appear no less real to us for all that. A human being does not act purely out of biological necessity: rightly or wrongly we are highly conscious of our freedom of action and hence of a need to define or justify ourselves. This is where the notion of self comes in. Beyond the physiological experiences of pain, pleasure, hunger, embarrassment, and so on, where is the I that experiences these sentiments? Or to put it another way, where is the seat of consciousness? Is it something separate from physiological processes? Unamuno had a lifelong obsession with locating his self, with discovering what drove him on. But in that case who is the self who is studying the self? The question is of course infinitely regressive, and Unamuno, predictably, never found an answer to the conundrum. What he did was to convert an ontological question into a linguistic, and ultimately a literary, one.

As we have seen, language, according to Unamuno, is a communal activity which we have to learn to use for our own ends: we are necessarily passive receptors and we cannot avoid falling under its dominion. So much so that a linguistic creation can become an alien object for the person who created it in the first place. In his essay 'Intelectualidad y espiritualidad' (1904), he describes, using third-person narration, the destabilizing effect of re-reading a piece into which he had poured his deepest feelings:

No, no comunica uno lo que quería comunicar –pensó–; apenas un pensamiento encarna en palabra, y así revestido sale al mundo, es de otro, o más bien no es de nadie por ser de todos. La carne de que se reviste el lenguaje es comunal y es externa; engurruñe al pensamiento, lo aprisiona y aun lo trastorna y contrahace. No, él no había querido decir aquello, el nunca había pensado aquello.

Fue singular y desasosegador el efecto que le produjo leerse como a un extraño, leer sus escritos como si lo fueran de otro.

[No, one does not convey what one wanted to convey—he reflected—; hardly has a thought become embodied in its word, and thus clothed emerges to the world, when it belongs to another, or rather to no-one because it is everyone's. The flesh of language is communal and external; it shrink-wraps the thought, it traps it, it even disturbs and disfigures it. No, he had not wanted to say that, he had never thought that.

Reading himself as a stranger, reading his writings as if they were someone else's, produced in him a singular and disquieting effect.]

(OCE I, 1138; OCA, III, 703)

This unnerving experience, which was to be repeated twenty years later in *Cómo se hace una novela* when Unamuno re-read and reacted to Jean Cassou's French translation of the original Spanish draft, shows Unamuno's discomfiture in having to admit that language does not belong to the individual who uses it, that it constrains and enslaves, forcing its users to express themselves in ways that may not reflect what they truly think or feel at that particular moment. ';Si fuera posible ir creando la lengua a medida que se habla lo pensado!' [If only we could create language as we utter what we have thought!] (OCE I, 1140; OCA III, 706), he exclaimed nostalgically, momentarily forgetting that in his linguistic philosophy language and thought were supposed to be indissoluble.

This indissolubility or togetherness of language and thought is an intrinsic part of our early formation as human beings. Since language programmes our brains as we develop in infancy and childhood, and since language is a public phenomenon that belongs to its community, it follows that when we absorb a language we are absorbing that community's disposition and outlook as ingrained in its language. There is, as it were, a communal brain that impacts upon each individual brain through the nature of language. This apparent constraint upon our ability to express our individuality in language was for Unamuno both a frustration and a challenge, for as he often repeated, and made some of his fictional characters echo, what was important to him was his awareness of himself as an individual, and he had no wish either to be someone else in life or to be absorbed into the godhead through Pauline apocatastasis upon death. For him selfhood was all important, and selfhood could only be studied through its manifestations; and in the case of a writer that primarily means his writings.

Unamuno's search for individuality within the ineluctable communality of language precisely mirrors the problem with identifying the self. As with language, the self is a social construct which we inherit, that is to say, we become conscious that other beings have a view of us, and our view of ourselves is conditioned by this external perception: 'Nadie se conoce sino en los demás' [No-one knows himself except in others] (Unamuno 1998: 46–7). This view of ourselves as a public persona or social self is the basis for Unamuno's complex permutations on the self, or personal identity, on which so much of his literature is built. At its simplest, the self, in Unamuno's ontology, develops in a social context as the individual establishes relations with his social group and acquires a role within it. This social self exists as a subject, but it is also an object because we are conscious of having an existence for others. The key point is that this integrated self is a reflection of a social reality: the public self impacts upon the private self. Both of these selves, internal and external, exist for us, and the individual who achieves equilibrium will be the one in whom these two dimensions engage in a harmonious dialogue. Where there is disharmony, alienation will supervene. The alienating phenomenon that, with reference to language, Unamuno describes in the passage quoted above and in *Cómo se hace una novela* is explored in terms of personality disorder in several of his novels, notably in *Niebla*, *Abel Sánchez*, *Tulio Montalbán y Julio Macedo*, and *La novela de don Sandalio*.

In *Niebla*, Augusto Pérez tries to forge an identity for himself through a double strategy, the physiological and the verbal, or the phenomenological and the metaphorical. It soon transpires that Augusto is much better at words than at sex, but his verbal musings lead not to self-cognition but to humiliation and disaster. He resorts to endless dialogue with others and with himself (or with his dog, whom he uses as his audience for his endless ruminations—Unamuno, in accordance with his theory of thinking makes his character speak his thoughts), but in so doing Augusto enters a labyrinth of words which ultimately prevents him from learning anything solid or reassuring about his own identity. As Paul Olson has explained in his Critical Guide to *Niebla*, language ends up by losing the subservience to its referent and acquiring its own autonomy (Olson 1984: 90–93). Ironically the only disinterested view of language in the novel comes from the mouth of one who cannot speak but, as his name Orpheus implies, can lament in song:

> [El hombre] en cuanto le ha puesto un nombre a algo, ya no ve este algo, no hace sino oír el nombre que le puso, o verle escrito. La lengua le sirve para mentir, inventar lo que no hay, y confundirse

> [As soon as man has given something a name he no longer sees this something, he only hears the name he gave it, or sees the name written down. Language is used to lie, to invent what is not there, and get confused].
>
> (OCE II, 680; OCA II, 996)

This canine view of man's linguistic fabrications is perhaps a more extreme version of the view that Unamuno upholds in his essays, but it nevertheless conveys the idea that language cannot lead us to the truth about our inner selves. If language creates its own reality, if it is born out of our need to establish links with other beings, if it is simply a social convention, it follows that our own individual existence cannot be underwritten by words. It is the receptor rather than the originator who is ultimately responsible for interpreting the meaning of an utterance, and this will apply even when we come across our own writing on a subsequent occasion. Indeed Unamuno was to go radically further in his explorations of language and to suggest that God is a consequence rather than a cause of our prayers, that He is, in other words, a linguistic creation: 'Es acaso Dios quien imita las obras del Hombre, del Hombre que le crea merced al lenguaje' (Unamuno 1998: 111)[7] [It is perhaps God who imitates the acts of Man, of Man who creates Him by the grace of language]. In the first of his collection of psalms, in which the poet desperately seeks God but can find him nowhere, he beseeches God to reveal his name, '¡Dime tu nombre! ¡Tu nombre, que es tu esencia!' [Tell me your name! Your name, which is your being!] (OCE VI, 219; OCA XIII, 284), thereby implying that it is the word that creates the reality of the object, an extreme form of nominalism, but understandable in the case of a poet, who creates ideal worlds through the power of his pen. For the poet, he says in one of his *Cancionero* poems, 'cosas' [things or objects] are but shadows of words (OCE VI, 965; OCA XV, 71). Man's world is metaphorical, and the supreme metaphor is the Word crucified. Theology, he writes in another poem, is nothing more than 'juegos de palabras' [word games] (OCE VI, 988; OCA XV, 109–110).[8]

In *Abel Sánchez*, Joaquín Monegro, instead of using the kind of interior monologue that Augusto employs in *Niebla*, uses autobiography, of which we get fragments in the wider third-person novel. This secret memoir is allegedly written for the benefit of his daughter, but Unamuno makes it clear that what Joaquín seeks is self-objectification, a projection of himself that will counter his uncertainties and self-loathing. It is in effect an artificial construct, a

---

7   The idea that religion, like myth, springs from language, was expounded by Max Müller in various parts of his sprawling work. See, for example, 'Semitic Monotheism' and 'Physical Religion'. For myth see the first of these two essays as well as 'On the Philosophy of Mythology'. All these essays are included in Müller. Unamuno mentions reading Müller in the 1890s.

8   There is an untitled poem in *Rimas de dentro* (1923), 'Cerré el libro que hablaba' (OCE VI, 534–5; OCA XIII, 864–5), which exactly concurs with Augusto Pérez's discovery that 'no hay más verdad que la vida fisiológica' [the only truth is that of physiological existence] (OCE II, 619; OCA II, 901), suggesting, that human language is a mere accessory, that it is inconsequential when compared to the natural language of a croaking frog as he goes about his nocturnal business in search of a mate.

response to the various ways in which others, his wife, his daughter, his son-in-law, his friend Abel, his cousin Helena, his patients, his fellow-academicians see him. Joaquín's self-creation is not spontaneous, as is his envy of Abel, it is reflexive, and it fails to reveal the source of his problem, of his Cain-like feelings of rejection. Once again we observe language, the social-bonding agent, failing us when we turn it in on ourselves. For Unamuno, it replaces reality instead of clarifying it.

Unamuno explores this theme also in *Tulio Montalbán y Julio Macedo*. Tulio Montalbán is the creation of a writer, the historian Henri Jacquetot. The effect of this verbal image is completely to displace the image of the 'real' Tulio Montalbán. The image becomes public ownership, each reader (represented in the novel by Don Juan Manuel Solórzano and his daughter Elvira) reading the biography in his or her own way. Both of these intradiegetic readers read according to expectations or desires, by which Unamuno seems to suggest that the images we create out of words tell us more about ourselves than about the referents. This point about the role of the reader in creating, authenticating, or giving plenitude to the verbal images that are found in books is given a further twist by Unamuno when he makes a character from a book come to life. For this character also turns out to be a reader, a reader of himself. The character Julio Macedo goes much further than Don Juan Manuel Solórzano. He dismisses Tulio Montalbán as a fictional being who is of no value compared to people of flesh and blood. In confessing that 'yo fui Tulio Montalbán' [I was Tulio Montalbán] (OCE II, 962; OCA IX, 401), Julio Macedo acknowledges that he is the victim of an external image which he refused to recognize, to answer to. For him the only authentic image is the internal one. He has 'killed' the public personality that was threatening to swamp the inner self; but in 'killing' him he has unwittingly opened the door to a legend. Through Henri Jacquetot's biography of him, which he calls 'esa fatídica historia' (OCE II, 962; OCA IX, 402) [that fateful history] his image and personality have become public property. He can no longer be perceived, worse, can no longer be loved, as the person he feels himself to be. When Elvira calls him Tulio, he replies: 'Has invocado el nombre, uno u otro, pero el nombre; no me has cogido al hombre, al de carne, al que está aquí, al animal si quieres [You have invoked the name, whether the one or the other, but merely the name, you have not chosen the man in me, the man of flesh and blood who is right here, the animal if you prefer] (OCE II, 962; OCA IX, 402). Language has replaced the reality of his being. He has been robbed of his natural identity and another extraneous one has been imposed on him through the interposition of words. Unable to come to terms with this 'inauthentic' image, desperate to recover a previous self, he will attempt flight and withdrawal, and when this is shown not to work, will resort to the final solution. Yet as we learn after his death, he too was obliged to resort to the written word in order to establish his counter-claim, the claim of the ordinary man against the claims of the heroes of history, or as he puts it, the man versus the personage. In writing 'The Memoirs of Julio Macedo' he too becomes what he had refused to be; another personage of history/fiction, a linguistic fabrication, like the protagonist of *Niebla* had discovered to his consternation.

The collection of twenty-three letters from an unknown writer to a virtually unknown correspondent (Felipe) that form *La novela de don Sandalio* is even more of a linguistic shell. The novel is full of linguistic signs placed there for the delectation of hermeneutically inclined readers, but by themselves these signs—a chess game, a hollow tree, the ruins of a house, waves upon the seashore—are devoid of meaning. The story is a mere accretion of signs and every scrap of information is countered by a corresponding absence of information. The letter-writer is running away from something, but from what we are not told. He is experiencing a deep crisis, but we are privy to neither its nature nor its origin. His sense of bitterness is ascribed to the loss of his home or family, but we learn nothing of that loss. He has retired to a place where he is unknown, but why he does not say. He admits he is driven by misanthropic sentiments, but the cause of his misanthropy remains shrouded in mystery. And most baffling of all, he wishes to befriend Don Sandalio and admits to being intrigued by him, yet he flatly refuses to be told anything about him. The novel continues in this vein right to the end, baffling and frustrating the receptor of the letters, Felipe, and by implication the conventional reader.

What most attracts the letter-writer about Don Sandalio are his silences, the fact that he plays the game of chess (or the game of life) without resorting to speech. When Don Sandalio falls ill, his substitute at the chess table is an inveterate talker, whose incessant chatter the letter-writer finds 'insoportable' [unbearable] (OCE II, 1171; OCA XVI, 651). The letter-writer's linguistic phobia is observable too in his scathing comments on all speakers, whether onlookers at the chess games, cardplayers making their bids, groups of 'tertulianos' [social gatherers] at the club, or simple conversationalists in the hotel. So much so that he rejects as unacceptable the version of a more garrulous Don Sandalio that the son-in-law reveals to him. The letter-writer, it transpires, is repelled by language, including the language of newsprint and advertisements. Truth is not and cannot be language-dependent. Language leads to falsehood and eventually to insanity. All the letter-writer will tolerate is 'a lo sumo, algún niño que no sepa aún hablar' [at most a child who has not yet learnt to speak] (OCE II, 1160; OCA XVI, 633). It is this linguistic repulsion that makes him reject all explanations about Don Sandalio's condition and fate: 'Tengo que mantener puro, incontaminado, a mi don Sandalio, al mío' [My Don Sandalio, the one who is mine, must be kept pure and uncontaminated] (OCE II, 1167; OCA XVI, 645). The letter-writer neither accepts nor is prepared to give explanations. Language contaminates, distorts, denatures; it does not give us the unembellished truth. In terms of language, *La novela de don Sandalio* is the final admission of defeat. The paradox is of course that the letter-writer, like his creator, cannot avoid using language; indeed he is, again like his creator, an inveterate writer of epistles. Even the rejection of language and what it conjures up has to be made through language. For a writer, silence is not an option. The most famous concluding remark in modern philosophy, 'whereof one cannot speak, thereof one must be silent' (Wittgenstein, *Tractatus*), is utterly unrealistic in the human context. If language is there we will use it, whatever its limitations. Unamuno might well have agreed with Wittgenstein's later finding that language is not stable, that words have not meaning but function or usage, in effect that language is a collection of games that govern our existence. In our search for truth about ourselves and others we may find that language can trivialize and dissemble, yet at the same time it is an addictive poison that compelled Unamuno to endless involutions of his tortured yet inventive self, as indeed it does to his many and dedicated critics who continue optimistically and unflaggingly to search for the truth of Unamuno's seductive wordgames.

Further Reading

Álvarez Castro (2005), Collins (2002), Ilie (1987), Larraín (1965), Longhurst (2009, 2011), Mermall (1990), Müller (2002), Olson (1984, 2003), Roberts (2000, 2004), Sinclair (1987), Unamuno (1993, 1998), Valdés (1982).

7

A Question of Ethics:
Exploring Issues of Right And Wrong in Unamuno

ALISON SINCLAIR

There is no doubt of the fundamentally ethical preoccupations of Unamuno. What is less clear is the degree to which he was ever concerned with the difference between right and wrong in any conventional sense, still less with the importance of acting upon it. His writings, whether fictional or non-fictional (and all variations in between), effectively challenge us – with unrelenting consistency – to think about right and wrong. Ethical or moral decisions are not necessarily central in his texts, but may emerge in ways that are consequential to other concerns of plot or argument. At times, as with the subplots of *Niebla* (Olson 1984: 68–75) they will be dealt with, or brought in as deliberately inconsequential matter, rather than being focused upon as the major issue. As far as the reader is concerned, it is deliberately not made clear what we are to do, or indeed to think, in the face of Unamuno's provocative drawing of new lines. His work is designed to push the reader into his or her own decisions about what is or is not ethical, or 'good', or 'wrong'. There is no such easy thing as 'telling' in the sense of informing and guiding. Instead there is the presentation of painful and complex situations to which we are invited to react. His concern, at least if we are to believe him, is not that we should think a particular thing, but rather *that* we should think.

Unamuno's concern with the individual as free-standing, responsible for taking his or her own decisions in life, follows in a broad European existentialist tradition. Most specifically we might contextualize his framing of the burden of individual choice within the work of two writers: Nietzsche and Kierkegaard. In the case of Nietzsche, an inevitable cornerstone of the intellectual *formación* of Unamuno and his contemporaries in Europe (not just in Spain), we find emphasis on those beliefs formerly held as absolute as being no more than human constructs. This forms part of the intellectual basis for Unamuno's philosophical approach with its focus upon the requirement that we all think for ourselves (see Guignon 1998). The anxiety that this inevitably provokes had been formulated, with no concessions to man's intellectual and ethical requirements, in the work of Kierkegaard, whose *Either/Or* (1843) was of clear inspiration to Unamuno, not least with its insistence on man's obligation to choose (Roberts 1986; Sinclair 1989; Wright 2004). Thus choice or liberty becomes the burden that Sartre would formulate a hundred years later in *L'être et le néant* (1943) (see Howells 1998).

My aim in this chapter is to look at a selection of Unamuno's writings, including fiction and the essay, and to look at them in terms of engaging the reader with issues of knowing right and wrong. To this end the discussion will be grouped under three broad headings: 'education', 'prohibition' and 'extrapolation'. In the first instance my intention is examine the primary texts selected for what, if anything, they tell us about Unamuno's sense of right and wrong, and how he conveys this to the reader. A further intention in this chapter, however, is to explore the degree to which Unamuno's engagement with the reader is not exclusively in terms of eliciting direct reaction to the text in hand, but rather to engage the reader's attention to a series of major discourses and master-narratives of his time: on education, eugenics, sexual ethics, feminism and national violence.

Education

In *Amor y pedagogía* (1902) and, *Niebla* (1914), the novel closely related to it (Ribbans 1971: 83–107), the process of education is made distinct from a simple learning of *things*. Indeed a perfunctory and ultimately dismissive treatment is given to the formal imparting of knowledge, while a broader learning is posited as desirable, but not obtainable via any direct route.

The method of imparting knowledge used by Avito with Apolodoro in *Amor y pedagogía* is based, *inter alia*, on a mixture of positivism and apparently progressive educational ideas, but his activity is flawed by the unthinking way in which he tries to apply method. It is more a case of importing than imparting. Minter has argued with great persuasiveness the close linkage between Avito Carrascal in *Amor y pedagogía*, and Pestalozzi, the eminent Swiss educationalist (1746–1827). This linkage is arresting for two reasons: for its closeness to what Pestalozzi believed and thought, and for the way in which it is arguably undermined by the facts of Pestalozzi's own family life. Pestalozzi's fundamental belief was that 'the child should learn in a more natural way, be encouraged to absorb sense-impressions from the world around her or him, and be led from the extrinsic qualities of objects to the intrinsic concepts which they represent' (Minter 1998: 82–3). These principles can be recognized in the subsequent theories and practice of Giner de los Ríos and his founding in 1876 of the

Institución Libre de Enseñanza. They can also be detected in the theories of Rudolf Steiner and his Waldorf schools, Maria Montessori and her methods for kindergarten, and Bernard and Dora Russell in their founding of the Beacon Hill School in 1927. The problem arises, however, when practice does not match theory, and when the desire to implement a method actually runs counter to the underlying theory of discovery and personal development. This is what Unamuno explores in *Amor y pedagogía* as he presents a ridiculous picture of the way Avito tries to apply Pestalozzi's entirely worthy theories. Additionally, as Minter points out, the corrosive attack on the faulty application of theory has a disturbing root in the model taken for his misguided educator. Pestalozzi's dealings with his own son were apparently as devoid of empathy as are those of Avito with Apolodoro (Minter 1998). In springing to rapid judgement of Avito, then, we need to be alert to the degree to which he embodies a principle rather than an exception, a human tendency to follow rules rather than a human ability to be creative and imaginative. At worst he embodies a lack of thinking, and a lack of discrimination of values. Avito's enthusiasm for 'method' indicates his deep underlying insecurity about virtually everything. His desire to control his child through the systematic application of theories of education is from the start pitiable rather than admirable. *Amor y pedagogía* is Unamuno's first major fictional text that offers doubt about knowledge being acceptable because it is offered by someone deemed to be in authority, a line of thought that will be pursued in the philosophical area in *Del sentimiento trágico de la vida* (1913), and repeatedly in relation to science (see for example Unamuno's 1907 article 'Cientificismo' (OCE III, 352–7; OCA IV, 521–9; Sinclair 2001: 50–69). Its roots can be seen in earlier writings such as his blistering 1899 essay 'De la enseñanza superior en España' [On Higher Education in Spain] (OCE I, 735–72; OCA III, 57–119).

The more programmatic the exposition of a set of ideas, the less persuasive they are likely to be: such, at least, is the conclusion one might draw about the exploration of new ideas in general, and certainly when seeing them in Unamuno's texts. Thus texts offering a simple view of eugenics (one of the master-discourses of Unamuno's time) are less likely to persuade readers to actually think critically about the subject than texts such as *Amor y pedagogía* that provoke questions (or laughter). Ridiculing pedagogical method, as happens in this novel, ultimately is capable of leading the reader to thought about what should be involved in pedagogy, whereas a straight exposition of ideas to be absorbed is unlikely to provoke such a thoughtful attitude (see Sinclair 2008). Learning by rote can also carry its problems over to learning by example. In general Avito makes no attempt to educate Marina, except during her pregnancy, when he requires her to eat 'alubias' [kidney beans] and to listen to the lives of great men (noted, perhaps caustically, as being 'biografías de grandes hombres *según don Avito*' [biographies of great men *according to don Avito*]. [OCE II, 327; OCA II, 454. Emphasis mine]). This practice echoes the intentions of eugenic publications, such as *Eugenical News* which began publication in 1916, and which regularly published the lives of men to be admired. Unamuno's point, we might infer, is that for this procedure, no thinking is required.

In relation to knowledge, Avito is not simply a perpetrator of a wrong approach. A telling retail is that he derives his knowledge of his own former existence as child from authority: 'Sí sé que lo he sido porque he tenido que serlo, lo sé por deducción, y sé que lo he sido por los que de mi niñez me han hablado, lo sé por autoridad, pero, la verdad, no lo recuerdo, como no recuerdo haber nacido... [sic]' [I *know* I was a child because I must have been, I know it by deduction, and I know it from those who have talked to me about my childhood, so I have it on good authority, but truth to tell, I don't remember my childhood, just as I don't remember having been born] (OCE II, 346; OCA II, 483). This suggests, in a manner that is ultimately engaging rather than alienating, that Avito has not simply become enthused by a wrongly understood pedagogical method, but is in fact an example of a victim.

Amor y pedagogía as a text is far from backward-looking, and Unamuno later seized the opportunity to indicate its contemporary applicability. Lest the text be interpreted solely as the tale of a misguided father who wants to create and raise a child by the book, Unamuno in his 1934 'Prólogo-epílogo a la segunda edición' [prologue-epilogue to the second edition] made it clear that there were links to be made with the educational ambitions of the Second Republic. With some edge to his tone, and conceivably even a note of bitterness, Unamuno declared, 'El niño es del Estado, y debe ser entregado a los pedagogos – demagogos – oficiales de Estado, a los de la escuela única. "¡Pobre conejillo! ¡Pobre conejillo!", exclamaba Apolodoro' [The child belongs to the state, and must be handed over to the official State pedagogues—demagogues—of the only type of school permissible. The poor little guinea pig!" Apolodoro cried.] (OCE II: 313; OCA II, 432). The whole is offset, however, by the spirit of the comic as the way through to understanding (see Cifo González 2005).

By contrast with this novel of pedagogy, *Niebla* (1914) appears at first sight not to have such obvious hooks to the social and cultural world. Its protagonist, Augusto Pérez, lives in an emotional and intellectual vacuum, unable to apprehend *how* to read the world, nor to learn to act within it. The idea that some actions might be 'wrong' is, in his case, more to do with whether or not he is being a proper human being (doing what others do) than whether there are moral or ethical rights and wrongs to be observed. The account of Augusto's education is given in Chapter 5 of the novel, where we learn that his mother sends him to the Instituto, and is then the one who 'hears his lessons' in the evening (OCE II, 571–2; OCA II, 826–7). This suggests a model of education (by no means unusual for the time) that is by rote and order rather than by discovery and understanding. It is noteworthy that the reaction of Augusto's mother to what she teaches is in some ways a pre-figuration of that 'asco' [disgust] felt by Tula in relation to the body and to what is sensual. What we can read as the retreat by Avito into a dry pedagogical system, fuelled by his inability to engage in difference and exploration, is followed in *Niebla* by an attitude of avoidance to the uncomfortable or unpalatable aspects of experience that is demonstrated by Augusto's mother. Small wonder that later on as Augusto embarks on his self-defined experience of 'love' with Eugenia he will try to discover knowledge less by experience than by asking for definitions: '¿Qué es el amor?' ['What is love?'] (OCE II, 569; OCA 822–3).

There are, however, passing references that situate Augusto in his time. As we first meet him in Chapter 1, he protests that he is not a *vago* [layabout]: 'Los vagos son ellos, los que dicen que trabajan y no hacen sino aturdirse y ahogar el pensamiento' [They are the layabouts, the ones who say they work and who only get confused and lost in their thought] (OCE II, 558; OCA II, 805). At first sight, this is simply a case of Augusto trying to persuade himself of his own substance and value. But it also demonstrates his attempts to define himself as a man of imagination, not a mere drifter. He is, of course, trying to give himself substance through definition, and his protests smack strongly of his being in denial. In addition to this, and as a passing reference, he is arguably distancing himself from that stratum of society most likely to fall into wrongdoing: the stratum of the *vagos*. Two years after the publication of *Niebla* the doctor Sanchís Banús, who would become one of the foremost psychiatrists in Spain, published his *Estudio medico-social del niño golfo* [Medico-social study of the vagrant child] in which he outlined a schema of the maladapted child. The 'vago', along with the 'pordiosero' [beggar] and the 'golfo' [street urchin], both of which appear in the novel,' was part of a group of 'antisociales', and, being on the margins, was considered a social danger (Campos, Martínez and Huertas 2000: 128–30). It will be for this group, understood as potential criminals, that the 1933 'ley de vagos' would be introduced.

In each of these works by Unamuno, the guidance that might be offered by the Church, or by some representative of religions, is so glaringly absent as to constitute a comment on the (lack of) relevance of such teaching. In *Amor y pedagogía*, spiritual education (which might include the discrimination between right and wrong) is troublingly located in Marina (all feeling and no intellect), while in *Niebla*, beyond the pedagogy employed for Augusto Pérez by his mother, and his self-help methods later (his consultations with his servants, or with Víctor Goti), there is little or nothing to assist him in the area of learning about morality in any conventional manner. For Augusto, the crucial step is not an intellectual or moral sort of discrimination but rather his grasp of the painful truths of personhood (pain, loss, outrage, being used by others, not having control over his being or his end) as brought to a climax in Chapter 31.

Prohibition

The above examples have concerned education in terms of learning, or the imparting of knowledge, and demonstrate a sadly empty vision of the process of education, and still less of learning to distinguish between right and wrong. They are notably secular in their focus: indeed the world of the characters of the novels mentioned so far is remarkably lacking the structure and customs of religion, or more specifically, Catholicism. At most, Catholicism is presented as a framework that might be a crutch, or one that can be used by the characters. It is true that Marina arranges for Apolodoro to be baptized (OCE II, 333; OCA II, 463), but we might note that on this topic the response of Avito concerns not right or wrong but power, in that his perception is that his 'principio de autoridad' [principle of authority] has been 'conculcado' [violated]. That is, his concern is with the affront to his sense of himself as a person (and one whose will is to be obeyed, presumably, particularly when exercising prohibition). In *Abel Sánchez* (1917) and *La tía Tula* (1921) we can read complementary accounts of an imposition of prohibition that springs from self-prohibition, without benefit of the intervention of others.

Psychoanalysis has traditionally given weight to the prohibitions that emanate from the father. Operating according Freud's theory of the Oedipus complex (for a discussion of Freud see Simon and Blass 1991) or to Lacan's reformulation of 'le nom du père' [the name/'no' of the father] (Lacan 1977: 67), psychoanalysis has posited that it is the threat offered by the powerful father (capable of castrating the child errant and uncontained in his desire for the mother) that makes the child desist from acting on his desires. Simple prohibition is, however, when one thinks it over, a remarkably primitive view of the possible source of an ethical or moral sense. It increases one's respect for Unamuno to see the degree to which he either avoids the instance of direct prohibition, or sends it up in a wave of satirical laughter (as exemplified in *Amor y pedagogía*).

Good or powerful fathers (who might be the source of prohibition, and hence of a rough and ready communication of right and wrong, or arguably of what is acceptable or unacceptable) are notoriously lacking in Western literature (Brewer 1980: 9–11), and Unamuno's fictions are no exception. Augusto Pérez's father has died before *Niebla* has opened; Tula's father (and mother) likewise; if Joaquín (Cain) of *Abel Sánchez* had a father, he is not mentioned, is presumably long gone by the start of the novel, and with no residual effects on Joaquín's being or actions. Furthermore, if God, according to the mythical framework, is Joaquín's father, there is no sense of prohibition from that quarter either.

Similarly, and at the level of prohibition within the family that might emanate from the father, in the short story 'El Marqués de Lumbría' of the *Tres novelas ejemplares y un prólogo* (1920) there is no evidence that either Carolina or Luisa consider their father's possible prohibition of their actions as deterrent.

As Unamuno is at pains to point out in the prologue to the *Tres novelas ejemplares*, his intention is first – in the tradition of Cervantes – to place emphasis upon aesthetic rather than moral exemplarity, and secondly, to focus not on the competing facets of real selves, but on the self that each of us desires to be (OCE II, 973; OCA IX, 415). In these stories, Unamuno is concerned not with right or wrong in any conventional sense, but with the integrity of being, and the lengths that his characters (and, by extension, we as human beings) are prepared to go to in order to secure or defend that integrity. The entire text of these stories thus works around axes of power, colonization, desire, and appropriation. What matters is what makes the person, and it is a fierce competitive world, with little or no mercy for the weak and vulnerable. In 'El Marqués de Lumbría' no sympathy is shown towards Tristán, the hapless male 'captured' by both Luisa and Carolina in their bid for a place in the family succession, nor is there sympathy towards Juan of 'Dos madres', except via the appeal to the reader. The possibility however, in the three stories of this fierce and unrelenting text, is that Unamuno is positing extreme examples of behaviour as a form of alert to the real uncivilized potential beneath the veneer of family and social conventions. What emerges is a strong message about the fragility of the morality of society, a structure that ignores at its peril the turbulent undercurrents of fear, desire and the compulsion not to be overcome by others.

A text that considers right and wrong most centrally is *Abel Sánchez*, with the powerful message from most of the narrative that 'wrong' has been done by the deity, in the form of injustice to Joaquín. It takes on the myth of Cain and Abel, that most powerful account of the Old Testament of judgement in relation to right and wrong, in which the utmost unreasonableness appears to be that of God. Here Unamuno explores the degree to which there is almost total inter-changeability of perpetrator and victim, of the malefactor and his prey. This treatment of the theme in the novel is consistent with the history of how this myth has been appropriated (Quinones 1991). Unamuno takes three new emphases, while exploiting all the reversals of perpetration, intention and responsibility possible between the two major players, and their wider families. The first is to emphasize being, not doing (Round 1974: 22). This virtually sidelines any question of intention of malefaction, or of will in relation to intention (which would imply some moral choice in the area of right and wrong). The second is to indicate, in his 1928 prologue to the novel written from exile in Hendaye, that the issue is not to do with the major figures presented in the novel, but with their inadequate copies. Hence his ultimate judgement about what is wrong concerns not a protagonist who is a malefactor (and his victim/antagonist) but those who are some inferior development or imitation of both: 'No es Caín lo malo; lo malo son los cainitas, y los abelitas' [It is not Cain that is evil; it is the Cainites and Abelites that are evil] (OCE II, 686; OCA II, 1006). The dating of this prologue (1928) also situates Unamuno in a time and place of his own sense of wronged but justified exile (and thus his experience is that of the marginalized one). That is, he writes from a position of being exiled for what he believes in, and believes himself justified, but is wronged by the authorities that have caused his exile. Thus marginalized, and thus akin to the Cain figure of the novel, Unamuno compounds the similarity between himself and his character by his refusal in July 1924 to accept re-admission to Spain (something which will be echoed and elaborated on in *Cómo se hace una novela*). His attitude resonates strongly with Joaquín's determination in the novel to retain his Cain identity and what he perceives as its superiority in the importance it gives to an attitude of rebellion and in its perceptions of unjust ill-treatment. The third emphasis that the reader can observe is on the degree of manipulative behaviour engaged in not only by Joaquín, but also by Abel, and by Helena. An overt narrative, particularly the one that comes from the interpolations of Joaquín's *Confesión* written for his daughter, talks of Joaquín being singled out for his wretched fate of being unloved. But what the narrative lays bare is the degree to which the three characters of the triangle Joaquín, Abel and Helena work on one another to inflict discomfort and to disavow any responsibility for so doing. There is no *raisonneur* in the text until the children are born, and Abelín and Joaquina (as they reach maturity and a state of judgement) add their perceptions to those of Joaquín's wife, the predominantly silent Antonia.

The Cain/Abel myth is one of envy, and emphasizes the degree of combined hate and helplessness that the competitive duo generates. It is fundamentally rooted in a dyadic relationship that denies all external witnessing, judgement or intervention (see Sinclair 2001: 166–7; 171–5). The Cain/Abel pair in the novel displays the degree to which identities existing only within a dyad are unformed and thus unable to participate in the narratives of adulthood where there is triangulation, witnessing, and the capacity to form and define the identity in relation to others. As Quinones has argued, what goes on in the Cain/Abel dyad is displacement for Cain's impossible relationship with his maker (Quinones 1991: 16; Sinclair 2001: 178), one in which we can assume no dialogue to take place. In the absence of power, manipulation steps in. Abel is the first to be presented as manipulative in his passive avoidance of decision; Joaquín is later manipulative in his actions concerning Abel and Helena). From the first page of the novel, the distinction is made between Joaquín as 'voluntarioso' [strong-willed], and of the complex attitude of Abel, who 'pareciendo ceder, hacía la suya siempre' [seemed to give in to others, but always got his own way] (OC II, 689; OCA IX, 1006). In Chapter 2 we see how Joaquín provokes the courtship and engagement of Abel and Helena, and his subsequent complaints about the results of his provocation in Chapter 3. In terms of moral choices and behaviour, they operate in a no-man's-land. All three are, each in their own way, unlikeable, depriving the reader of any simple option of identification, and thus stimulating him or her into thinking *about* the plot, and the rights and wrongs of action, rather than simply following it.

A further spur to the interruption of identification with Joaquín derives from his *Confesión*. When he talks of his 'odio' [hate] for Abel (the emotion identified by Freud [1915] as the most primitive reaction to the other) he is self-indulgent in his depiction of the state. He is passive, enveloped by the 'ice' of hatred (OCE II, 699; OCA IX, 1022). But how are we to take this? His account of himself at the wedding of Abel and Helena borders on the style of a Romantic novelette, as he recounts how his heart stops as they say their vows, and as Helena turns to look at him (OCE II, 699; OCA IX, 1023). Is it conceivable that Unamuno intended the reader to pick up the novelistic notes of this discourse, this telling of a fiction to present the self to others that is couched in traditional formats of pulp fiction? The narrative of the *Confesión* as a whole is multi-faceted: it purports to having sincerity of presentation, with Joaquín presenting – it has to be said – his 'best' self to his daughter, 'best' here indicating most worthy of her pity and respect. If she respects she may understand and forgive.

A different, and partly complementary, view of Joaquín as the self-justifying wrongdoer who presents himself for his daughter's understanding consists in Unamuno's highlighting of pathology rather than criminality. In part we can read this as a further dialogue with his time, specifically with the increasing interventions of psychiatry into the field of criminology (see Huertas 1987). Joaquín may ultimately succeed as a criminal when he knowingly prompts Abel's fatal attack of angina, but we have also learned earlier how he had been distracted from his professional occupation when he lets a woman die (OCE II, 704; OCA IX, 1031–2). His 'diagnosis' of himself is of a pathological example. His idea is that a wrong has been visited upon him, so that he sees himself as a rather admirable 'desgraciado' [wretch, or literally, one who has 'fallen from grace'] (OCE II: 716; OCA IX, 1051). This is a more modern (and more forgiving) version of 'pecado' [sin] (an interpretation he also espouses in his unconvincing adoption of the practices of the Church in an attempt to defend against his hate for Abel). Joaquín's off-loading of the pride of the sinner on to the unfortunate maid of the household, in Chapter 18, is finally articulated clearly by both his wife and the humble maid, and is clearly a desperate strategy of avoiding what he cannot recognize, still less tolerate, within himself. Discrimination and insight are, however, left to the reader, rather than bestowed upon the character. That Joaquín is ultimately and tragically narcissistic still places in question the rights and wrongs of his behaviour.

Unamuno did not confine his writing on the Cain myth to this novel, and across his various essays and fictions one can discern an evolution in his ideas of Cain (Sinclair 2001: 178–82). Abel, originally a shepherd in the myth, counts on God, and arguably thereby loses any claim to existential angst. Cain, in his marginalization through his envy and eventually through the wrongdoing of killing his brother, achieves at least status in the eyes of the world, and – according to the myth – will become the founder of cities, of modern civilized life (Sinclair 2001: 180–187). This would be emphasized by Unamuno in his 1933 essay, 'La ciudad de Henoc' [The City of Enoch] (OCE VII, 1093–1095; OCA XVI, 873–876).

A more extreme case of the envy that is explored in *Abel Sánchez* is presented in the play *El otro* (1926). In keeping with the lateral shift of focus from murder (the sin of Cain, and the technical wrongdoing of Joaquín) towards the discomforts of envy, and the experience of injustice, *El otro* in its turn manages to subvert customary gradations of the hierarchies of actions that are considered to be wrong. Thus a surface text invites us to consider the murder of a twin by his identical brother. But there are two strong alternative strands that prompt us to see this more as an outcome than as the primary or most important wrong. The unthinking possessiveness of the two women, Laura and Damiana, who compete for the remaining twin, is matched only by their Damiana's disregard for the personhood of the two men displayed in her attempt, in a chilling spirit of enquiry, to deceive the twin she had married with the twin she had not married (OCE V, 693; OCA XII, 842), an attempt neatly foiled by the twins themselves. Even more chilling, however, is the initial wilful blurring of the boundaries of personhood by the mother of the twins and the Ama, who swapped the babies one to the other without regard for their separateness (OCE V, 678–9; OCA XII, 818). This disregard for the confines of the person sets the central note of the play as involving not murder, but betrayal.

La tía Tula (1921), the 'sister' novel to *Abel Sánchez*, is a novel of insistent prohibition, but contained within the family. When its dominant note is not of prohibition, it is of unreasoning requirement. 'Because I say so' is how we could summarize the *dicta* of Tula (occasionally backed up with statements about purity and the need to keep the pure and innocent safe from the contamination that derives from the body and its desires). In Tula's attitude we can recognize that form of reasoning, or rather, of response, used by adults at the end of their tether when faced with a recalcitrant child, and from the insistence with which this response appears in the novel we might infer that it would draw little support from Unamuno. It does not brook discussion, still less the idea of learning through exchange and experience. And yet, despite these negative aspects of Tula's behaviour, we can see the level to which Unamuno dismisses participants on the other side of that exchange, those that would submit to the emphatic ordering. Characters like Rosa are barely better than those in the style of Abel in their passive acceptance of a role, in this case a woman's role of reproduction and the containment of masculine sexual urges. Tula responds with fury and indignation to the pressures of her confessor (that she should marry, that she should be the solution to the incontinent desires of her suitor), but in this she is a lone (female) voice.

In Unamuno's letter of 3 November 1902 to Juan Maragall he speaks of the nascent plot of *La tía Tula*, a novel that would only reach publication in 1921. It would tell of a spinster who lives with her widowed brother-in-law, looking after the children of her dead sister. In condensed manner he indicates the central concern: she will not marry the man 'pues no quiere *manchar* con el débito conyugal el recinto en que respiran aire de castidad sus *hijos*. Satisfecho el instinto de maternidad, ¿para qué ha de perder su virginidad? Es virgen madre. Conozco el caso' [because she does not want her conjugal duties to *stain* the environment where her *children* should be breathing in only the most chaste air. Once her maternal instinct has been satisfied, why should she have to lose her viriginity? She's a virgin mother. I'm familiar with the case.] (OCE II, 41; OCA IX, 31–2; see also Carlos Longhurst's comments in his edition of *La tía Tula* [Unamuno 1987b: 13–14).

What is striking about this quotation, and indeed about the entire novel, is how we are presented with key words ('virgen madre' [virgin mother], 'castidad' [chastity]) that suggest a context of Catholicism, and yet the framing of the central concern of the novel lays most emphasis on social practice. The division between purity and danger outlined by the anthropologist Mary Douglas (1966), based on the practices and beliefs of numerous primitive societies, is one that underpins Tula's precepts, both positive and negative. Tula's course of action is self-determined, not in submission to a set of precepts and prohibitions that emanate from the Church, but because they suit her urge for personal independence. They are what we could deduce to be convenient prohibitions, and helpful in presenting a public face to the world, thus conveying Unamuno's modern perception of the place of traditional prohibitions within society. It is true that Tula's original guardian is her uncle, a priest, and it is true that she has periodic contact with a confessor. But in the spirit of Santa Teresa (the link with whom is emphasized by the prologue that was composed rather later than the novel rather than by the main text: see Ribbans 1987), Tula picks and chooses the pastoral advice that she proposes to follow. When Tula deals with others, however, this selectivity in relation to advice or admonishment is not countenanced.

Tula's framework for behaviour, her own and that of others, is based on polarities that suggest extremes of right and wrong, or rather of what is to be rejected on the one hand and what is to be espoused on the other in order to make that rejection effective. Lannon has set out in detail the gap between an image of Catholic Spain, and the realities of a patchy practice of Catholicism that varied regionally, and according to wealth and politics (Lannon 1987: 9–35). Although *La tía Tula* lacks an overt sense of class (contrary to what we find in Lorca's character Bernarda Alba), it is clear that the household Tula runs is moneyed rather than otherwise, respectable rather than marginal. Indeed, her freedom to establish the unconventional household she does suggests a style of conservative Catholicism coincident with security of social and financial standing.

Lannon argues that the area in which Catholic tradition in Spain found its main target in resistance to European progress was within the behaviours of sex (Lannon 1987: 49). In this context, Tula's avoidance of sex through her creation of an aunt/mother/spiritual guardian role is superficially in accord with Catholic tradition at the same time as it makes it glaringly obvious that there are problematic consequences for society in an overall avoidance of sexuality. What is important in Tula is not that she avoids sex because there is a negative tradition towards it in the Church, but rather that she uses, or mis-uses the authority of the Church to justify a behaviour that suits her. The reader is struck by the sheer oddity of the behaviour that Tula espouses, and that is relentlessly documented by Unamuno. Reading her repeated parrying of questions or enquiries conveys the questions surrounding cultural practices that embrace equally the importance of the family and the primacy of celibacy. If there is religious observance in the novel it is of the routine practice of communal prayer ('Ahora, hijos míos, un padrenuestro y avemaría por papá también' [Now children, an Our Father and a Hail Mary for daddy too] [OCE II, 1070; OCA IX, 567]) rather than attendance at Mass. What we see in Tula is not an implementation of official religion, but her use of it, and the creation of her own world of authority. Questions of wrong, therefore, are – if articulated by Tula – apparently what the Church teaches, but the mode of expression and the areas of prohibition are such that the reader will be led to question her prohibitions.

What source, if any, is there for the extreme attitudes of Tula? She avoids all contact with sex, the body, and even the emotions. For her, all of these are somehow 'wrong', a judgement she justifies through prohibitions derived from a framework of a Catholicism against which she nonetheless takes a markedly independent stand. Tula's speech, and her desire for *her* form of purity, her need to separate herself and the children from sex and sensuality signal behaviours that will become eerily familiar in the Sección Femenina and its discourse. This movement, set up in 1934 by Pilar Primo de Rivera, was founded some twelve years after the publication of Unamuno's novel. But its beliefs and maxims (as recorded, for example, in Martín Gaite's novel, *El cuarto de atrás* (1978), and as conveyed further in the advice to young women that she details in the *Usos amorosos de la posguerra española* (1987) are strikingly of a piece with the attitude of Tula. It was a movement that had particular devotion to Santa Teresa. Indeed the adoption of Santa Teresa by conservative and Catholic Spain (see Di Febo 1988), not least in the Franco years, goes some way to undermine the apparently positive claims for the link between Tula and Teresa articulated in Unamuno's prologue to the novel. There has been no identification of the 'caso' [case] mentioned by Unamuno on which his novel was based, but there is an interesting coincidence between the novel and the family life of José and Pilar Primo de Rivera. The six children born in six years to Miguel Primo de Rivera were left without a mother when she died in 1908 after the birth of Fernando. The children, José then five, and Pilar two, were cared for by their grandmother and two aunts, one of whom, Maria Jésus Primo de Rivera y Orbaneja, came to be known as Tía Ma by all members of the Falange (Rambaud 2011). If Tula seems from the novel to be both extreme and anguished (her self-questioning lending some humanity to the less than human mode of external behaviour) it is a portrayal of an attitude to wrong that is both chilling and compelling. It is the more so given its roots in extremes of social reality that are used by the protagonist to shore up her independence, and given the extremes of repressive discourse and behaviour that will succeed it in the Sección Femenina.

Extrapolation

There are simple equations in relation to Unamuno's views that provide a starting point for thinking about his attitude to making the reader consider ethical issues. Indeed, Olson's book *The Great Chiasmus* (2003), is based on the either/or tendency within Unamuno's thought and fiction, a precept that derives also from Kierkegaard's *Either/Or*. The point of Kierkegaard's pair of alternatives, however, is that it obliges the reader to evaluate, to think, and neither alternative can be considered as 'the answer'. This obligation to evaluate is one that is a constant for Unamuno: for him there are no easy answers, or at least not if one is to have full merit as a human being.

Unamuno did not keep his ideas in neatly labelled boxes of 'fiction', 'essays', 'philosophy'. We have seen how some of the ideas in the primary fictional texts discussed above can be extended outwards into general principles: on *vagos*, on the criminal, on the repressive *mores* of early twentieth-century Catholicism. Whether or not we allow others to lay down the law to us is arguably a litmus test for Unamuno of the strength of identity.

This litmus test also applies to the requisite qualities of nationhood. Tula's rebellion against being ordered about (conveniently not allowed for those others

that she orders herself) would appear to call up some of those attitudes Unamuno
had discussed in 'Sobre el marasmo actual' [On the current state of paralysis]
at the end of *En torno al casticismo* (1902). In his summary of what is wrong
with Spain, he rails against the 'espíritu ordenancista' [rule-bound spirit] (OCE
I, 856; OCA III, 283), its organizational mania, but also its tendency to a willed
fatalism. These warning notes about what is wrong in Spain are given flesh in
the middle-period narratives, *Abel Sánchez* and *La tía Tula*, discussed above.
Abel Sánchez displays through Joaquín the ills of willed fatalism, and Joaquín
and Tula share other traits of the worst in Spain: extreme individualism, the
refusal to obey, dogmatism.

There are apparently issues of gender here, or at least the use of gender-related
stereotypes in order to set up questioning about discrimination, judgement and
action. In 'La tradición eterna' [the eternal tradition], the first part of *En torno
al casticismo*, Unamuno had posited his famous opposition between history
and what was intra-historic, a contrast that effectively is a masculine/feminine
opposition. In this, history is the passing surface text of time and politics, and
which stands in opposition to the more important (and unchangeable) subtext
of what is intra-historic. The 'below' of the latter is associated with the *pueblo*
[the people], a part of society regularly romanticized by the generation of 1898,
and regarded – in the form of a stereotype of the feminine – as the storehouse
that contains culture. The text of history is typically associated with the masculine
world of public politics and events. By contrast, the text of the intra-historic is
inscrutable, beyond recording. It is the archetypally feminine, boundless, full
of riches for the future, the storehouse to which one must descend in order to
find the 'ideas madres' [foundational or core ideas (literally 'mother' ideas)],
something which is satirized through Don Fulgencio Entrambosmares in *Amor
y pedagogía* and his *Ars magna combinatoria* (OCE II, 337; OCA II, 469) (a
gendered term again). The feminine connotations of the intra-historic emerge
in such passing famous phrases of nurturing as 'lo que pasa queda, porque hay
algo que sirve de sustento al perpetuo flujo de las cosas'[what passes continues
to be, because there is something that sustains the perpetual onward-flowing
of things] (OCE I, 792; OCA III, 184). By implication, and consonant with
Marina of *Amor y pedagogía*, and Antonia in *Abel Sánchez*, if not with either
Eugenia of *Niebla* or Tula, the feminine does not distinguish, choose or
discriminate: it accepts, and it allows things to flourish.

In Platonic terms, what Unamuno foregrounds here is the essential part of
the *materia* of the Spanish national identity, which perhaps needs to be placed
in contact with the *forma* of history and the masculine. This seems to be
evidenced by what he sees as the dead text of (bad) *tradición* against which his
new *tradición eterna* needs to be understood. In his summary of this new genre
of *intrahistoria*, Unamuno again uses gender-inflected language: 'Volviendo el

alma con pureza a sí, llega a matar la ilusión, la madre del pecado, a destruir el yo egoísta, a purificarse de sí misma, a anegarse en Dios' [As the soul comes back to itself in a state of purity, it is able to kill illusion, mother of sin, and to destroy the egoistical self, purifying itself, and dissolving itself into the Divine] (OCE I, 798; OCA III, 193). The feminine is again associated with the getting rid of false delimitations and boundaries, but also (the feminine always stands to be blamed) as the *madre del pecado* [the 'mother of sin'], the non-limited view of the world seen through illusion and hence a danger to practical achievement. Right and wrong are here not a question of moral choices, but of modes of survival. In evolutionary terms, 'right' is what will allow for survival and growth, and it is not completely clear that the feminine will lead the way.

This curiously unquestioning opposition in the guise of masculine and feminine terms that we see in *En torno al casticismo* is arguably repeated and yet undercut by Unamuno's presentation of the *pueblo* in *San Manuel Bueno, mártir* (1930). In a text where he foregrounds the issue of faith (or loss of it) in the protagonist, and raises questions about whether belief has to match action, Unamuno appears to be prepared to let some of us, at least, off the hook. This is displayed in the strikingly pragmatic understanding of Christianity as conveyed in the dealings of Manuel with his parishioners. The poor and ill-educated villagers of Villaverde are offered solutions (and often obligations) consistent with a Catholic message of good living, of social interactions that are for the good of others, and at times for the good of all. But although value is apparently given by Manuel to the lives of the villagers, it is not clear where they stand as *persons*. That category is reserved for those who take on less simple options: Lázaro in his ambiguous continuation of Manuel's work, and Angela in her construction of Manuel for posterity, in a narrative intended to stand in opposition to the official documentation of his saintliness.

For whatever reason, there seems to have been some simplification in this relatively late work, conceivably resulting from experience. Unamuno had in 1930 visited Sanabria, where there was a lake at the bottom of which was Villaverde de Lucerna. Sanabria was a village that would be visited in 1933 by the Misiones Pedagógicas, and Unamuno's visit there echoes the visits of others to Las Hurdes, for example. Just as there is an element of the idealization of the *pueblo* in *San Manuel, mártir*, so too there would be in the publications of the Misiones (Sinclair 2004; Sinclair 2009: 164–6). Yet the poverty, extreme social conditions and lack of education of the villagers in *San Manuel*, addressed directly by Lázaro (even if to be dismissed by Manuel), places in question the simple option of viewing the *pueblo* as a site of blessed innocence.

Conclusion

Where does Unamuno wish to leave his reader: discerning and understanding, or troubled and uncertain? It is clear that being at peace is perceived as a fundamental human desire, a longing that we are likely to entertain, but that being at peace is dangerously close to a state of unthinking passivity. In principle, from an early age, we might need to learn to engage with difficulty and decision, yet the processes of education (whether intellectual or moral) do not necessarily proceed in a way to teach us to discriminate. Readers are well aware of the degree to which Unamuno chose to provoke thoughtfulness about what happens beyond the grave, the immortality that we might yearn for, yet of which there is no guarantee. But he was also engaged repeatedly with the questions of being in and of the world, of the experience of living with which we contend on a daily basis, and in which there are inevitably judgements about value and action. We live with others, and in response to others. Learning to tread the lines between right and wrong, while wrestling with problems of the self, is part of life's richness, and significant in our path through what is known (life) before encounter with the unknown (death). Speaking of Unamuno in relation to Kierkegaard, Sarah Wright has neatly shown the link between Unamuno's habitual procedures and the traditions of the classical Greek culture that was his professional life. She argues that it is maieutic, a word derived from the Greek *maia* for 'midwife' and reminds us that this refers to the 'Socratic method of allowing the listener/reader to come to his/her own conclusions from a myriad of different points of view' (Wright 2004: 124/494–125/495). This points us towards a thoughtful and engaged understanding of the onslaughts made on us by Unamuno's frequently abrasive texts, and provides the ultimate container of an intention of integration.

Further Reading

Blanco Aguinagua (1964), Hannay & Marino (1998), Magnus & Higgins (1996), Ouimette (1974).

8

The Necessary Enemy or the Hated Friend:
Self and Other in Unamuno

GARETH WOOD

Unamuno's theorization of 'envidia' [envy], like so many other aspects of his imaginative world, is far from straightforward. His vision of interpersonal rivalry suggests that, at its best, it can play a vivifying role in the life of both the individual and the community, helping the former to define him- or herself in the context of the latter, giving rise to compassion, and fellow-feeling. And yet he also believed envy to be a torpid, knee-jerk response to those around us, one produced by a spiritual death in life that he made it his mission to circumvent through his public role and published writings. He had, in that sense, taken very much to heart Kierkegaard's injunction that 'The very maximum of what one human being can do for another in relation to that wherein each man has to do solely with himself, is to inspire him with concern and unrest' (1968: 346).

We find the former of these attitudes epitomized in his first, and subsequently atypical, novel, *Paz en la guerra*, and in his most important philosophical exploration of faith and doubt, *Del sentimiento trágico de la vida*. The latter, destructive vision of envy, on the other hand, he explores most clearly in the celebrated diagnostic essay 'La envidia hispánica' [Hispanic Envy] (1909), written in response to Alcides Arguedas's study of Bolivian society, *Pueblo enfermo* [An Ailing People] (1909). There, Unamuno argues that the fatal cancer of envy, identified by Arguedas as endemic throughout the Latin American country, is no more than a lingering hangover from imperial rule: hatred of others' success, resentment of any departure from stifling social norms, an unremitting urge to denigrate even those one professes to admire, all of these pernicious traits Unamuno sees as coterminous with Spanish – and hence Hispanic – social life. Such 'íntima gangrena' [intimate gangrene] is born of 'ociosidad espiritual' [spiritual idleness]: it was central to his role as a public intellectual that he wished to live a life combating this particular social ill and also that as a creative writer he should develop an understanding of how fictional and dramatic works might be harnessed to help in that same endeavour. And yet, as his career progressed, the tensions between his private self and his public role appear to have given him an acute awareness of where his own theories might break down. Both the *Diario íntimo* and *Cómo se hace una novela*, albeit at distinct crisis-points of his adult life, attest to tormenting doubts over the authenticity and coherence of his public and private roles. Hence it is that his best novel, *Abel Sánchez*, and his most rounded dramatic work, *El otro*, depict the breakdown of the mutually reinforcing struggle between the self, self-image, and the other, leaving in its wake only suffering and seemingly ineluctable destruction.

Unamuno was of course far from alone in diagnosing envy as a key factor of the Spanish malaise at the turn of the twentieth century. When writing an updated and morally more responsive version of the 'romance de ciego' [The Blind Man's Ballad] in the form of 'La tierra de Alvargonzález', Antonio Machado developed the action around parricidal and fraternal jealousy among a rural farming family. Two of the eponymous patriarch's three sons kill their father while their youngest sibling is away in America seeking his fortune, only for their grasping jealousy to prove their undoing when it becomes clear that, in seeking to circumvent the natural rhythm of inheritance, they have entered into their birthright too soon. It is only the return of the prodigal son, Miguel, that saves the farm from ruin, while the older brothers sicken into depression and suicide for what they have done. Machado declared that his ballads 'look at what is elementally human, at the Castilian countryside and at the first book of Moses, known as Genesis' (1989: 275). Unamuno was of course to find key inspiration in all three elements of this triad, the last of them above all.

Nor have some of the most prominent anthropologists to study Spain in recent times been blind to the crucial role envy plays in determining the outlook of rural communities in particular.[1] In fact, their conclusions mirror Arguedas's in striking ways. The life of a humble provincial community entails scarcity of resources, competition for limited goods, and eking out an existence alongside others whose trajectory is inevitably close to one's own. Such scarcity and hermeticism provoke, in the words of Timothy Mitchell, 'mistrust of fellow ecological competitors', to the point that 'suspicion [is] endemic in many parts of rural Spain – suspicion not of strangers, in this case, but of those one knows all too well: the neighbors' (1988: 99). David Gilmore paints a picture of rural life that could be the implicit backdrop to Lorca's rural tragedies, even referring to the community's collective voice as a Greek chorus, just as the famous dramatist deliberately portrayed the washerwomen in *Yerma* (Gilmore 1987: 34) This is a world in which individuals fear the censure

---

[1]   As well as those cited below, see Renshaw (2011: 92–110).

of their community as much for any conspicuous good fortune as for their transgressions: 'success in these societies is a form of moral deviance: it sets one apart and it inspires the hostility of the others' (170).

What unites Arguedas, Unamuno, Lorca, Mitchell, and Gilmore as observers of Hispanic envy is their shared sense that it arises out of frustration. As mentioned above, Unamuno describes such envy as the product of spiritual idleness, with the implication that the human spirit needs to find an outlet for its energies lest it should turn in on itself and lash out in anger. That sense of the soul and body as an economy in need of regulation underpins his understanding of the dynamic between self and other throughout his career. No less a figure than Pedro Salinas was aware of this continuity in Unamuno's thought, drawing attention to the links between *Paz en la guerra* and the play he was then reviewing, the 1932 production of *El otro* (1970: 70–71). We need to remember that, although 'it would never again be important to Unamuno to put into a novel what he had found important to put into [his first] one', his attitudes to certain dialectics of human personality and political activity remained consistent for the rest of his career (Round 1989: 101). Evidently, what he moved away from in subsequent fiction were the trappings of circumstantial realism: specificity of temporal and spatial setting, the sense of human agents acting against the backdrop of wider historical narratives, efforts towards realistic representation of detail, and prolonged exposition of character through an omniscient narrative voice.[2] And yet, although he came to believe that such features were no more than distractions from the true drama of human emotions presented in the cold light of day, he retained a quiet pride in his first novel, claiming that 'If I am leaving anything to the literature of my country, this novel will not be the least of all' (Unamuno 1983: 6; OCE II, 92; OCA II, 74). That same prologue just quoted makes clear that the novel represented a hymn to his homeland and the Bilbao of his childhood, the background against which his earliest conception of how self and other interact was forged. Fundamental to that backdrop was his experience of the Second Carlist War and the siege of his home city in spring 1874, as detailed in Jean-Clade Rabaté's chapter in this volume. His novelistic recreation of that period becomes a potent autobiographical exposition of how he began to understand the stifling narrowness of political causes when they are used as markers of personal, regional or even national identity.

---

2   His reasons for this shift in priorities are of course laid out most notably in the 'Prólogo' to his *Tres novelas ejemplares y un prólogo* (1920) (OCE II, 971–977; OCA IX, 413–423). He also gives them a substantial and clarifying exposition in remarks on the follies of Naturalism, scientific determinism, and the observational/psychological schools of nineteenth-century realism in a footnote to 'La regeneración del teatro español' (1896) (OCE I, 902–3; OCA III, 350–351). Two excellent summaries of Unamuno's more characteristic fiction are to be found in Macklin (1–18) and Round (1974: 12–24).

Paz en la guerra: mutually self-creating adversaries

Critics have long puzzled over where the central focus of *Paz en la guerra* lies. On first reading, the novel is likely to strike us as an uneasy hybrid of the historical novel, the 'intrahistorical' novel, the thesis novel, and the *bildungsroman*. As Round observes, the 'story flows restlessly, indeterminately on, losing its way in a haze of vivid but largely unrelated detail' (1989: 103). But for all its extraneous, meandering passages on the Carlist campaigns of the early 1870s, a coherent picture does emerge of its central figures and of how we should understand their relationship to wider national and ideological narratives. Central to Unamuno's preoccupations is the depiction of the opposing political identities pitted against one another in the siege of Bilbao. Each is represented, conveniently and conventionally enough, by a family dynasty: on the Carlist side Pedro Antonio Iturriondo, his wife Josefa Ignacia, and their son Ignacio; on the Liberal side Juan Arana and his son Juanito. Political allegiance runs in the blood for these families, not least because Pedro Antonio has brought his son up on his tales of derring-do from the First Carlist War of the 1830s. When the cause comes calling once again, Pedro Antonio not only plunders his savings to pay a subscription in support of the war, he also makes the dearer sacrifice of allowing his only and late-born son to take up arms in the name of the pretender to the Spanish throne. Ignacio is eager to emulate the long-cherished paternal example but his experience of the sporadic skirmishes and furtive retreats of a guerrilla campaign does not stir in him the unalloyed certainty of fighting for truth and justice. At the moment of his death, unheroically cut down by a stray bullet, he appears on the point of rejecting any such absolute ideology in favour of a more plural vision of the national future. A clue as to why this should be comes early in the novel when we find two secondary characters arguing in their regular evening gathering:

> They parted, one mumbling "aggressive brute!", and the other "What an old codger!" But by the next day each would feel a need for the other, the one who arrived first at the *tertulia* would impatiently await the other's arrival. [...] On days in which one would seem to get the better of the other, the one who had lost would go away in smoldering silence, but the truth was that they cared for each other, in an affection that took the form of rancor, a sign of the solidarity between belligerents who complemented each other.
> (Unamuno 1983: 107; OCE II, 147–148; OCA II, 166)

Such adult sparring is merely a more civilized version of the rough and tumble Ignacio and his friends engage in on the city's streets as they grow up. The narrator draws deliberate attention to the fact that after such scraps 'the [...] combatants

[went] off together, without obvious rancor' (Unamuno 1983: 25; OCE II, 102; OCA II, 91). Only once rivals have squared up to one another in combat, be it physical or verbal, can they truly experience, understand, and empathize with each other as human agents. Hence it is that Ignacio the young soldier finds himself discomfitingly estranged from his comrades in their ramshackle regiments:

> Though they were all joined together in a fighting force, something nevertheless separated them. Come together in a united cause, each man lived within himself and for himself. Concurring in a common action, they remained each in his own little world, his spirit impenetrable.
> (Unamuno 1983: 145; OCE II, 168; OCA II, 199–200)

Although this might sound like a repetition of ideas to be found in Galdós, Ganivet, and others on the subject of the Spaniard's inaptitude to the demands of military discipline due to his essential individualism, Unamuno is in fact tracing a theory of how the individual defines himself in opposition to the other that will gain its fullest expression in *Del sentimiento trágico*. If fighting for a common cause leaves Ignacio and his brothers-in-arms divided, it is precisely because they have each subsumed their being, their tussle for self-definition, in an imposed unity of purpose that squashes dissent. But nor does fighting the enemy with the tools of modern warfare lead to any more satisfying enactment of that struggle:

> Compared to the high-spirited spontaneity of a childish stone-throwing contest, what a farce this was! What an empty illusion that turned to dust at the slightest touch! The very size of the field of combat made it meaningless.
> (Unamuno 1983: 15; OCE II, 174; OCA II, 209).

Battles fought over wide areas and at long distance through the sights of a rifle leave no room for the experience of the enemy as a human being, epitomized by the startling passage in which Pachico kills his first enemy in battle:

> Fijóse en un muchacho, apuntóle con cuidado, y diciéndose: ¡a ver si acierto! – disparó a él. Al retirarse con la masa, dirigió una última mirada al pobre muchacho, que de rodillas en el suelo, parecía beber en un pequeño charco de sangre.

> [Concentrating on one of the attackers, he took careful aim, said to himself "Let's see if I'm lucky!", and squeezed the trigger. When he withdrew with the rest of them, he cast a last glance towards the poor enemy boy, on his knees, appearing to drink from a puddle of blood].
> (Unamuno 1983: 281; OCE II, 243; OCA II, 322)

Notice how much Unamuno achieves unobtrusively here with his choice of adjectives and nouns, the work that 'muchacho' [boy], 'masa' [mass], 'pobre' [poor], 'pequeño' [poor] do to convey Ignacio's awareness of the littleness of his actions, how far they are from the heroism evoked by others.

His experience of the war thus departs radically from his expectations and his mind cannot but return to another of the companions alongside whom he grew up, Pachico Zabalbide. The latter is a dissenter and a sceptic, one reluctant to endorse a given cause or programme but ready to debate indefatigably on both sides of any argument. Were this not already ringing enough bells for those familiar with Unamuno's political non-allegiances and habit of developing 'monodiálogos' [monodialogues], the sketch we get of Pachico's early life betrays key coincidences with that of his creator, confirming that the character is at least in part an avatar of the author himself. Pachico it is who is given centre stage at the novel's lyrical finale, reflecting that the Carlist struggles are no more than the ripples on the surface of a deeper intrahistorical harmony. Martin Nozick is not alone in finding Pachico's late emergence as the novel's fulcrum unhelpfully abrupt but, read attentively enough, the text makes clear that Pachico is left to be the spokesman for a generation that Ignacio might have been (1971: 144). As Victor Ouimette has pointed out, 'the tragedy of his death is owing to the fact that Ignacio dies at the moment of his greatest lucidity, when he is most conscious' (1987: 370). The Ignacio who evokes Pachico's scepticism in the long intervals between battles comes to see the Carlist cause as no more than an effort towards self-definition in opposition to a discernible 'other'. That process begins shortly after his ascent into the hills, seen here in its incomplete early stages:

> Ignacio one night remembered how Pachico had said that both sides were right and neither was right, that victory alone decided who was right. But when they all set off at dawn, he felt himself to be part of the whole, part of the mass: reality took over, living reality. The enemy: there was the final meaning. The enemy? And who was the enemy? Why, the enemy! The Other!
> (Unamuno 1983: 155; OCE II, 173; OCA II, 208)

Weeks later and in the wake of fraternization between combatants during a ceasefire, Ignacio comes full circle, seeing that the shadow-play of modern warfare is the least generative means of resolving differences:

> Pero era brutal y sobre todo estúpido, realmente estúpido, totalmente estúpido. Se mataban por otros, para forjar sus propias cadenas, no sabían por qué se mataban. Formaban en dos ejércitos enemigos, y asunto concluido. El enemigo era el enemigo, y nada más; el de enfrente, el otro. La guerra era para ellos la tarea de oficio, la obligación, el quehacer.

[But it was brutal, and what's more stupid, truly stupid, absolutely stupid, all of it. They were killing each other [themselves] for the sake of others, and they were forging their own chains. They didn't even know why they were killing each other. They made up two enemy armies. That was that. The enemy was the enemy, nothing more; the man on the other side, the other. War was their obligation, their job].

(Unamuno 1983: 299–300; OCE II, 254; OCA II, 339).

Note the polysemy of the phrase 'Se mataban por otros' with its dual sense that they are killing in the name of others' causes but also that they are killing each other because they are 'the other'. Hence Pachico's emergence on the hillside as the voice of his generation is more closely woven into the fabric of the novel than might at first appear. As Ouimette has suggested, Unamuno/Pachico reject '[t]he falsity, levelling and depersonalization implicit in every ideology, which can never be more than a means of provoking blind and ignorant support' (1987: 374–75).

And yet, that need not always be the case. Unamuno appears at pains to show the ways in which that same collective identity rejected by Ignacio and Pachico can be a living source of both comfort and meaning. A grief-stricken Pedro Antonio retreats into himself following his son's death, finds no solace in so great a sacrifice to the cause, and instead worries about never seeing again the money he invested in victory. It is not until later, the siege of Bilbao having ended in defeat, when he attends the ceremony at which the pretender Carlos pledges allegiance to the 'fueros' [foral/customary laws and privileges] at the foot of the tree of Guernica, that he is able to reconcile himself to his loss. Unamuno writes the scene with a powerful but contained emotive force, Pedro Antonio reconnecting with the collective identity that had proved so important to him for so long and from which his son's death had estranged him. The tears he sheds are observed by two 'muchachas alegres' [lighthearted girls] who laugh at his – to their eyes at least – ridiculous fervour. Their inclusion is curious but at the same time artistically apt. Perhaps Unamuno wishes to contrast the spectacle of a man truly at one with his community with the sneering superciliousness of the outsider. Pachico's pledge at the end of the novel is not of that aloof, unproductive nature. He will remain deeply engaged with his fellow men and the struggles of their existence but will also keep an eye on the larger picture of the eternal truth that 'guerra' [war] is but the passing form of 'paz' [peace].

Pedro Antonio's consoling absorption into a larger collective identity, presented as it is without authorial undercutting (what else do the 'muchachas' convey but that their reaction will not do?) mirrors other paradoxical aspects of Unamuno's thought. Not the least of those was his yearning for the automatic faith of childhood despite living a life tormented by religious doubts that nevertheless underpinned his sense of authenticity. It is a truism of Unamuno studies that shortly after *Paz en la guerra* saw print the personal crisis of 1897 precipitated a step-change in both his vocation and his aesthetics. At least where the latter is concerned, we ought perhaps to add some nuance to that familiar narrative.

Self, self-image and the other in Unamuno's theatrical writing 1898–1909

If his first novel had taken somewhere between seven and twelve years to complete, we perhaps ought not to be surprised to find that its author's literary sensibility had evolved in the meantime.[3] The slow-burn of a sprawling historical novel would never again be his chosen route to his reader's sympathies, a change of tack anticipated, even partially announced, in 'La regeneración del teatro español' (1896). Though too extensive to summarize in full here, that essay sows the seeds for the shift in his aesthetic theory by decrying the tendency for Spain's theatre companies to be hermetic and nepotistic environments.[4] Learning their craft among practitioners and in the shadow of fusty traditions, Unamuno believes Spanish playwrights produce 'teatro de teatro' [theatre from theatre], a banal palimpsest of all that has gone before, suited to the tastes of a bourgeois paying public whose main interest is to see and be seen in the auditorium. If the contemporaneous essays of *En torno al casticismo* offer the at times puzzling juxtaposition of diffuse philosophical abstraction with sensible practical suggestions, 'La regeneración del teatro español' is very much in the same vein. It rounds off a series of tendentious arguments about – among other things – Lope de Vega as mouthpiece of the Spanish 'pueblo' [people] with calls for state-subsidized theatre and open-air performances of the great Golden Age tragedies in rural villages. In fact, he was to see the latter of those ideas made flesh, albeit thirty-eight years later, when he attended a performance by Lorca's travelling company La Barraca at the International University in Santander in the summer of 1934.[5] The two dramatists shared a sense of needing to create an audience for the sort of drama they wanted to produce on Spanish stages and Unamuno appears to have reinforced his sense of finding a worthy disciple in Lorca later that same year by attending both the rehearsals and première of *Yerma*. He was reported

---

[3]   Unamuno tended to add years onto the 'heroic' labours he expended over his first novel, to the point that the seven years he reported it had taken him in 1896 had, by 1933, become twelve. See Francisco Caudet's 'Introducción' to *Paz en la guerra* (Unamuno 1999: 11).

[4]   For an excellent summary of the historical context in which Unamuno wrote 'La regeneración del teatro español', see Gagen (1989).

[5]   Unamuno recorded his enthusiastic reaction to these efforts to bring theatre to the 'pueblo' in 'Hablemos de teatro', published in *Ahora*, 19th September 1934. See Unamuno (1959: 1193–96).

in the press as having likened it to his own drama of frustrated motherhood, *Raquel, encadenada* (1921), only done better (Gibson 1998 II: 334–35).[6] It ought to be no surprise that he admired the claustrophobic atmosphere, clipped dialogue, and stark tragedy of Lorca's play. He had, after all, been advocating just such a pared-down and unremitting aesthetic – art stripped of artifice – since 1896, two years before Lorca was even born and one year before the crisis that is said to have precipitated the change of direction.

Nevertheless, his first effort to dramatize the conflict between self, self-image, and other, *La esfinge* (1898), finds its roots in that same crisis. The play explores the dilemma confronting Ángel, a charismatic political leader whose sense of vocation has deserted him. He craves only a retreat from the hurly-burly of party activism into a solitary, pantheistic religious faith. Instead he finds himself pulled in the opposite direction by the twin claims of his comrades and his wife, Eugenia, for whom the prospect of power offers a palliative against her frustrated maternal longings. Most, if not all, critics of Unamuno's drama agree that *La esfinge* displays significant shortcomings, notwithstanding the fact that it enjoyed a successful and lucrative season when it premiered at the Teatro Pérez Galdós in Las Palmas de Gran Canaria in 1909 (Unamuno 1959: 51–58). Donald Shaw's even-handed analysis points out that the contrasting choices facing Ángel are never truly presented as competing viable options: Ángel has made his mind up before the play begins and so Unamuno is forced to incarnate the political life he has already rejected in the competing claimants who vie for supremacy over him (1977: 253–56).[7] In spite of which Ángel comes across as a petulant, egotistical, even childish figure, his speeches attesting to a relentless self-absorption that only alienates him from the audience. Moreover, we never see him in action as a political rhetorician (Unamuno's dislike of elaborate staging or spectacle dictated that the play should begin in the moments immediately after what becomes Ángel's final apotheosis in front of his adoring supporters) and the result is that he never appears truly credible in that role. In short, *La esfinge* epitomizes what some have taken to be a wider problem with much of Unamuno's drama: the fact that 'it does not entirely cover the route which runs from the dynamic schema of the action to the realization of that schema' (Ruiz Ramón 1989: 80).

There is, however, one moment in the play which does succeed in giving dramatic, that is active, physical shape to Ángel's dilemma. And, not surprisingly, it was one the dramatist took directly from personal experience of the 1897

---

6   Nicholas Round has suggested that the stark setting and harsh tones of the dialogue in Lorca's play may have derived at least in part from the influence of Unamuno's *El otro*. See his 'Introduction' in García Lorca (2008: x)

7   See also Shaw (1979). A further worthwhile study of the play is to be found in Heil (2009).

crisis. The relevant passage from the *Diario íntimo*, which records Unamnuo's struggles in the spring of that year with such unsparing detail, is as follows:

> I remember from time to time having looked at myself in the mirror until I became doubled and saw myself as a strange/alien subject, and once, in that position I softly said my own name out loud, and heard it as another's voice calling me, and I was terrified and overcome—as if I felt the abyss of nothingness and as if I were a vain passing shadow. I felt such sadness then! It seems as if one submerges oneself in unfathomable waters which cut off all one's breathing, and as everything dissipates while nothingness, eternal death, advances.
>
> (Unamuno 1998: 46)

Thus we find this scene transposed onto the stage at the climax of Act 1 of *La esfinge*. The Ángel who is finding it increasingly difficult to distinguish between the face he presents to the world and the core of his being regards himself in a mirror situated at one side of the stage. Coming as it does before a curtain fall, Ángel's (self-)questioning of the image in the mirror 'A shadow? No! No! I'm alive! I'm alive!' (OCE V, 67; OCA XII, 250) is the essence of his torment, strikingly realized as dramatic spectacle. It is no accident that Unamuno was to return to the motif in his best play *El otro*. As Stephen Roberts has suggested, '[o]ne of the terms which recurs most insistently in Unamuno's *Diario* is *comedia* [play/drama], a term that Unamuno uses in order to contemplate matters pertinent to the playing of roles, the self and sincerity' (2007: 77). So it is that Ángel questions the honesty of his own actions, wondering whether he is not playing to the gallery of his political supporters, violating in the process his deepest needs. His self fragments as he contemplates the competing impulses that ebb and flow, conscious all the time of watching his own actions for signs of inauthenticity. Although Katrina Heil is right to suggest that 'the self of existential philosophy is best expressed subjectively in the first person. [...] [D]rama is in many ways the ideal genre to portray a philosophy concerned with subjective existence, as well as relationships with others who, in turn, also exist subjectively', Unamuno has not yet found the necessary balance of stagecraft and character (486). The dilemma Unamuno was to formulate and develop more fully as his career progressed has had its first, albeit imperfect, airing.

Roberts contends that Unamuno emerged from the 1897 crisis reinvigorated with intellectual and spiritual purpose. Thus the first of the *Tres ensayos* [Three Essays] (1900), '¡Adentro!', alerted the Spanish public to the nature of his new role as an 'agitador de espíritus' [agitator of spirits] announcing his intention to explore his ontological doubts so publicly and straightforwardly as to expose his readers' own identical struggles (Roberts 2007: 67–91): 'Catch each one, if you can, on his/her own, in his dressing room and make him uneasy inside, because he who has never known unease will never know rest' (OCE I, 951; OCA III, 425). Clearly matters of technique were uppermost in his mind. It is to this change of direction which we must ascribe the eradication of all 'extraneous' detail from his subsequent fictional and dramatic works. *La esfinge* was therefore a significant early outing for the new approach but, thanks to the archival work of Manuel García Blanco, we know that its reception by at least two of the readers to whom Unamuno entrusted the perusal of the first draft was anything but positive. In fact, one of them, Pedro Jiménez Ilundain, replied with a critique so devastating it could only have come from the best of friends or the worst of enemies, containing as it did such phrases as '[f]rom the point of view of stagecraft, it is the work of someone who has never seen a drama and has rarely read one' (OCE V, 15; OCA XII, 22). Although he waited four months before replying, Unamuno expressed gratitude for his friend's candour and was equally magnanimous in accepting the criticism that he had written an undramatic drama, replying that this was precisely what he had been seeking:

> I want to be clear that I am not seeking dramatic success if, in order to achieve it, I have to sacrifice what, in my opinion, cannot be sacrificed. I don't care if I am not understood, [...] Rather than write plays for the audience, I want to create an audience for the plays. A dozen attentive readers will do for me.
> (OCE V, 29; OCA XII, 44)

Nor did he contradict the suggestion that he was a theatrical novice. Indeed, he was sufficiently unembarrassed by his lack of theatre-going experience as to mention it in several of his essays, including those about the state of contemporary drama.[8] In 'Soledad' (1905), he made clear why he attended the theatre so seldom and what effect theatrical artifice usually had on him:

> Mankind interests me so much and my heart becomes so agitated when I hear his eternal 'ohs', that I cannot resist a dramatic performance. It seems like a pure lie to me. I cannot hear one man talk to another, or even less in front of a crowd. I wish to hear him on his own, when he talks to himself.
> (OCE I, 1253; OCA III, 885)

What he is responding to here is doubtless the declamatory style of delivery favoured by actors of his day. But it also points towards the intimate and stripped-back dramatic works he was to create. Such is after all the stage

---

[8]   See, for example, the first sentences of 'De vuelta del teatro' and 'Impresiones de teatro' in Unamuno 1959: 1171 & 1176).

practice implicitly advocated in 'Teatro de teatro' (1899) and '¡Adentro!': the intimate communication from the depths of one soul to the depths of another. In the former, he had laid emphasis on the 'teatro de ideas' [theatre of ideas] he wanted to see flourish in Spain, and outlined that one crucial step towards achieving it was the creation of characters stripped of all markers of social position, regional identity, or recognizable 'type'. The last thing he wanted was for members of the audience to be able to identify them with any preconceived expectations and thereby dismiss them (Unamuno 1959: 1160–61). That idea fed into the development of subsequent fictional prose and became a key tenet of how he would seek to harness the theatre in the service of his larger project, a labour that continued for the remainder of his career. Replying to Jiménez Ilundain in 1899, he had stated defensively that theatrical success was not his priority – 'A dozen attentive readers will do for me' (referenced above). Whether disingenuous or merely self-justificatory, that response is at odds with the emphasis he had placed on the collective nature of theatre-going experience in 'La regeneración del teatro español'. But the tension over whether plays could speak to individuals or groups was to remain one with which he grappled. It resurfaced in response to *La esfinge*'s successful stage run in 1909, when he observed to a correspondent that its reception had caught him by surprise: 'I speak and write for each of those who hear me and not for them collectively. And in a theatre audience, the individual 'I's dissolve into a 'we'' (Unamuno 1959: 52). Perhaps buoyed by the validation of his ongoing project, the following year he replied somewhat tartly to a correspondent who had asked him whether there was a printed edition of *La esfinge*: 'No, I have not published *La Esfinge*. I am unwilling to publish dramatic works, which are written to be seen and heard, not read' (Unamuno 1991: I, 270). We should bear this in mind when looking in detail at *El otro*. As Roberts has suggested, the outcome of the 1897 crisis was, paradoxically, to reinforce Unamuno's faith in the public role he had forged hitherto. Did the validation of his theatrical practice in the case of *La esfinge* leave him unhelpfully wedded to an outmoded dramatic theory? What did Unamuno learn in subsequent years about harnessing the theatre as theatre to engage the sympathies of each member of his audience?

The fact that Unamuno was able to accept and act in response to Jiménez Ilundain's criticism (by maintaining their correspondence and redrafting sections of *La esfinge*) also adds further complexity to the picture Alison Sinclair paints in the first chapter of her study of how the Spanish writer interacted with European scientific and philosophical debates. There, Sinclair uses evidence from his correspondence to show how poorly he coped at times with dissent from his idiosyncratic views, closing down friendships and cutting off communication with those who challenged them (Sinclair 2001:

13–30).[9] That prickliness sits at odds with the exhortation to the readers of *Del sentimiento trágico*:

> All of us--each of us, can and ought to determine to give as much of himself as much as he possibly can—nay, to give more than he can, to exceed himself, to go beyond himself, to make himself irreplaceable, to give himself to others in order that he may receive himself back again from them
> (Unamuno 1954: 269–270; OCE VII, 267–8; OCA XVI, 393).

Faced with the need for a God who could not be generated by rational means, Unamuno advocated the extension of the individual's own sense of ontological doubt to his fellow sufferers. Only on the basis of such empathy could fellow-feeling and community be forged. And yet, that empathy had to be reinforced by a continued awareness of the root problem, hence the mutually self-creating struggle for supremacy of one individual over another needed to remind each of their ontological insecurity. To be so reminded was positive because it encouraged the expansion of the spirit:

> Evil blurs the conscience, and not only the moral conscience but also the general psychical consciousness. And everything that exalts and expands consciousness is good, while that which depresses and diminishes it is evil.
> (Unamuno 1954: 291; OCE VII, 280; OCA XVI, 414).

As it stands, the theory advocated allows for one self potentially to be consumed by another. What happens when one individual cannot or will not enter into the spirit of that struggle? It is just such a breakdown of mutual understanding and tussle that Unamuno recreates so successfully in *Abel Sánchez*.

---

9   Gonzalo Sobejano makes equally insightful remarks on Unamuno's public pronouncements about Nietzsche. Sobejano suggests that Unamuno's frequent claims to have read little and enjoyed less of the German philosopher owed more to envy and to similarities in their thought than to sincerity on the Spaniard's part. Particularly striking is the passage Sobejano quotes from 'La pureza del idealismo [The Purity of Idealism]' (1915), in which Unamuno asks himself '¿no crees tú que [...] si fueses hijo de un imperio, como el de Alemania, cuya voluntad es la justicia para cada uno de sus miembros, no crees que entonces esa tu novela *Niebla*, pongo por caso, o cualquiera otra de tus obras filosófico-literarias y joco-serias, habrían sido recibidas de otro modo, y las que llaman tus paradojas, pasarían por profundas concepciones? ¿Qué se diría de un Nietzsche portugués o guatemalteco, o siquiera español?' [Don't you think that [if you were the offspring of an empire like Germany's, whose will is justice for each and every one of those who make it up, don't you think that in that case, that novel of yours, *Niebla* for the sake of argument, or any other of your philosophical-literary and jocular-serious works, would have been received differently, and what are referred to as your 'paradoxes' would pass for profound conceptualizations? What would be said about a Portuguese, Guatemalan or even Spanish Nietzsche?] (Sobejano 2004: 316).

Doubles, brothers and enemies: fiction and drama 1908–1929

Drawing inspiration from the contemplation of a divided self in his own mirror, Unamuno developed a number of fictional scenarios in which to explore further his understanding of human personality. Among his first attempts in fictional prose was the short story 'El que se enterró' (1908), in which an anonymous narrator describes the mysterious and terrifying experience of his friend Emilio, a young man whose formerly gregarious demeanour has changed abruptly to that of an introverted and sorrowful loner. His friends quiz him as to the cause of his anxieties, with Emilio eventually yielding to the narrator's entreaties to divulge what has happened to him. He reveals that all savour has gone from life since he was visited one day by a double of himself who calmly sat down in the chair opposite him and stared him in the eye. So overwhelmed was he by 'the height of resigned desperation' that he died, only to awake a short time later seated where his double had previously been. His original body now lay inert before him, his consciousness apparently having transferred to the intruder. Under cover of darkness, he buried his former body in a corner of the garden and tried to pick up his former occupations, only to realize that they no longer held any meaning for him.

Early in the story, one of Emilio's friends provides a recondite literary parallel that attests to the breadth of Unamuno's reading:

> One of our friends, an assiduous reader and decipherer of Browning, remembering the strange composition in which Browning tells us about the life of Lazarus after he was brought back from the dead, used to say that poor Emilio had visited death'
>
> (OCE II, 817; OCA IX, 194)

The reference is to Robert Browning's 'An Epistle Containing the Strange Medical Experience of Karshish, the Arab Physician'; and the characterization of it as 'extraña composición' is not unjustified. The poem takes the form of a letter from Karshish, an Arab physician travelling in the Holy Land at an unspecified time in the 60s AD, addressed to his mentor and relating, among other things, an encounter with Lazarus, a man apparently brought back from the dead by a healer named Jesus. Why his account (and Browning's poem) suit Unamuno's purpose so well is because Lazarus is described as a man seemingly no longer of this earth:

> So here – we call the treasure knowledge, say,
> Increased beyond the fleshly faculty –

> Heaven opened to a soul while yet on earth,
> Earth forced on a soul's use while seeing heaven:
> The man is witless of the size, the sum
> The value in proportion of all things,
> Or whether it be little or be much.

According to what value system Lazarus now views the world remains a mystery when he can look with equanimity on the death of a child:

> While a word, gesture, glance from that same child
> At play or in the school or laid asleep,
> Will startle him to an agony of fear
> Exasperation, just as like.
>
> (Browning 2009: 190)

It is one of the poem's great strengths that it offers no explanation other than that a view of the infinite divine has left Lazarus incompatible with life on earth. That sense of mystery and awestruck contemplation extends into Unamuno's tale, where Emilio's friends cannot make rational sense of their friend's experience of doubling, merely look upon it in fearful wonder.

Browning was far from the only source Unamuno would draw on when exploring the self through fiction. Byron's *Cain* and Stevenson's *Dr Jekyll and Mr Hyde* would feature within the fictional worlds of *Abel Sánchez* (1917) and 'Artemio, Heautontimoroumenos' (1918) respectively, while critics have argued for the implicit influence of further texts whose focus is broadly similar, among them Dostoevsky's *The Double*, Gorky's *Cain and Artyom*, James's 'The Jolly Corner', Poe's 'William Wilson', and Wilde's *The Picture of Dorian Grey*.[10] However, as Julia Biggane (2000) has argued in relation to *El otro*, the pursuit of literary debts real or imagined can at times be a reductive exercise, driven by unacknowledged anxieties over the quality of Unamuno's works. Her reservations echo those of Nozick who asserted that, while Unamuno:

> has with justification been called one of the most extensively "related" thinkers of Western culture [...] if his frame of reference is of astounding

---

10   Rebeca Martín (2007) speculates that Poe's 'William Wilson' should also be added to this list Martín speculates that Unamuno could have read Stevenson in the first Spanish translation of *Dr Jekyll...* which appeared in 1920 (122). In fact, he had no need of it, already owning an English-language edition which he annotated. He had almost certainly read Stevenson before 1920 in any case, making reference to Stevenson's novel in the 1918 short story 'Artemio, Heautontimoroumenos'.

comprehensiveness, he mainly favored those writers and moralists who struck him as foreshadowings or duplications of himself' (1971: 26).[11]

While the latter verdict may be crying out for clarification and nuance, it is with Biggane and Nozick in mind that I intend to focus in what remains of this discussion on *Abel Sánchez* and *El otro* as reading and theatrical experience. Where I comment on his literary debts it will be with the specific aim of showing how his reading of others' works has sharpened his literary and dramatic sensitivity.[12]

The ultimately fratricidal struggle unveiled in *Abel Sánchez* makes for a visceral reading experience.[13] Joaquín Monegro and Abel Sánchez grow up together, their paths inexorably intertwined, and with the former always conscious of living in the latter's shadow. In each of the important early arenas – the school playground, the first steps towards a career, their first love affairs – Abel beats his friend to the prize. That he does so apparently without effort or conviction only enrages Joaquín the more, his life reduced to a series of non-choices of what is left after Abel has won the spoils. The novel follows their trajectories through life: Abel's career as a celebrated artist, his marriage to the beautiful Helena, the birth of his son, Abelín; Joaquín's career as a doctor, his disappointing marriage to Antonia following Helena's rejection of him, the birth of his daughter Joaquina, and her later marriage to Abelín. He wages quiet war on Abel, consumed with envy and resentment at the other's achievements, unable to enjoy his own in consequence. Their struggle for supremacy comes to a head as they vie for the affections of their grandson, Joaquín unable to contain his anger at Abel's taunts over his 'mala sangre' [bad blood], seizes his rival by the throat, only to provoke a fatal heart attack.

As early as Chapter 1, the anonymous narrator interpolates the first of many fragments from Joaquín's 'Confesión', a private diary of his miseries in which he:

[11]   Certainly, Unamuno would disagree, claiming in 'Divagaciones de estío' that '¿Qué nos dice el mar? Lo que queremos que nos diga. Es como la música. Y yo quiero que las cosas – los hechos y los misterios – me digan no lo que yo quiero, sino lo que quieren ellas, y que me obliguen a resistirlas. Y he aquí porque [*sic*] no leo los escritores que supongo han de decirme lo mismo que yo pienso' [What does the sea tell us? Whatever we want it to tell us. It's like music. And I want things—both facts and mysteries—to tell me not what I want to know, but what *they* want, and that they make me resist them. And that is why I don't read writers that I think will tell me the same things I think]. (OCE III, 406; OCA IV, 598–599.

[12]   Those seeking further information of Unamuno's use of sources in relation to *Abel Sánchez* and *El otro* can consult the following: Gullón (1965); Hudson (1991); Ilie (1961); Jurkevich (1990); Lee (1979); Marbán (1976); Orringer (1986); Round (1974); Smith (1972).

[13]   Readers wishing to gain the fullest understanding of *Abel Sánchez* can do no better than consult Round (1974).

embarks upon a process of self-creation [where] he reflects upon and recounts his experience and feelings, he creates a version of the self that he aspires to, which is itself part of what makes him a person'

(Macklin 1999: 24).

But Joaquín has never reached an acceptance of his identity and personality. By seeking out self-affirmation through his interaction with others, he has introduced a crucial lack into his own make-up, one filled only with spite due to Abel's refusal of mutual sympathy or struggle. The reason why this should be the case is left open-ended, the narrator commenting in Chapter 1 that Joaquín 'siguió fiel a su propio natural' [remained faithful to his natural self], with its inscrutable implication that Joaquín has simply been born into this state of being. In that regard, the novel proves unsparingly bleak. Round's assertion that '[I]t is the purpose of all Unamuno's novels to mount an imaginative attack on [...] the refusal to acknowledge that the business of being human at all is a deeply problematic one' could not be more apt (1974: 20). This is also crucial for the choice of paired-down novelistic form:

Man minus his social dimension exists in the context of a set of relationships which we are compelled to regard as somehow unconditioned and primary. Thus the fact of Joaquín's insecurity, for which no explanation of a social kind if available, compels the reader to think of insecurity in these terms. It throws into relief the idea of insecurity as something which can very well arise from no other reason than the challenge of having to live in the world with others

(Round 1974: 20–21)

Unamuno had reflected in the *Diario* íntimo on the contradiction between divine and human responses to criminality:

God hates the sin and loves the sinner; man loves the sin and hates the sinner, he exploits the crime and condemns the delinquent. A hatred for the criminal is one of the saddest human feelings

(Unamuno 1998: 125).

Thus his empathy with Joaquín extends beyond the limits of his novel to what Machado had called 'lo elemental humano' [what is elementally human], whose most emblematic encapsulation both he and Unamuno found in the Book of Genesis. In *Del sentimiento*, Unamuno had already suggested that the motivation behind Cain's slaying of his brother was the thirst for immortality, the desire to live on in the divine memory which he saw crucially threatened by God's preference for Abel's offering over his own. It is the insertion of *Abel Sánchez* within such timeless quandaries over how we might live a meaningful existence alongside our fellow man that give it the unsettling impact it delivers. Alison Sinclair's reading of the novel would extend that impact further beyond the confines of the text by encouraging us to reject the face-value anonymity of the narrator. Taking *La novela de don Sandalio, jugador de ajedrez* as the Unamunian precedent for a novel in which the putative outcome is called into question by the narrative frame, Sinclair suggests that Abel Sánchez is not only key protagonist but also narrator of the text (2001: 170–190). Were her interpretation to be correct it would make *Abel Sánchez* not just, in Macklin's words, an 'unforgettable contribution to the twentieth-century literature of the self', but also one of the great literary depictions of cruelty. As Unamuno made clear in his 1928 prologue to the novel's second edition, Joaquín's envious struggle is self-destructive and self-defeating; but it is still a struggle for existence, meaning, and self-definition that Abel Sánchez cruelly refuses. Were he the narrator of the novel, it would leave us with the desolating knowledge that Abel had it in his power to aid Joaquín in the resolution of his divided self but chose not to do so.

When it comes to discerning how Unamuno ensures that *El otro* becomes a fully realized theatrical experience, we might begin by questioning Ricardo Doménech's suggestion that our responses are driven by predisposition: 'Those who share that tragic feeling usually like Unamuno's plays [...] Those who are insensitive to that tragic cosmology notice only the spareness of his stagecraft' (Doménech 1998: 115). Were that to be true it would be a sorry indictment of Unamuno's writing for the stage. Instead, it will be argued that *El otro* works as a murder mystery, but one in which the audience's imagination is engaged to move out from the resolution of the crime into ontologically more much unsettling territory. The 'Autocrítica' [Self-Criticism] Unamuno penned to mark the play's première shows Unamuno to be more (self-) aware of the techniques he is employing and of their inherent dangers:

> Perhaps some spectators will think that not a breath of fresh air, nor a hint of humour runs through this dark mystery, and s/he is not wrong. [...] I am aware of the risks entailed in always keeping the thread pulled tight, and keeping the audience on tenterhooks, but I also know the --perhaps greater—danger of loosening the tension for even a moment
>
> (OCE V, 654; OCA XII, 802)

That sense of pervasive tension is established early: the play opens with Ernesto and Juan on stage, discussing the shadow that has fallen over the marital home of the former's sister, Laura, and her husband Cosme. The two men convey a sense of their creeping unease, with Ernesto declaring 'This seems part-prison, part-cemetery, part-...' only for Juan to complete the phrase for him with the exclamation 'Madhouse!' (OCE V, 655; OCA XII, 803). The latter is an 'alienista', [an alienist] a term pregnant with unsettling associations, and we learn that he has been summoned to the house by Ernesto to get to the bottom of the mystery that has engulfed it. Cosme has seemingly lost his mind, will not see his wife, and insists on calling himself El Otro [The Other]. Strangest of all is Laura's reaction:

> JUAN: And the most worrying thing of all is that she, Laura, doesn't seem to mind such bizarre obsessive behaviour, as if all this about 'the Other' had some kind of meaning that was hidden to the rest of us
>
> (OCE V, 656; OCA XII, 804)

As in the best crime dramas, the audience gains a sense of whom to trust. And yet, it is also part of Unamuno's strategy to confound that expectation when it becomes clear at the play's conclusion that the doctor is the most literal-minded and flat-footed interpreter of events, encouraging the audience to move beyond his blunt rationalism into richer metaphysical territory.

Unamuno has also learned to allow his audience greater participation when it comes to the conjuring of dramatic tension. El Otro makes his appearance in Act 1 Scene 3, consenting in the next scene to give Ernesto an account of what has occurred. Their conversation contains the macabre irony of the latter's words 'No, don't get upset or be afraid', an inlaid stage-direction indicating that the actor playing Ernesto should show considerable discomfort, not helped by El Otro's declaration that '[p]eople are as afraid to be left alone with someone they take to be mad—always dangerous—just as they fear going into a cemetery at night' (OCE V, 660–661; OCA XII, 809–10). What might otherwise appear to be Unamuno's wearisome penchant for paradoxical wordplay

ERNESTO: ¡Acaba!
OTRO: ¡Pero si no he empezado!...
ERNESTO: ¡Pues empieza!
OTRO: ¡Empiezo!

ERNESTO: Stop!
OTRO: But I haven't even started!...
ERNESTO: Well start then!
OTRO: I'm starting!

(OCE V, 661; OCA XII, 810)

becomes instead an expression of Ernesto's squirming fear. El Otro it transpires is a murderer: he has killed his twin brother after a lifetime of jealous personal and sexual rivalry. He gives the first of two descriptions of the crime, his speech characterized by a rising note of panic until he declares that he can see the corpse right before his eyes. Unamuno is requiring skill of an actor but is also engaging the audience's imagination in the generation of horror. The latter point is illustrated by Adolfo Bioy Casares in his prologue to the *Antología de la literatura fantástica* [Literary Anthology of the Fantastic] he edited in collaboration with Jorge Luis Borges and Silvina Ocampo. There, he relates an anecdote about the stage adaptation of a horror story by John Hampden:

> One of the spectators said after the performance that the horrible ghost seen when the door opened was an offence to art and good taste, and that the autor should not have shown it, but instead have let the audience imagine it, which was exactly what he had done.
>
> (Bioy Casares: 9).

The fear generated by the audience in their minds is far more effective than anything produced by any amount of stage trickery. El Otro takes Ernesto to the cellar where he has hidden the body, the stage left empty in their absence, and the only sound being Laura's voice heard from the wings demanding entry to the room: it is one of the most dramatic moments of the play, precisely and paradoxically because the action lies beyond the audience's purview. The extensive quotation from 'The Murders in the Rue Morgue' Unamuno included in his essay 'Sobre el ajedrez' [On Chess] (OCA IV, 906–908; OCE III, 605) tells us that he had read Edgar Allan Poe by at least 1912 and the fact appears crucial to the staging of these scenes in *El otro*. The dramatist is exploring the possibilities offered by the body that lies just beyond the boundaries of the physical space of the setting, just as the American does in 'The Black Cat' and 'The Tell-tale Heart'. As all three texts demonstrate, it becomes a powerful motif, a potent symbol of an uneasy conscience, and the reminder of a horror that rapidly engulfs the protagonists. The main character in each clings to his remaining fragments of sanity long enough to leave an account behind of his misdeeds before quitting the world for good.

Following in the footsteps of Arturo Fox, Sinclair gives a striking account of the play's psychoanalytical resonances, highlighting the extent to which the early life of Cosme and Damián has laid the foundations for their inability to forge individual identities (Fox 1991; Sinclair 2001). The audience of the play need not necessarily be familiar with the Freudian, Lacanian, and Kleinian theory on which Sinclair draws to perceive the role that their psychosexual development has played in laying the foundations for the tragic outcome to their lives. Conversations at either end of Act 2 between Laura and Ernesto, El Otro and the Ama confirm that neither of the formative experiences of female affection the twin brothers enjoyed has allowed them to forge a self as distinct from each other. Not only did the two women who supplied them with maternal affection – their mother and their nursemaid – treat them interchangeably—their first romantic attraction was to a woman, Laura, who refused to choose between them: the brothers came to an agreement between themselves that it would be Cosme, but clearly it could (tragically for their sense of self) have been either. Nor – as we learn at the beginning of Act 3 – did the marriage of Damián to Damiana help matters, since her sexual curiosity extended in the days after her wedding to Cosme; El Otro defensively alleges that her efforts to sleep with each twin separately and in secret failed because they counter-conspired to ensure she only enjoyed one of them, though it is impossible to know if this is true.

The failure of these formative relationships to permit differentiation and reinforcement of stability is partly a perversity of human character in desiring what we cannot have and partly a dereliction of maternal duty. But it makes utterly real to the audience the ontological doubt the brothers experienced:

> EL OTRO: 'We made each other evil between the two of us…When one
> is no longer one, that person becomes evil…To become evil,
> there is nothing like always having a mirror in front of one,
> and even more so when that mirror is alive and breathing'
> (OCE V, 679; OCA XII, 830).

Were we in any remaining doubt, it is realized on stage not just through the struggle of the two women over what's left of the spoils – El Otro – but also through another mirror scene, this time at the start of Act 3. Unamuno has improved on previous employment of the device, placing the mirror 'in the background' (OCE V, 682; OCA XII, 832) (not to one side, as in *La esfinge*), thus in front of the audience who will see their own presence reflected back at them just as El Otro sees his own disintegration of self in that same mirror. It is this scene that gives meaning to the Ama's potential speech in the epilogue (Unamuno leaves it to the director to choose between the formulation 'the historian does not know who he is' and 'Unamuno does not know who he is') on our radical insecurity of identity (OCE V, 709; OCA XII, 862). When we hold the list of binaries implied by Cain and Abel so closely intertwined within the single self, on what basis can we truly determine a meaningful thread of existence?

Further Reading

Heil (2009), Ouimette (1987), Roberts (2007), Round (1974), (1989), Shaw (1979).

9

From Separate Spheres to Unilateral Androgyny:
Gender and Sexuality in the Work of Unamuno

JULIA BIGGANE

Given that his writing career spanned more than forty years, it should not come as a surprise that the representation of gender and sexuality in Unamuno's work changed as the horizons of women and men in Spain, and their social and personal relations, shifted dramatically over the course of the late nineteenth and early twentieth century. Born into an era in which educational opportunities, civil-society rights and legal protections were starkly differentiated according to gender, and in which the Catholic Church dominated the (limited) discourse on sexuality and marriage, Unamuno lived to see the entry of women into higher education, the rise of secular birth-control organisations, the incorporation of middle-class women into the workplace on an unprecedented scale, the introduction of female suffrage and the legalisation of civil divorce.[1]

Unamuno's fiction, drama, poetry and essays certainly register such changes, if idiosyncratically and at times obliquely. But he did not just chronicle such change, directly or indirectly; as a legislator in the first months of the Second Republic he enabled it too, voting to grant women suffrage at the end of 1931. But we should not conclude from this last fact that Unamuno was a supporter of feminism; as this chapter will argue, though Unamuno's representation of women altered notably over the course of his career, it remained deeply conservative. Nevertheless, this conservatism is far from uncreative or monotonous; indeed, much of his work may be read as a series of sometimes ingenious attempts to symbolically contain or resolve the transformations wrought by the departure of bourgeois women from the domestic sphere in ever greater numbers. His representation of male figures is no less interesting:

---

[1] For incisive studies in English of how economic and social change in the early twentieth century affected women, see Davies (1998: 99–103) and Shubert (1990: 23–43).

as Jo Labanyi has pointed out, his work may be read as a 'very self-aware exploration of masculine anxiety' (2010: 96).

This chapter argues that representation of male and female figures may each be divided into three approximate, not entirely consistent periods. It will map the characteristics of gender representations and relations in his work to wider social change in Spain. The chapter will also explore the way in which questions of gender and sexuality in Unamuno's work have only relatively recently become areas of interest for scholars of early twentieth-century Spanish culture: they remain under-studied and the object of contradictory assessments. The chapter will demonstrate the importance of a gender-based approach, which helps us reframe the significance of his work and historicises it more richly than some traditional critical approaches.

1897–1911: telluric women; struggling fathers and sons

Although feminist ideas had been circulating in Spain, albeit on a local or relatively small scale, since before the mid-nineteenth century, and although a proposal for limited women's franchise had first been submitted to the Spanish parliament in 1877, it was not until the late 1880s/early 1890s – precisely the period in which Unamuno began his writing career – that feminism began to occupy a more prominent place in public debate. There were still no national organised movements at this time: feminist ideas and arguments continued to be disseminated largely by small groups, or a few notable figures such the social campaigner and essayist Concepción Arenal and the writer Emilia Pardo Bazán. It was not until the beginning of the twentieth century that the issue of women's civil rights and suffrage became a more substantive issue in Spanish political life: the campaigns of the British suffragettes received widespread international press attention; the extension of the franchise to women was debated in the Spanish parliament – though again without success – in 1907 and 1908, and new pro-suffrage commentators and journals began to emerge.

Nevertheless, organised feminism was still not able to gain a foothold at this time, so it is not remarkable that before 1914, the figure of the feminist or modern emancipated woman is absent from Unamuno's fiction and dramatic work. In Unamuno's earliest, turn-of-the century novels and plays, the significant female characters tend to be demure, deeply Catholic, traditional figures. They are intimately associated with nature and *intrahistoria*:[2] the village girl who bewitches Ignacio in *Paz en la guerra* is described as the 'daughter of air, water and sunshine. She had the same calm joy as did the countryside. […] She was

---

[2]   See Jean-Claude Rabaté's chapter in this volume for an analysis of this concept.

as elegant as an ashtree, as solid as an oak, and as full of plenty as a chestnut. And the peace of the mountains was reflected in her eyes, those large cowlike eyes' (Unamuno 1983: 103; OCE II, 145; OCA II, 162); Marina in *Amor y pedagogía* is described by her suitor Apolodoro as 'nature, instinct, unconsciousness, the material' (OCE II, 322; OCA II, 446), and although Apolodoro's views are ironised, Marina is not vastly different from this characterisation.[3] These early female characters all remain firmly within the domestic sphere: their realm is that of affect and tradition rather than intellect and enlightenment. They are represented in unambiguously positive terms, and their most striking feature is a deep and all-encompassing maternal feeling: they mother not just their children, but also act as healing motherly figures to their husbands or fiancés as well. Both the 1898 play *La esfinge* and *Amor y pedagogía* end with women cradling their afflicted husbands: Avito addresses Marina as '¡Madre!' before fainting into her arms (OCE II, 395; OCA II, 561) and in his 1912 essay *Del sentimiento trágico de la vida*, Unamuno asserts that 'woman's love is all maternal [...] Women yields herself to the lover because she feels that his desire makes him suffer' (Unamuno 1954: 136–137; OCE VII, 190; OCA XVI, 264–265).

Aside from the coquette Clarita who plays a minor role in *Amor y pedagogía*, the only other female type that appears in the early work is the prostitute and the maid. In *Paz en la guerra*, Ignacio's adolescent desire drives him to the brothel; the *Vida de don Quijote y Sancho* comments on the prostitutes la Tolosa and la Molinera who help Don Quixote arm himself. The representation in both texts is sympathetic: in the *Vida de don Quijote y Sancho* the narrator exclaims 'Poor women who, without any cynical showiness, give in to the necessity of vice and the brutality of man, resigning themselves to a bad name in order to earn their crust. Poor guardians of other women's virtue' (OCE III, 76; OCA IV, 101). In short, female types in this early period, whether mothers or prostitutes, are either subjects or objects of compassion, and tend to be presented as asexual.

The anguished, doubting, self-divided male figure, so characteristic of Unamuno's creative output as a whole, is present from his earliest work. In varying ways, all the early male characters struggle to break free from tradition, inheritance or what they perceive to be atavistic impulse, while simultaneously being drawn to such forces, which usually triumph: for example, a utopian political realm proves to be existentially insufficient for Angel in *La esfinge*, who reverts to his childhood religious faith; in *Amor y pedagogía* Christian faith, tradition and superstition are embodied by Marina, to whom Avito is so

---

[3]   It is true that the minor character of Don Fulgencio's wife is a more worldly and assertive figure, but her function seems primarily to make Fulgencio an even more quaintly parodic figure as a hen-pecked husband rather than to represent a modern woman.

powerfully attracted. As the closing lines of the tale make clear, Marina's simple, traditional Christianity ('amor') defeats Avito's reverence for positivistic modernity ('pedagogía'). Such struggle is also staged in terms of Oedipal conflict in works such as the 1910 play *El pasado que vuelve*, which depicts three successive generations of sons rebelling against their fathers, in each case by reverting to the beliefs of their grandfathers. There is elsewhere also a particular emphasis on the difficulty of successfully escaping or challenging the influence of fathers or father-figures. The fathers' overbearing influence or interference has not just counter-productive, but also destructive results on their sons: we think of Apolodoro's rebellious cleaving to Romantic tropes to the point of suicide in *Amor y pedagogía*; in *Paz en la guerra*, Ignacio's disillusionment with the Carlist programme, and with war as political solution, notwithstanding his continued cleaving to the military path followed by his father – a path that leads to the young man's death. But the fathers are far from being tyrannical or distant, authoritarian figures: they are well-intentioned and loving – if misguided – figures, at times as anxious and vulnerable as their sons.

It is possible that there is also an autobiographical dimension to Unamuno's early male characters' struggle with authority and tradition. Still young at the time – he was in his thirties when all the texts discussed above were published – Unamuno was trying to establish himself as a public intellectual. As Roberta Johnson has noted, Spain had a small reading public and a closed publishing world dominated by established figures (1993: 4). The resulting struggle for patronage is lampooned in the prologue of the later novel *Niebla*. In addition, in part because of his membership of the socialist party between 1894 and 1897, and also because of his criticism of the Church, he encountered considerable hostility in establishment circles, particularly those with close links to Catholic institutions.[4] At the same time, Unamuno was himself a figure of authority as a university professor and socially conservative bourgeois paterfamilias by the end of the 1890s; furthermore, the painful struggle with his own religious faith at this time may also have prompted a reassessment of the place of inherited tradition in his life and thought – he had been brought up in a strictly religious household.

Of course the family is a social institution as much as an intimate emotional unit, and representations of relations between husbands, wives, parents and offspring may also be a proxy for the working-through of broader questions and problems about social reproduction or change. The recurrence of the theme of failed struggle against paternal(istic) authority alongside the sympathetic representation of paternal anxiety and vulnerability may be not just an expression of the contradictions or ambivalences of Unamuno's own personal position, but

---

[4]   See Jean-Claude Rabaté's chapter in this volume for further information on Unamuno's early intellectual and political work, and the obstacles he encountered.

may also reproduce the wider socio-political tensions of the Restoration system which permitted only limited change to traditional, conservative structures. The only character in Unamuno's early fiction who successfully reaches accommodation with both tradition and progress, escaping lasting Oedipal struggle or scarring from the past, and able serenely to contemplate the future, is Pachico Zabalbide in *Paz en la guerra*. It is perhaps no coincidence that, at the novel's conclusion, he is unencumbered by paternal authority,[5] and is unmarried and childless. Pachico's serenity, then, seems at least in part to be a function of his freedom from familial obligations, which may themselves encode wider oppressive forms of power and inheritance.

Notable from Unamuno's earliest work is a strong distaste for brute masculinity and its pernicious social effects (OCE I, 862; OCA III, 292). He was particularly scornful of the literary embodiment of womanising lawless, violent, egotistic masculinity, Don Juan. This was a figure reappropriated by a range of early twentieth-century Spanish writers and intellectuals in various, at times conflicting ways as part of the cultural response to changing gender roles and norms, but none of Unamuno's early male characters resemble or critically adapt the Don Juan archetype, and for Unamuno during this period Don Juan remained a reactionary and 'completely and utterly stupid braggart' (OCE III, 289–293; OCA IV, 429). Of course Don Juan was not the only literary character revived at this time of rapid change. The tercentenary of the publication of Cervantes's *Don Quixote* in 1905 produced a panoply of commentaries and creative rewritings that used the Quixote figure partly as a vehicle for examining Spain's recent loss of empire, its economic problems, the growth of mass society and the figure of the modern hero. In common with other turn-of-the-century rewritings of the character, Unamuno's own 1905 commentary, the *Vida de Don Quijote y Sancho*, presents Don Quixote's ingenuousness, faith, idealism and indomitable will not as simply comic traits, but as qualities with the potential to lift contemporaneous Spain from its diminished role in the world and its economic malaise; such qualities could also potentially counter narrowly materialistic values, poverty of spirit and ambition as well as unthinking or reactionary traditionalism.[6]

Unamuno constructs Don Quixote as both a Christ-like figure and a national hero, but what stands out in his portrayal is the importance of gender and sexuality as determinative factors in his enterprise. The Unamunian Quixote's thirst for lasting glory and renown through brave chivalric deeds is attributed entirely to his timorousness in love and therefore his inability to produce heirs: Unamuno asserts that 'the anxiety for immortality is nothing but the fruit of

---

5   Pachico is orphaned as a child.
6   See J.A.Garrido Ardila and Julia Biggane's chapter in this volume for a fuller account of Unamuno's engagement with Don Quixote.

an anxiety for lineage', and that 'only unhappy/frustrated love is fecund in fruits of the spirit; only when the natural, normal course of love is closed off does it find issue in aiming for the heavens; only temporal sterility yields eternal fecundity' (OCE III, 101; OCA IV, 142). Unamuno's reducing women/ female figures to their maternal capacity may be unremarkable for the time, but his parallel reduction of men/male figures to their capacity for paternity is a little more unusual. Unamuno's preoccupation with reproductive capacity as the defining element of male and female character and achievement may be a vestige of his early interest in Spencerian evolutionism. But it was also of course shaped by his more consuming anxiety about the endurance of the person beyond his (or, less commonly, her) mortal span, an anxiety discussed in more detail below.

Don Quixote remained an important ideal and reference for Unamuno throughout his writing career. Roberta Johnson has also noted that it shaped his earlier male fictional characters: she refers to *Amor y pedagogía*'s Avito Carrascal as an 'odd modern Quixote whose ideal is a doomed-to-fail outmoded positivism', and claims Augusto Pérez, the protagonist of *Niebla* (published in 1914 but begun years before) as a quixotic figure because of his philosophical idealism (Johnson 2003: 71). We could also adduce *Paz en la guerra*'s Ignacio Iturriondo: his childhood reading of heroic legends is a contributory factor in his enlisting to fight in the Carlist wars. While these male characters may share some traits with Don Quixote, they are presented in a significantly less heroic register than in the 1905 commentary *Vida de Don Quijote y Sancho*, perhaps partly because all are more firmly enmeshed within the modern material and social world or family ties; they are represented sympathetically, but are certainly not presented as models for national renewal.

While a major axis of struggle and conflict in the early work may be between fathers and sons, relations between husbands and wives are not characterised by any mitigating happiness or understanding: although the female characters may provide surrogate maternal comfort to their husbands when the latter are distressed, there is in most of the texts an unbridgeable distance between them in values and behaviour that results in incomprehension and isolation: Pedro Antonio and his wife Josefa Ignacia in *Paz en la guerra*, Avito and Marina in *Amor y pedagogía* and Eufemia and Angel in *La esfinge* are alienated from each other by their profoundly different aspirations, intellectual horizons or reaction to adversity. Sexual desire is represented only outside conjugal relations, and is a cause of anguish and suffering: in *Paz en la guerra*, Ignacio's own faith and obedience to his pious family means that he is wracked by guilt when his adolescent sexual energies drive him to the brothel; Unamuno also represents anguished, taboo female desire in his 1910 reworking of Racine's *Phèdre*. These representations are notable less for the unhappiness that sexual life causes characters than for the fact that, as Unamuno's fiction progresses, heterosexual desire is replaced by apparent asexuality or spiritual androgyny in the significant male figures.

1912–1923: the 'new woman', male existential anxiety, interdependence and the threatening Other

As elsewhere across Europe, in Spain it was the far-reaching consequences of the First World War that accelerated changes to the hitherto gradually and unevenly shifting situation of women within society, even though Spain was a non-belligerent country. The increase in war-related industrial production for export, and the rise in price of basic commodities and consumer goods brought more Spanish women into the workforce in traditional but also new roles. The second decade of the new century also saw the official opening up of higher education to women. The question of women's legal status and civil, educational and professional capacities or rights became ever more prominent, and the first national feminist and mass women's associations began to appear at this time.

When the figure of the non-traditional woman who left the home – or who was otherwise diverted from a conventional maternal or religious path – began to be registered in Unamuno's fictional work in the second decade of the twentieth century, the representation was not flattering. The 'new woman' Eugenia in *Niebla* who insists on her independence, and works to support herself financially, is a coldly selfish, manipulative and deceitful figure. And as the number of women entering the workforce or higher education grew during this decade, so the female figures in Unamuno's fiction who ventured into civil society, or who made use of civil law and contract, became more monstrous. Their maternal vocation is as strong as the early, traditional figures, and it is indeed precisely the fierce protectiveness of or loyalty to their offspring that is shown to be incompatible with other roles within society: the characters' maternal drive consumes and indeed annihilates any sense of civic or wider ethical responsibility they might have.[7] For example, the widow Raquel in *Dos madres* (1920) is shockingly ruthless in pursuit of her maternal ambitions. Unable biologically to have children, she uses her financial and contractual expertise to arrange what is, in effect, surrogate motherhood, destroying the life of the innocent, young woman she uses for her scheme, and driving the father of her acquired baby to his death. The figure of Carolina in *El marqués de Lumbría* (1920) is similarly cruel: she is

---

[7] The only apparent exception is *Niebla*'s Eugenia, whose lack of maternal feeling may be a function of her youth.

dismissive of tradition and propriety, and is utterly unconcerned about betraying and destroying her wider family in order to secure advantage for her son, born out of wedlock. It is significant that both figures, a widow and (initially) a single woman respectively, are not subject to the Civil Code, a body of law which, amongst other things, severely restricted married women's activity outside the domestic sphere: the two women are in this sense 'outlaws', uncontainable and free to manipulate civil society and its rules in the service of their blind, anti-social maternal devotion to their offspring, unburdened by broader moral considerations. In these two tales, female participation in civil society is portrayed as pernicious because women seem unable to detach their maternal drive from a wider, disinterested good. Conversely, the protagonist of Unamuno's 1921 play *Raquel, encadenada*, who renounces a prestigious professional career as a musician to adopt a small child, is presented in positive and highly sympathetic terms.

Unamuno's representation of female characters in the period up to the mid-1920s may have had its basis in traditional social Catholic teachings on men and women's roles (although hostile to some aspects of the Church's teachings, his views on gender and sexuality were not notably discrepant), and may also have been shaped by elements of the social philosophy of Hegel, a thinker who had exercised great influence on the younger Unamuno.[8] An important defender of the separate-spheres thesis, Hegel argued that women's natural attachment and loyalty to family made her unsuitable for participation in civil society, let alone in the life of the state.[9] Certainly the equation in Unamuno's work between the positive representation of domestic mothers and the negative representation of women – particularly mothers – who enter civil society is consonant with this division. And in 1920, Unamuno had made the rather Hegelian assertion that '[w]omen lack a sense of the civic and substitute the domestic for it: for women, the family *is* the fatherland'.[10]

---

[8]   To be sure, much of the mature Unamuno's tragic philosophy was fundamentally incompatible with that of Hegel's idealism, and he was already gently parodying Hegel's systematicity by 1895, in the essays that would subsequently be published as *En torno al casticismo*. Nevertheless, Unamuno retained respect for Hegel's work and traces of, or references to, Hegelian thought are to be found throughout his later writing.

[9]   Hegel famously argued that 'man has his actual substantive life in the state, in learning, and so forth, as well as in labour and struggle with the external world and with himself'. Because of her natural passivity and subjectivity, '[w]oman, on the other hand, has her substantive destiny in the family, and to be imbued with family piety is her ethical frame of mind.' He notes that 'family piety [is] principally the law of woman and [...] law of a substantiality at once subjective and on the plane of feeling, the law of the inward life [...] a law opposed to public law, to the law of the land (1952: 114–115).

[10]   Reproduced in Robertson (1996): I, 382. Whether this condition was, in Unamuno's opinion, innate to women or was historically contingent was a question he did not address explicitly here or elsewhere in his work.

But Unamuno's representation of women during this period is not entirely reducible to a binary division between virtuous domesticated females and the deviant characters who enter the civil sphere. As the 1921 novel *La tía Tula* suggests, Unamuno's position on women shifted significantly during this period. Like Raquel in *Dos madres*, Tula hungrily takes on a proxy motherhood role. She exhibits qualities both of the staple domestic angel figure of Unamuno's earlier work, and of the more emancipated characters of his post-1914 fiction: she can be ruthless, cruel and inhuman in pursuit of her maternal urges and in order to protect her own autonomy; she can also be tender and nurturing; she has a keen intellect and quick wit; she can be emotionally manipulative; she can, too, be a vulnerable figure of great pathos. She is not simply a Hegelian domestic mother, but is also far from being a new or emancipated woman.

In separate important readings of the novel, Geoffrey Ribbans (1987) and Carlos Longhurst (1989) argued that Tula can be seen as embodying the position that Unamuno laid out in *Del sentimiento trágico de la vida* whereby, in the absence of the guarantee of an afterlife, each individual should strive to become irreplaceable, and should instead pursue a vocation with such conviction and will that a lasting mark be left on others.[11] Carlos Longhurst's reading places particular emphasis on the religious dimensions that, for Unamuno, a task such as Tula's entailed: he follows the Lutheran argument that a religious vocation was not to be understood as being confined to an ecclesiastical or cloistered role. Fulfilling one's own particular role in secular society with the utmost ethical commitment and will to be irreplaceable, and to leave a lasting trace on others, could be just as much a religious vocation as being a priest. For Longhurst, Tula clearly exemplifies the pursuit of a religious vocation through the uncompromising embrace of a lay role – here the care and nurture of children (Longhurst 1989: 147). Furthermore, as Roberta Johnson later astutely pointed out, Tula 'exhibits the same existential anxieties as her male counterparts' (2003: 166). Tula is the first of Unamuno's female figures to possess such qualities and such anxieties. This is an important development: Unamuno is now prepared to admit an intellectual and existential complexity previously denied to his female characters, and in this sense *La tía Tula* may represent a change in Unamuno's views perhaps arising from wider shifting perceptions of women's capacities.

---

[11]   It may be worth noting that the examples Unamuno uses of vocations being exercised in society are all professions or trades that were exclusively masculine at that time. It is not easy to say whether Unamuno was simply illustrating his point by drawing on existing practice or convention, or whether he felt that such an existential enterprise was limited to men. There remains, then, a potential difficulty about the translatability of the figure appearing in *Del sentimiento trágico* to the female sex, despite the importance and attractiveness of Longhurst's and Ribbans' readings.

Nevertheless, *La tía Tula* is far from being a feminist text: rather than opening up the civil sphere to its female characters, *La tía Tula* expands domestic spatiality, whose organization provides what appears to be a substitutory, or compensatory mimicry of work outside the home, at times even reproducing the logic and terminology of economic modernisation and industrial rationalisation: the text enacts a division of labour between the material maternal procreator and the spiritual and emotional nurturer (Tula); it refers to a married couple as being as 'at full productive capacity' (OCE II, 1058; OCA IX, 549) and to the 'production plant' of a pregnant woman's body (OCE II, 1084; OCA IX, 588). This expansion of the domestic sphere may plausibly be read as part of a conservative 'solution' to the rise of feminism and female civil-society participation. But it may be serving other, wider, socio-political ends too, particularly if considered in the light of the striking religious agency with which Tula is endowed. In Unamuno's early novels, female characters act largely as simple, intuitive repositories of traditional religious values; after 1914, the – sympathetically represented – female characters in Unamuno's fictional texts often take on roles more traditionally associated with institutionalised male vocations. Joaquina in *Abel Sánchez* acts as a confessor-figure to her father; Angela Carballino also acts as a confessor-figure to San Manuel Bueno, and becomes his unofficial deaconess in the later novella *San Manuel Bueno, mártir*; Tula takes on a confessorial role too.

This transfer of sacerdotal agency may be another dimension of the text's drive to provide a compensatory substitute for women's continued lack of civil agency and the very narrow channels of civil participation open to them. But it might also provide an imaginary solution to another social problem that was exercising Unamuno in the first two decades of the twentieth century: the power of the Church in Spanish civil and political life. In *Del sentimiento trágico de la vida*, Unamuno had argued for the 'deseclesiastización' [disecclesialisation] (OCE VII, 268; OCA XVI, 394) of the Church as part of the widening out of the concept of a religious vocation into secular civil life as discussed above. There was another welcome aspect to such disecclesialisation: it also entailed the weakening of the social and political power of the Catholic Church in Spain. Unamuno was enduringly hostile to the Church's influence on political life, and there seems to have been a parallelism between the threat posed to the healthy, well-functioning liberal state by both Church *and* women. Here it becomes possible to see how *La tía Tula* could in part represent an ingenious solution to Unamuno's problems: in laying out an expanded role for the (intelligent, questioning) chaste woman to be part of disecclesialisation by taking up in the domestic sphere some of the hitherto institutionalised clerical male tasks, secular civil life is insulated from both women and Church, while agency and prestige is added to women's domestic role as a substitute for greater civil rights.

Despite the shift in the conceptualisation of women's capacities and possibilities in *La tía Tula* though, the representation of women continues to be undergirded by traditional assumptions, even towards the end of the period. For example, in the play *Soledad*, written just a year before the publication of *La tía Tula*, the female characters are reduced to binary cyphers representing death (Soledad) or transitory earthly achievement and renown (Gloria). And throughout the period, although the women depicted sympathetically may occupy a greater variety of roles than in the earlier period (as artistic muse, artist or confessor-figure, say, in *Soledad, Raquel, encadenada* or *Abel Sánchez* respectively), they are never social actors. Nevertheless, women occupy a more prominent place in the fiction or drama of this period, and Unamuno registers their greater presence not just outside the home, but also as important cultural consumers. In the preface to the 1920 collection *Tres novelas ejemplares y un prólogo*, Unamuno asserts that the principal readers of novels were 'señoras y señoritas'. He is insulting about such readers, characterising them as superficial, distastefully sexualised or else passive figures under the thumb of their confessors, but is careful to distinguish them from 'mujeres'—implicitly more substantial, serious figures (OCE II, 977; OCA IX, 423). Of course this characterisation might be read as a form of flattery of his female readers, who may be expected to align themselves with the 'mujer' figure, but flattery is not a feature readily associated with Unamuno's rhetorical style, and this splitting off of serious women from frivolous or mindless *señoras* or *señoritas* may be seen as a further indication that Unamuno's representation of women becomes increasingly responsive to major social change during these years.

The representation of male figures in Unamuno's work also changes during this middle period; how much this change was conditioned by the dramatically shifting horizons of women's place in society is of course not determinable, but is unlikely to have left the masculinity of the narrative and drama untouched. Certainly male characters are weak or vulnerable to manipulation by 'new women'—Augusto Pérez in *Niebla*, Ramiro in *La tía Tula* and Don Juan in *Dos madres*—which suggests a certain traditionalist zero-sum conceptualisation of the balance of power in gender relations. But there are wider shifts too. Although there are vestiges of the conflicts between young men and paternal/authority figures that characterised the earlier work – perhaps most notably in Augusto Pérez's confrontation with Unamuno the author-figure, but also in Abel Sánchez, where Abelín reacts against his artistic father and embraces science instead – it is peer relationships that predominate in this period.

However, such relationships do not take place in a space of horizontal fraternity or homosocial bonding; they are characterised by the struggle for individual recognition, favour or power over others. In these texts, although the ostensibly immediate object of competition is the love of a woman, Unamuno emphasises the intensity of the affective relationships between male characters underlying their struggle. This is most explicitly represented in Joaquín's corrosive envy in *Abel Sánchez*, which is stronger even than his desire for Helena. It is also present in *Niebla*, where, even after apparently prostrating himself before Augusto, Mauricio then triumphs in winning Eugenia from him; the visceral reaction that Augusto suffers when bested by his rival over both Eugenia and Rosario, and the shame and embarrassment he feels at being tricked, are as strong as his grief at losing Eugenia (OCE II, 659–661; OCA II, 964–967). It also appears in *Nada menos que todo un hombre*, where Alejandro sets out to humiliate utterly el Conde de Bordaviella. Although the struggle between male characters is usually over a woman, this is not always the case: even the self may be divided, part of it split off into a hated other, vying for power, as in *Julio Macedo y Tulio Montalbán*.

The intensity of affect between male competitors may tempt the reader towards a Girardian reading of the triangular relationships or envy in the texts, particularly in *Abel Sánchez*. Rather than any diverted homosexual undercurrent though, what prevails is a herostratic desire to achieve distinction or elevation in the eyes of others. Abel Sánchez is explicit about his need for renown, and his scorn for the undistinguished masses; both Alejandro Gómez as a self-made *indiano*, and Mauricio as a lowly hanger-on without Augusto Pérez's financial and class security, can find all-important recognition in amorous victory over others. The ironised author-figure Unamuno in *Niebla* is also anxious that his power over Augusto, and Víctor Goti, be recognised by both characters (and of course, by extension, by the readers of *Niebla*). It is not difficult to see how this preoccupation with distinction and fame, and with a herostratic standing out from the crowd, might be understood in terms of a modernist preoccupation with the rise of mass society and 'mass man', and what this might mean for the way that the individual perceived himself and was perceived by others.[12] Such a reading is certainly plausible, and, like many other modernist writers, Unamuno seems to conceptualise it as an exclusively masculine preoccupation. Although female characters may feel envy (Tula, for example), or destructive rivalry and will-to-power (Raquel in *Dos madres*, Carolina in *El marqués de Lumbría*), they are unconcerned about recognition and glory for themselves; moreover, they are represented as being driven by atavistic maternal desire—any modern traits they might possess are overshadowed by instinct and traditional maternal instinct.[13]

---

[12]   Alison Sinclair's psychoanalytic study of *Abel Sánchez* explores this interpretation of the text in an illuminating way (2000: 170–190).

[13]   The most extreme example is Raquel in *Dos madres*: when she cradles the baby she has 'purchased' from Berta, the narrator notes that she sings strange songs that seemed to come from a distant world, lost in dreamy mists (OCE II, 994; OCA IX, 449–450).

Unamuno's explorations of man in modern society are distinguished by the depth of sympathy they show for those male characters anxious to achieve recognition and make a lasting mark on their environs. It is not that the male characters' efforts or aspirations are presented in approving or heroic terms: the wracking self-doubt and torment that Joaquín suffers in *Abel Sánchez*, the cripplingly high price that the eponymous Tulio Montalbán/Julio Macedo pays for his glory, the lack of satisfaction and consolation that Agustín's achievements bring him in *Soledad* and the ironising self-representation of Unamuno-the-author-figure's pretentions to power in *Niebla* put paid to any such reading. This failure of Nietzschean overcoming is accounted for in large part by what might be described as the 'pathos of interdependence' in the representation of male characters and their struggles to gain recognition. This exceeds any Hegelian master-slave dialectic. The Cain and Abel narrative is rewritten in tragic key in *Abel Sánchez*: Joaquín (Cain) is unable to exist without Abel after the latter's death, so structured is his own sense of self around his hated rival; Alejandro Gómez's grotesquely destructive dependence on Julia in *Nada menos que todo un hombre* means that he, too, expires when she does. Even when recognition and glory have been achieved, they are not fulfilling—the self is never *accurately* recognised by others, as Tulio Montalbán discovers, and the gulf between one's persona and one's intimate sense of self causes further anguish. What distinguishes the male protagonists of this period, then, is their desperate need for the other, even though the other is insufficient or destructive to the self.

These male characters are profoundly lonely figures, not uncommonly afflicted by loss, or bereavement pre-dating the beginning of the narrative/drama: we think of the death of Agustín's son in *Soledad*, of Augusto's mother in *Niebla*, of Tulio Montalbán's fiancée and of the loss of homeland for Tulio and for Alejandro Gómez in *Nada menos que todo un hombre*. This loss or absence at the centre of the male characters' lives may be read as a fictional thematising of Unamuno's highly idiosyncratic existential thought as laid out in *Del sentimiento trágico de la vida*, where man is also conceptualised in terms of an originary lack.[14] For Unamuno, as is well known, this lack is an 'hambre de inmortalidad' [hunger for immortality]. In the absence of any guarantee of life after death (except through religious faith, which, in Unamuno's conception, was not reconcilable with another primordial human quality – reason), men are driven to seek substitutes or proxies, either through procreation, or through the seeking of recognition or glory as a way of leaving a tangible or transmissible trace to ensure some form of perdurance after death. It may be for this reason

---

14   This characterisation is perhaps one reason that Unamuno's work has seemed so conducive to psychoanalytical readings, perhaps particularly those of the Lacanian school: see, for example, Navajas (1985), Fox (2001), and Sinclair 2001: 111–125.

that so many of the male protagonists are creative artists (the playwright Agustín in *Soledad*, the novelists Víctor Goti and Unamuno-the-author-figure in *Niebla*, the painter Abel Sánchez); even those that are not artists in the strictest sense of the term conceive their vocation in such terms (Joaquín Monegro in *Abel Sánchez* regards his practice of medicine as an art, Tulio Montalbán creates a republic as leader of an anti-colonial national liberation movement. Within Unamuno's fiction, aesthetic practice is represented not as an attempt to create the beautiful or ineffable, nor is it an act of self-realisation or critical engagement with social mores; most often focalised through the perspective of the artist himself, it is above all an attempt at leaving a record of the self, a protest against annihilation. This is entirely in keeping with Unamuno's assertion in *Del sentimiento trágico de la vida* that 'If the man who tells you that he writes, paints, sculptures, or sings for his own amusement, gives his work to the public, he lies [...] He wishes, at the least, to leave behind a shadow of his spirit, something that may survive him' (Unamuno 1954: 51; OCE VII, 139; OCA XVI, 179), but the fictional representation imbues this reductive view with considerable pathos.

It seems likely that this preoccupation with man's yearning for immortality also accounts, in part at least, for the prominence of procreation and parenthood across Unamuno's work as a whole: there can be few Spanish writers who explore so persistently the topics of fatherhood and motherhood, although this topic is a surprisingly under-researched one in Unamuno studies. For Unamuno, parenthood is not limited to biological reproduction: in this period there is a recurrent interest in adoptive and proxy parenting (one thinks of Tula, Raquel in *Dos madres* as well as her—very different—namesake in *Raquel, encadenada*, and of don Antonio in one of *Niebla*'s intercalated tales). Nor is parenthood always gender-delimited: in Unamuno's later texts, the priest Don Manuel Bueno, spiritual father to his congregation, is also represented by the narrator of the tale as a 'varón matriarcal' (OCE II, 1129; OCA XVI, 583), as is the eponymous hermano Juan. This detaching of parenthood from biological reproduction, and the importance given to 'spiritual' maternity and paternity in texts such as *La tía Tula*, *San Manuel Bueno, mártir* and *El hermano Juan o el mundo es teatro* suggest that the questions of immortality and perdurance after death (rather than, say, dynastic succession or social reproduction) lie at the heart of Unamuno's preoccupation with motherhood and fatherhood.

His fiction and drama provide no determinate or consistent conclusion about the degree of success or consolation achievable from the male characters' efforts to gain some form of immortality on their own terms, though the prospects seem to become more bleak towards the end of this period under examination, as *Soledad* and *Tulio Montalbán y Julio Macedo* suggest. Procreation does not appear to offer a straightforwardly reliable route, at least in relation to male offspring, who do not appear to offer a reliable guarantee of continuity for their fathers. To the extent that sons are examined in this period, they tend to rebel against their fathers, as in *Abel Sánchez*. Elsewhere, sons are not close to their fathers (one thinks of Augusto Pérez's alienated recollections), or the father-son relationship does not feature in the narrative (*Tulio Montalbán y Julio Macedo* or *Nada menos que todo un hombre*, for example).

The effectiveness of immortality through artistic creation is also far from certain. The survival of an author through his creations is of course an explicit theme of *Niebla*, though the novel leaves irresolvably open the question of who the ultimate author is: Víctor Goti and Unamuno-the-author-figure tussle for supremacy in the Prólogo and Post Prólogo, each claiming to possess (different) truths about the climactic encounter between Augusto and Unamuno-the-author-figure, and there are sporadic suggestions within the text that the novel the character Víctor Goti is writing *is Niebla* (or a version of it); Augusto Pérez also asserts to Unamuno-the-author-figure that what readers engage with and remember above all are the characters: if a text survives, the characters are far more real to readers than the author, who becomes a subordinate, dependent figure, ontologically at the mercy of his textual constructs. Of course by conceptualising this existential struggle so explicitly and distinctively in the metafictional encounter, Unamuno the author (as distinct from the fictionalised author-figure) has achieved a lasting afterlife in the canons of modern literature in Spain and beyond, though the likely small degree of consolation this would have afforded him means that this is far from a simple irony. In a not entirely dissimilar way, in *Abel Sánchez*, although the publication of Joaquín's writings on what he sees as the 'art of medicine' is not realised, his confession – a textual creation registering the struggle for lasting recognition – *does* survive his death. But later works of this period seem to foreclose even this possibility. In *Tulio Montalbán y Julio Macedo*, all traces of Julio Macedo are lost by the end of the narrative: all that survives is the fame of Tulio Montalbán, a persona that Julio has come to hate and fear. Oblivion can come in more than one form: here the self is irrecoverably buried under the distorting mask of fame and public reputation. And in *Soledad*, though the question of the posthumous survival of Agustín's plays is left unexplored, as the tragic denouement indicates, an Agustín deranged by grief turns away from what he sees as failure in both his political and artistic enterprises, and instead comes to embrace death (Soledad): immortality through literary creation, or any other endeavour, has become meaningless to him.

Within Unamuno's narrative fiction and drama, this consciousness of a hunger for immortality is gender-specific. With the partial exception of Tía Tula, as discussed above, female characters are untroubled by the kinds of existential anxieties afflicting their male counterparts during this period. They are certainly not represented as being interested in the pursuit of fame or glory. Partly this is a function of the gendered public-/private-sphere division in Unamuno's thought. When, in the prologue to *La tía Tula*, Unamuno cites Aristotle's assertion that '[el] hombre es *zoon politicon*' [man is a social/civic animal] (OCE II, 1042; OCA IX, 526), is it clear that 'man' is not a stand-in for a universal 'mankind'; for Unamuno, women are by rights domestic creatures. They are exempt from the frustrations of seeking public recognition, and from the distortions and misrepresentations that such recognition brings because their own contribution to the *civis* is made from the private sphere. Consonant with this division, they find greater satisfaction and influence in parenthood than the male characters, and the absence of a need for public recognition perhaps accounts in part for the lack of female creative artists in Unamuno's work. Music is the only artistic field in which the female characters participate, and neither Eugenia in *Niebla*, nor the eponymous protagonist of *Raquel, encadenada* view their professional musicianship as a creative vocation; both are happy to give up their jobs.

When viewing this period as a whole through a gender-focused lens, it is notable that male characters become more thwarted, anguished and tragic as the period progresses, while female characters tend to become more complex, bold and successful in achieving their desires (or at least imposing their will). As noted above, it is tempting to correlate these opposing trajectories, even if an explicit, detailed social context may be absent. But a simple comparison would be misleading: *La tía Tula* aside, the female characters are outlined more sketchily than the male characters, who tend to be at the centre of the narratives and the drama during this period.

And of course gender is only one of the socially-focused perspectives through which we might view Unamuno's work of this period. Even though they lack an explicit, detailed context, the struggles of the philosophical subject of *Del sentimiento trágico de la vida* and the ever-bleaker vicissitudes of his male protagonists might equally easily be correlated to wider social shifts and sharpening political conflicts in Spain at this time; the potentially usurping, but in some cases interdependent 'other' may be read as a figure obliquely representative of any number of growing threats to the liberal bourgeois subject, from organised labour to reactionary religious politics.[15] It is difficult to abstract Unamuno's tragically uncertain philosophical subject or his lonely, frustrated characters, from the broad dislocations of the second decade of twentieth-century Spanish life, and shifts in gender roles and relations are one amongst a constellation of such dislocations. At the same time, the intensity, idiosyncrasy and pathos of Unamuno's male protagonists prevent us from reducing them to simple cyphers of social and political change.

---

[15]   For good accounts of such threats, see the essays by Jacobson & Moreno Luzón; Radcliff; and Arranz, Cabrera & del Rey in Alvarez Junco and Shubert (2000).

1924–1936: unilateral androgyny; the emergence of a woman's voice

The last dozen years of Unamuno's life were characterised by two dramatic changes of circumstance: first his six years of exile, during which time he absconded from Fuerteventura to Paris, subsequently settling in what for him was the less alienating location of the border between France and his native Basque country, and then, shortly after his eventual return to Spain in 1930, the social and political transformations of the Second Republic. Unamuno's creative writing reduced in length and frequency during this period, particularly his narrative fiction. Perhaps reflecting the disruptions of exile, and the commitments of Unamuno's anti-Primo de Rivera campaigning, the shorter forms of poetry and drama prevailed during the time he was away from Spain, and the one prose composition, *Cómo se hace una novela,* was a portmanteau of also brief component-forms: diary, partial sketched-out novel and essay.

In this and the work after his return to Spain, when novellas become his preferred fictional form, there were important continuities with or returns to the themes and preoccupations of previous years: male characters all too painfully aware of their mortality appear again in *Cómo se hace una novela* and *San Manuel Bueno, mártir*; those tortured by envy, oppressive interdependence, the conflict between persona and personality and its resulting misrecognition also continue to appear (in *El otro, Sombras de sueño* – a dramatisation of *Tulio Montalbán y Julio Macedo* and *La novela de Don Sandalio*). There is some leavening of the bleakness of the exile work immediately after Unamuno's return in the gentle tale *Un pobre hombre rico,* and the ambiguity and irresolution of *La novela de Don Sandalio, jugador de ajedrez* relieves the tale somewhat from the tragedy of Tulio Montalbán's inescapably distorted persona in *Sombras de sueño.*[16] The creative writing across this period also continues to focus heavily on male characters. With the exception of *San Manuel Bueno, mártir*, women appear as minor or one-dimensional characters, at times reprising previous roles—monstrously ruthless and amoral maternal figures in *El otro*, for example. But there are also some significant developments and novelties in terms of the conceptualisation and representation of gender roles, and it is on these aspects that the final part of this chapter will concentrate.

The first is Unamuno's embracing of a (carefully limited) androgyny in his later work. As noted above, he had long been critical of bellicose or excessive masculinity, arguing that it needed to be tempered with the qualities he associated with femininity. After 1923, this criticism became one plank of his trenchant

---

16   See Pedro Ribas's chapter in this volume for incisive readings of *Un pobre hombre rico* and *La novela de Don Sandalio*; see C. Alex's Longhurst's chapter for a further reading of *La novela de Don Sandalio.*

opposition to the Primo de Rivera dictatorship. We remember that the manifesto of the 1923 coup which brought the regime to power explicitly excluded those who lacked the 'virility' to contribute to its political mission, and Unamuno reserved some of his most mordant criticisms for the regime's exaltation of masculine values.[17] Primo de Rivera's directory also embraced a reactionary form of Catholic nationalism which Unamuno vigorously attacked too. Although the 1925 essay *La agonía del cristianismo* which Unamuno was commissioned to write not long after he was first exiled is to a significant extent a revisiting of the themes of *El sentimiento trágico de la vida*, the 'androgyny' of faith is a new concept. In a chapter entitled 'La virilidad de la fe' [The Virility of Faith], Unamuno criticises Hyacinthe's Loyson's equation of religious doubt with a lack of virility, insisting that a truly living faith must actually incorporate qualities that he genders as feminine:

> Faith is passive, feminine, the daughter of grace; it is not active or produced by free will. A truly living faith [...] is a will to know which is converted into a desire to love, a will to understand that becomes an understanding of will; it is not a will to believe which, driven by virility, ends in nothingness. Faith occurs agonistically, in struggle. Virility is will; faith is feminine, is woman [....] Virility on its own is sterile.
>
> (OCE VII, 333–334; OCA XVI, 506–507).

This spiritual androgyny is present also in Unamuno's 1929 play *El hermano Juan o el mundo es teatro*. As noted above, Unamuno had long been critical of the Don Juan figure, dismissing him as stupid, socially and politically reactionary as well as brutish in his masculinity; he directly compared those responsible for the 1923 coup to figures from the Don Juan canon (cited in Rabaté y Rabaté 2009: 439). His 1929 play rewrites Don Juan, stripping him of his aristocratic arrogance and replacing it with the levelling fraternity of a religious vocation. Don Juan's sterile hypermasculinity is substituted with a more fertile androgyny: el hermano Juan refers to himself as a 'nodrizo' [a male wet nurse] and a 'madrino' [a male godmother] (OCE V, 809; OCA XII, 978). Instead of seducing women and killing men, he nurtures loving monogamous relationships amongst those he knows (OCE V, 809; OCA XII, 978). The play may be read in part as a form of poetic redress against the Primo de Rivera regime, with el hermano Juan's virtuous androgyny countering the vicious masculinist praetorianism of the regime.

---

[17] The manifesto notoriously proclaims 'This uprising is a manly one: he who cannot match its masculinity should wait on the sidelines and not disturb the joyful days that we are preparing for the fatherland. 'Manifiesto de *Miguel Primo de Rivera*', *La Vanguardia*, Barcelona, 13 de septiembre de 1923. See also the articles 'Mi pleito personal' (1927d), and 'De nuevo lo de las responsabilidades' (1928) for examples of Unamuno's criticism of 'political masculinity'.

Mary Lee Bretz sees el hermano Juan as 'flaunting a transgendered subjectivity' and as giving birth to a new model and transformed possibilities for gender relations (2001: 488). But if we explore Unamuno's representation of material, or lived – rather than spiritual or politically useful – androgyny, a much more conservative picture emerges. In a gloss accompanying a 1924 sonnet he wrote about 'mariquitas' [pansies] and 'marimachos' [butch women] witnessed in a bohemian café on the Boulevard Montparnasse, Unamuno asserted that 'The bad thing is not that pansies and butch women are not fathers and mothers but that they actively avoid becoming parents. They do not properly try to procreate' (OCE VI, 721; OCA XIV, 569). This is hardly celebratory of androgyny as a lived social practice, and there seems little possibility here of the positive transformation heralded by Bretz. Indeed, beyond its oppositional potential in relation to the Primo de Rivera directory, rather than the vanguard of any new social model, el hermano Juan's spiritual or disembodied androgyny may be seen as part of a wider defensive move in Unamuno's late work which served ultimately to *reinforce* socio-sexual boundaries between genders rather than blur or erode them. We need to remember that in *El hermano Juan* (as in *La agonía del cristianismo*), the androgyny is strictly unilateral: it seems that only men need be spiritually imbued with feminine qualities (in order, amongst other things, to curb what Unamuno sees as the innate aggression and violence of masculinity in the realm of politics, which mar the civic virtues of the liberal state). In contrast, it is not deemed appropriate or necessary for women to receive an injection of masculinity in order to be better citizens: indeed, a highly unflattering picture of the modern androgynous woman is presented in *El hermano Juan* by Antonio:

> Instead of cutting Samson's hair off, the modern-day Delilah has her own hair cut short and then goes to the football to shout herself hoarse like a manic fishwife, or goes to a boxing match and shouts (I've heard it myself!) 'Kill him!', and she becomes a member of parliament in order to make herself manly
>
> (OCE V, 780; OCA XII, 946).

Although Elvira responds by suggesting that such behaviour is simply women's reaction to the feminisation of men at the time, neither she nor any other character defends this modern Delilah. The unilateral androgyny that marks out Unamuno's final works reflects the difficult position in which the author found himself in relation to the question of gender roles and relations in the late 1920s: if he was repulsed by the hypermasculinity of praetorian politics, the new urban models of modern femininity were equally distasteful to him. Unilateral androgyny was a tactical device allowing a theoretical remodelling of a male political subject fit for an ideal liberal *res publica*. Pace Bretz, Unamunian androgyny has nothing to do with new material or lived possibilities for equality or the emancipation of the genders: it represents less an attempted subsumption of women than a homeopathic defence against the 'new woman'.

A trace of this androgyny may also be found in Unamuno's most famous late text, *San Manuel Bueno, mártir*, where, as noted above, Don Manuel is described as a 'varón matriarcal'. For many years, criticism focused almost exclusively on Don Manuel, the significance of his anguished lack of faith and his response to it, with much work reading the priest as a vehicle for the articulation of Unamuno's own struggles with religion and its place in society at a crucial political juncture.[18] It was not until the 1970s and beyond that critical attention turned to the narrator of the tale, Angela Carballino. An illuminating article by C.A. Longhurst (1981) argued that Angela's unreliability as a narrator is a manifestation of the post-realism so central to much of Unamuno's literary work, and that the text is a reflection on 'man's limited access to knowledge of others' (597); a decade later, Pamela Bacarisse's psychoanalytic reading also insisted on the importance of the text's narratorial perspective, given that it 'emanates from an unusually complex, interested and insecure psyche' (1991: 66). While both articles argued forcefully that the meaning of the text remained indeterminate, both articles were crucial for formulating new questions about the text that acknowledged the importance of a gender-focused perspective: Bacarisse explored what she saw as the text's 'sexual substratum' (69), and Longhurst was the first to ask why Unamuno chose a female narrator for the tale (1981: 582).

If we build further on Longhurst and Bacarisse's valuable insights and consider the historicity of the text's representation of gender roles and relations, further intriguing (though still unanswerable) questions emerge. The text was written at a time when pressure for meaningful democratic reform of the country was becoming irresistible, and women's suffrage was an issue that would need to be addressed by any post-dictatorship reform (partly because female suffrage was gaining ground internationally, and partly because the dictatorship had itself introduced provision for the female vote in municipal elections).[19] Might the ambiguity and ambivalence with which the character of Angela is invested not, at least in part, be a projection of Unamuno's own wider ambivalences about the scope of women's place in society, particularly in relation to religion and politics? I have argued above that these topics were integral to *La tía Tula*: they remain important in *San Manuel Bueno, mártir*. The narrative is, amongst other things, the account of a shifting power relationship between Angela, Don Manuel and her brother, Lázaro: Angela chronicles her growing role as the priest's unofficial

---

[18]   See Pedro Ribas' chapter for a study of this juncture.

[19]   Concha Fagoaga notes that this granting of limited suffrage raised expectations for further reform, and provided a fillip for campaigning groups (1985: 181).

deaconess, and she also becomes a confessor-like confidante-figure to him before being displaced by her brother. Both Lázaro and Don Manuel are dismissive of women's intellectual capabilities, yet Angela's account indicates that she is far from a simple, naïve or powerless figure, and, as Bacarisse and Longhurst have pointed out, she holds Don Manuel's posthumous fate and reputation in her hands.

As a narrator who is unwilling to report the truth about Don Manuel's struggles with his faith to the Church authorities, but who is driven nevertheless at the same time to commit a 'confesión' of her thoughts and anxieties about this and other matters to paper even though she cannot be sure of its eventual fate (OCE II, 1129; OCA XVI, 583), Angela's story is poised uncertainly between the private realm of confession and the public arena of disclosure. Although her choice derives from and mirrors that of Don Manuel's own dilemma, it is hard not to read her character, at least in part, as an oblique embodiment also of Unamuno's doubts and reservations about the position of women vis-à-vis the public and private realms more widely. If she is, as Longhurst has argued (1981: 587), and Bacarisse suggested (65), an unreliable narrator, perhaps this status reflects broader questions that Unamuno harboured about women's reliability as civic subjects; the issues of political education and participation, and their interrelation with religion, are raised explicitly in the text, and although they are dealt with only in relation to the rural poor, they had a charged pertinence to the situation of women in 1930 too. Ultimately, *San Manuel Bueno, mártir* is too intractably ambiguous for any confident interpretation. But even if the character of Angela is ultimately unreadable, the late construction of a complex first-person female narrator is itself meaningful when we map it against the starkly simple, unidimensional female characters of his earlier work.

Looking at Unamuno's work through the lens of gender produces a very different vista from that offered by a perspective focused on ideas and themes. It provides perhaps the most vivid illustration of the fact that, for all that Unamuno pursued a set of fundamental existential concerns with dogged consistency over a long writing career, and for all that his fiction eschewed temporal and geographical specificity after 1897, it was, willy-nilly, intimately engaged with the major social changes taking place in early twentieth-century Spain. Indeed, the conceptualisation of gender is perhaps the most plastic aspect of Unamuno's work as a whole. One of Unamuno's most important and enduring conceptual figures was the 'hombre de carne y hueso' [man of flesh and bone], defined in the opening chapter of *Del sentimiento trágico de la vida* as:

> [...] the man who is born, suffers and dies [...] the man who eats and drinks and plays and sleep and thinks and wills; the man who is seen and heard; the brother, the true brother
>
> (Unamuno 1954: 1; OCE VII, 109; OCA XVI, 127).

The man of flesh and bone is invoked by Unamuno to counter the ideal or abstract figure constructed by science (*homo sapiens*), much philosophy, and socio-economic theory (the *homo economicus*), which, for Unamuno, was:

> A man neither of here nor there, neither of this age nor of another, who has neither sex nor country, who is, in brief, [...] a no-man
> (Unamuno 1954: 1; OCE VII, 109; OCA XVI, 127).

By this definition, the men that Unamuno created in his fiction were certainly not 'no-men': they were shaped by their age, their nation and by gender-specific forces. Unamuno never specifically conceptualised 'the woman of flesh and bone', but, as his fiction and drama show, she is not only a crucial shifting figure in his work, but also a major conditioning force in relation to her male counterpart, if not in ways that Unamuno always recognised or welcomed.

Further Reading

Bretz (2001), Johnson (2003).

10

Quixotic Unamuno:
Cervantes in Unamuno's Thought and Fiction

J.A. GARRIDO ARDILA AND JULIA BIGGANE

A defining feature of the early-twentieth-century Spanish writers known as *noventayochistas* (the 'Generation of 1898') is their auto-didacticism, the wide cultural, philosophical and scientific knowledge they each acquired by reading independently and eclectically. Unamuno's philosophical and literary works are particularly rich in allusions, references to and influences from classical and contemporary authors. Of course as a professor at Spain's oldest university, Unamuno had access to one of the largest libraries in the country, but his intellectual curiosity also led him to purchase a large quantity of books published abroad, some of which included works in German philosophy and Scandinavian literature, which were little known by his fellow countrymen. Indeed, the rich intertextual dimension of Unamuno's works is perhaps unparalleled in the literary and philosophical history of modern Spain.

Barry Luby (2008: 13) has suggested that Carlyle, Kierkegaard and William James were the three philosophers that exerted the deepest influence on Unamuno; in his 1913 article 'La Generación de 1898', Azorín (1969: 39) thought that Ibsen, Tolstoy and Amiel were the foreign authors that had marked Unamuno's literary works most profoundly. To condense Unamuno's intellectual influences into a list of a few authors would decidedly misrepresent the scope of his intellectual ambitiousness, but perhaps Kierkegaard and Ibsen are the authors with whom he felt the most passionate or sympathetic affinity; within Spain, Ganivet and Galdós are perhaps the authors who most inspired his literary development. Yet one obvious name is absent from Azorín and Luby's lists—Cervantes. His masterwork *Don Quixote* is clearly at the centre of Unamuno's philosophical and literary production. The Cervantine elements in Unamuno's work have been competently studied by several scholars. However, as is the case with many other aspects of Unamuno's works, his thought and his creative writing have often been studied in isolation from each other. This chapter examines Cervantes's presence in both Unamuno's essays on ontological and historical questions, in his literary output and the way he conceived the novel.

Popular and scholarly interest in Cervantes and *Don Quixote* had been growing in Spain since the second half of the eighteenth century, and the tercentenary of the publication of part I was one of the factors that further renewed its currency in the early 1900s: the novel was appropriated by intellectuals in diverse ways to (re)assess Spain's modern history and to envisage possible future directions for the nation. Whether explicitly or more obliquely, figures such as Maeztu, Castro, Ortega and Madariaga re-examined Don Quixote to discuss pressing contemporary political and social issues: the loss of the last remnants of empire after 1898; the much-criticised Restoration parliamentary system and its social effects; the uneven development of the country and the rise of nationalist movements in the Basque country, Catalonia and Galicia; the national character.[1] Unamuno was the pioneer in this regard – his *Vida de Don Quijote y Sancho* appeared in 1905, the exact year of the tercentenary.

By that point, he had already been writing regularly on the figure of Don Quixote for a decade,[2] and he continued to study him afterwards, notably in *Del sentimiento trágico de la vida*, where Cervantes's hero appears as a seminal cultural and philosophical icon, crucial for an understanding of Spain and the Spanish people, but also in his exilic writings in the second half of the 1920s. Unamuno's engagement with Cervantes and Don Quixote is, then, not just earlier, but also deeper and more sustained than his contemporaries. Indeed, in Cervantes's novel Unamuno found a philosophy of Spain and of life, though his representation of Don Quixote changed as his own thinking about Spain and about existence changed. There is not, then, one Unamunian Don Quixote, but several, as this chapter will show.

'Death to Don Quijote!' Early representations in Unamuno's work

Unamuno's first sustained engagement with *Don Quixote* is to be found in the 1895 essays that would later be published as *En torno al casticismo*. As detailed

---

[1]   For example, José Ortega y Gasset's *Meditaciones del Quijote* [Reflections on Don Quixote] (1914), Américo Castro's *El pensamiento de Cervantes* [Cervantes's Thought] (1925), Salvador de Madariaga's *Guía del lector del Quijote* [A Guide to Don Quixote] (1926) and Ramiro de Maeztu's *Don Quijote, Don Juan y La Celestina* (1926).

[2]   See for example, 'El caballero de la triste figura' [The Knight of the Sorrowful Countenance], (1896) (OCA III, 364–385; OCE I, 911) '¡Muera Don Quijote!' [Death to Don Quixote] (1898) (OCA V, 712–716; OCE VII, 1194–1196) 'El fondo del quijotismo' [The Essence of Quixotism] (1902) (OCA, V, 725–729; OCE VII, 1203–1206), 'La causa del quijotismo' [Quixotism's Cause] (1903) (OCA, V, 730–736; OCE VII, 1206–1210), 'Sobre la lectura e interpretación del *Quijote*', [On Reading and Interpreting *Don Quixote*] (1905) OCA III, 842–860; OCE I, 1227–1238, and, of course, *En torno al casticismo*, as detailed below.

in Jean-Claude Rabaté's chapter in this volume, *En torno al casticismo* is an attempt to explain Spain's problems in terms of its *Volksgeist* and to indicate a feasible solution for its problems at the end of the nineteenth century. For Unamuno, Spain needed to free itself from a harmful and isolating official culture, forged over centuries, in order better to find its place in a broader *tradición eterna* of European civilisation. Although it contains some of the positivistic tendencies characteristic of Regenerationism, *En torno al casticismo* avoids the scientific or medical discourse used in Regenerationist 'diagnoses' of Spain's ills, and Unamuno's discussion of Spain's historical problems draws significantly on culture and the arts instead.

For Unamuno at this time, *Don Quixote* embodied both one of Spanish history's problems and provided a solution for its future. He insisted on the distinction between Don Quixote and Alonso Quijano, the modest *hidalgo* who only became Quixote after having been driven mad by reading accounts of derring-do and glory in chivalric romances. Alonso Quijano and his avatar provide an analogy for Spain's historical and civilisational development: Don Quixote represents the Castilian spirit, which includes both militant hierarchical regimentation and anarchism, and the heroic will to impose its values on other cultures (see, for example, OCE I, 791–2; OCA III, 181–183);[3] Alonso Quijano represents the more universal being underlying the specific historical identity—he is eternal human tradition rather than Castilian historical tradition. Unamuno lauds the final chapter of *Don Quijote* where the self-styled knight errant regains his sanity, and original identity, on his deathbed:

> In the sublime ending to his *Don Quixote*, Cervantes shows Spain—our Spain of today—the path to its regeneration in Alonso Quijano the Good [who....] as the purest kind of Spaniard, attained a kind of renunciation of his official Spanishness ['españolismo'] and attained the universal spirit, the spirit of mankind that lies dormant within us all
> (OCE I, 791; OCA III, 183).

Like Don Quixote, then, Spain must regain its sanity by throwing off its particular martial heroic national history in order to rediscover its deeper common human values. It is for this reason that, towards the end of the text, Unamuno declares 'Don Quixote must be killed in order that Alonso Quijano el Bueno may be resuscitated' (OCE I, 854; OCA III, 279). This was a call that Unamuno repeated three years later in the wake of Spain's disastrous defeat in the Spanish-American

---

3   Unamuno elaborates further on the inseparability of Don Quixote and Castile in the first essay he devoted exclusively to Don Quixote 'El caballero de la triste figura' [The Knight of the Sorrowful Countenance] (1896) (referenced above).

war: in his 1898 article, ¡Muera Don Quijote! [Death to Don Quixote!], Quixote
is more explicitly equated with Spain's imperial history, and is set apart from
Christianity. Unamuno argues that:

> We must forget the life of adventures, that going forth to impose on others
> what we thought best for them and that seeking overseas a deceptive empire.
> We must reflect, above all, on the profoundly unchristian nature of the
> chivalric ideal [...] the mission of a people is to realize justice and become
> Christianised in itself, *ad intra*
>
> (OCA V, 715; OCE VII, 1195–1196).

Also evident in Unamuno's early study of Don Quixote is the rejection of what
he sees as an untenable opposition between fiction and reality, as manifested in
the public reception and understanding of literary characters and their authors.
In an 1896 essay entitled 'El caballero de la triste figura' [The Knight of the
Sorrowful Countenance], he asks '[d]id Homer make Achilles, or was it the other
way around? (OCA III, 374; OCE I, 918); referring to Don Quixote's 'biographer'
Cide Hamete, on whom Cervantes claimed to have based his novel, Unamuno
argues that 'the transient, contingent world gradually produces the permanent,
necessary world of our spirit, and this is its greatest reality: all of history is the
idealisation of the real by means of the realisation of the ideal' (OCA III, 374;
OCE I, 917–918). Don Quixote becomes more real in this sense than either
Cervantes or Cide Hamete, an argument later rehearsed many times, not least
in the confrontation between Augusto and Unamuno-as-author-figure in *Niebla*.

The Vitalist Quixote

The study of Don Quixote's existence as autonomous from Cervantes, and of
his melancholic character, was further developed in Unamuno's book-length
essay *La vida de Don Quijote y Sancho*, published in 1905. By the beginning
of the twentieth century, there was an established tradition of Cervantes studies,
though Unamuno disdained the academic approach to Cervantes's work, and
the *Vida* is less of interest for what it might tell us about Cervantes scholarship
than for what it reveals about Unamuno's own preoccupations. The *Vida* is an
idiosyncratic mixture of chapter-by-chapter commentary on Cervantes's novel,
meditations on the state of Spain, particularly after the 1898 defeat to the U.S,
and reflections on Unamuno's own role as a Quixotic 'agitator of spirits'. Most
strikingly of all, it reverses Unamuno's previous position: rather than calling
for his death, the *Vida* now proclaims ¡Viva Don Quijote!
    The very personal nature of Unamuno's interpretation, and the volte-face of
his views on the character should not lead us to think that the *Vida* is not a

serious or major text. Although it has been rather under-studied in relation to Unamuno's other essays, Pedro Cerezo Galán is right to note that it occupies a fundamental place in his thought (1996: 312). It is where Unamuno first substantially sets out his irrationalist, vitalist and voluntarist views on existence, and where he explored the 'hunger for immortality' that became such a cornerstone of his later thought. If for Unamuno scholars the *Vida* is important to understand the evolution of Unamuno's mature thought, for more traditional Cervantes scholars it is one of the most passionate examples of the so-called 'Romantic' approach to *Don Quixote*, which, following German Romantic interpretations, saw Don Quixote as a heroic, rather than simply comic character. Certainly Unamuno idealises Don Quixote's 'hunger for glory and renown' (OCE III, 228; OCA IV, 232), which is presented not as simple vain search for fame; he is driven by his need to extend his personality across space and time, defying mortality, and is driven not by egotism but by a particular, deeply cordial philosophy:

> the philosophy of not dying, of believing, of believing the truth. And this philosophy is not learned in the university lecture, nor can it be laid out through inductive or deductive logic, nor does it emerge from syllogisms or laboratories; instead it rises up from the heart
>
> (OCE III, 232; OCE IV, 349).

The truth this philosophy aims for is similarly set apart from the academic: it is, instead, vital: 'Truth is what makes us live, not what makes us think' (OCE III, 210; OCA IV, 314). Unamuno also lauds Don Quixote's great fortitude. Addressing the knight directly, he says 'your greatness lay in never recognising when you were defeated' (OCE III, 80; OCA IV, 108).

In the *Vida*, Quixote is compared to Ignatius Loyola, the founder of the Jesuit order, and to Teresa of Avila: for Unamuno: all three are 'caballeros andantes' [knights errant] (OCE III, 157; OCA IV, 230), and Don Quixote does not fight to right wrongs, or help the needy, but to conquer the spiritual kingdom of faith (OCE III, 79; OCA IV, 106). Unamuno rewrites him as a sacrificial, selfless Messianic figure, who, like Christ in the Gospel of St Matthew, came not to bring peace on earth but with a sword (OCE III, 142; OCA IV, 207). Critics disagree as to how this messianising should be read. For Anthony Close, Unamuno's views:

> are the lament of a man who has evolved an agnostic existentialism in the shadow of orthodox Catholicism, transforming secular action and fame into a substitute for traditional piety and casting many a wishful backward glance at the untroubled assurance of childhood faith (1978: 154).

Unamuno did indeed lose his faith as a university student in Madrid, but this loss was itself shaken in 1897 after an existential crisis. The precise status of Unamuno's religious belief was perhaps less easy to categorise than Close implies, but, even if, as Cerezo Galán notes, the 'faith' that Don Quixote possesses and Unamuno exalts in the *Vida* may not have a determinate content, it militates for a spiritual realm and a transcendent immortality, distancing it from mere herostratism (1996: 328). Certainly Quixote's actions seem to have a genuine religious valence for Unamuno: addressing the knight towards the end of the text, he claims that:

> [t]he root of your madness for immortality, the root of your yearning to live for centuries unending [...] was your goodness. [...] The good man does not resign himself to his own dissipation because he feels that his goodness is a taking part in God ['hace parte de Dios']
>
> (OCE III, 245; OCA IV, 368).

That Don Quixote is raised to the status of a Christ-like figure by Unamuno does not mean that his representation is not also conditioned by more secular, local and contemporaneous concerns. The knight's heroic idealism and faith are presented as qualities which could help Spain overcome its present-day problems and regenerate. The text presents early twentieth Spain as a country dominated by Sansón-Carrasco types, preoccupied with facile reason and a desire for conformity (OCE III, 95; OCA IV, 132). Such figures also predominate overseas, and the essay is a call to arms for irrationalists and idealists to use their faith against the growing might of positivism and materialism. The essay has to be read in the context of the rise of other nations when Spanish imperial and economic power was at a low ebb. Unamuno argued that the windmills that Don Quixote tilted against were, at the turn of the twentieth century, engines and turbines (OCE III, 86; OCA IV, 118), but if Don Quixote (Spain) could not best them materially, he could triumph in terms of spiritual strength and faith. Unamuno proclaims that 'those giants may be able to break our weapons, but they can't break our hearts' (OCE III, 87; OCA IV, 119). The legacy of 1898, and the rise of other nations' imperial and economic might haunts the pages of the *Vida*, and the text is, in part, a defiant nationalist credo in the wake of defeat, pitting will, faith and spiritual superiority against technological and military might. It also contains bitter criticism of Spain's civic and political life: the Restoration monarchical regime, for Unamuno a regime with little credibility, is compared with Maese Pedro's puppet show, and a Don Quixote was needed to destroy it (OCE, III, 177; OCA IV, 262); civic debate remained a dialogue of the deaf, closed to nuanced discussion, such disunity opening the country to the possibility that 'our enemies will slit our throats' (OCE III, 96; OCA IV, 133).

As Javier Blasco has observed (2009:79) Unamuno also identified with Don

Quixote in his own idealistic mission to right wrongs in Spain: in 1905, Unamuno had not entirely established himself as one of Spain's first public intellectuals; moreover, his views had met with considerable hostility in conservative circles in Salamanca. It is not difficult to see how the figure of Don Quixote as a lone crusader and misunderstood, ridiculed figure might have resonated with Unamuno, and the *Vida* opens by observing that if Don Quixote were to return to present-day Spain, ignoble, simplistic or cynical intentions would be wrongly imputed to his desire to correct injustices (OCE III, 51; OCA IV, 70–71). Unamuno also writes bitterly of being whispered about or denigrated by people who had not even read his work, and notes that Don Quixote suffered a similar fate, being ridiculed by those who knew nothing of his deeds (OCE III, 221; OCE IV, 331). As Friedrich Schurr has observed, Don Quixote allowed Unamuno to create a myth for himself and to reflect on himself through the knight (cited in Cerezo Galán 1996: 313); for Ricardo Gullón, '[i]n *Don Quixote* the novel and with Don Quixote the hero, Unamuno found spiritual solace and inspirational encouragement) (Unamuno 1987: xviii); the functions that Don Quixote fulfilled for Unamuno personally are certainly evident in the *Vida*.

Unamuno's Tragic Agonist: the Quixote and *Del sentimiento trágico de la vida*

Unamuno developed further the analogy between Don Quixote and Christ in his most well-known essay, *Del sentimiento trágico de la vida,* where Don Quixote and his beliefs raised to even further heights. In its concluding chapter, entitled 'Don Quixote in the Contemporary European Tragicomedy' Unamuno proclaims that:

> Quixotism [...] is a whole method, a whole epistemology, a whole esthetic, a whole logic, a whole ethic, whole religion—that is to say, a whole economy of things eternal and things divine, a whole hope in what is rationally absurd
> (Unamuno 1954: 325; OCE VII, 299; OCA XVI, 446).

In this wide-ranging chapter, Unamuno provides a robust and defiant defence of Spain and its historical achievements on the world stage. In following its own very distinctive path, Unamuno notes, Spain has been slandered because it championed the Counter-Reformation. Displaying the agonistic current underlying all his mature thought, Unamuno responds with the question: '[w]as there no importance [...] in the Counter-Reformation? Without the Counter-Reformation, would the Reformation have followed the course that it did actually follow?' (Unamuno 1954: 307; OCE VII, 289; OCA XVI, 420–1). He notes also that Spain's intellectual achievements have also been under-valued, reproducing Carducci's judgement that 'even Spain, which has never attained the hegemony of the world of thought, had her Cervantes'. Again Unamuno questions this evaluation, asking '[b]ut was Cervantes a solitary and isolated phenomenon, without roots, without ancestry, without a foundation?' (Unamuno 1954: 306; OCE VII, 289; OCA XVI, 429), partly agreeing with Carducci that Spanish thought was to be found in its literature, but also arguing that it was found elsewhere too: '[o]ur philosophy, the Spanish philosophy, is liquescent and diffused in our literature, in our life, in our action, in our mysticism, above all, and not in philosophical systems' (Unamuno 1954: 309; OCE VII, 290; OCA XVI, 431).

Unamuno then goes on to explain that Don Quixote is of crucial importance because he encapsulates Spain's philosophy and its precious legacy to the world. In the nineteenth century – 'an unphilosophical and technical epoch' – the ideal of progress, science and reason had become a nothing more than pseudo-scientific vulgarity (Unamuno 1954: 298; OCE VII, 284). Unamuno does not disdain material progress or science, but sees them as insufficient on their own. He agreed with Brunetière that science was bankrupt because it could not answer mankind's most fundamental questions and yearnings: the *maladie du siècle*, announced in Rousseau and voiced most clearly in Senancour's *Obermann*, was caused by the loss of faith in the immortality of the soul (Unamuno 1954: 298–299; OCE VII, 284; OCA XVI, 422). For Unamuno, here Don Quixote embodied the tragic conflict between reason and faith, a conflict essential to the Spanish people:

> The philosophy in the soul of my people appears to me as the expression of the inward tragedy analogous to the soul of Don Quixote, as the expression of a conflict between what the world is as scientific reason shows it to be, and what we wish that it might be, as our religious faith affirms it to be
> (Unamuno 1954: 321; OCE VII, 297, OCA XVI, 442–3).

To underline the unique nature of this legacy, Unamuno is careful in *Del sentimiento trágico de la vida* to mark out Don Quixote's philosophy as 'not strictly idealist—he fought for the spirit' (Unamuno 1954: 314; OCE VII, 293; OCA XVI, 436), in order, presumably to differentiate him from modern Kantian and neo-Kantian philosophies' valuing of rationalism. Don Quixote fights against the modern age: he is a medieval spiritual warrior (Unamuno 1954: 326; OCE VII, 300; OCA XVI, 448).

As in the *Vida*, Unamuno once again identifies himself with Don Quixote. Like the knight, he was on a spiritual crusade, fighting to uphold faith in his agonistic and voluntarist vision:

> My work—I was going to say my mission—is to shatter the faith of men here, there, and everywhere, faith in affirmation, faith in negation, and

faith in abstention from faith, and this for the sake of faith in faith itself; it is to war against all those who submit, whether it be to Catholicism, or rationalism, or agnosticism; it is to make all men live the life of inquietude and passionate desire
(Unamuno 1954: 322; OCE VII, 297–298; OCA XVI, 444).

Consonant with Unamuno's divinisation of the knight, the chapter concludes by prophesying what seems to be a second coming for Don Quixote:

What, then, is the new mission of Don Quixote, to-day, in this world? To cry aloud, to cry aloud in the wilderness. But though men hear not, the wilderness hears, and one day it will be transformed into a resounding forest, and this solitary voice that goes scattering over the wilderness like seed, will fructify into a gigantic cedar, which with its hundred thousand tongues will sing an eternal hosanna to the Lord of life and of death
(Unamuno 1954: 329; OCE VII, 301–302; OCA XVI, 450).

Towards the end of this concluding chapter, Unamuno states trenchantly: 'the world must be as Don Quixote wishes it to be' (Unamuno 1954: 327; OCE VII, 300; OCA XVI, 448). It certainly true that Don Quixote was always as Unamuno wanted (or needed) him to be at different points in his life: as we have seen, from symbol of imperial folly in the 1890s article '¡Muera Don Quijote!' he becomes the object of patriotic apotheosis in the first two decades of the twentieth century. Later still, when Unamuno was in exile, in the notes that he compiled for an unfinished volume entitled 'Manual del Quijotismo', his Quixote undergoes yet another metamorphosis, becoming the champion of a kind of divinised liberalism as Unamuno himself sought to challenge the authoritarian conservative modernising of the Primo de Rivera regime (Unamuno 2005a).

Quixotic fictions

Just as *Don Quixote* lies at the heart of Unamuno's philosophy, its literary innovations are central to the way Unamuno conceived the novel. And although the *Vida* does not explore the literary aspects of Cervantes's work, it is irrefutable that Unamuno's novels were deeply influenced by them. One of the most salient features of Unamuno's compositional technique is what he termed *escribir a lo que salga* (to write without a plan).[4] Both the technique and the expression

---

4   At times Unamuno referred to this type of writing as 'vivíparo' [viviparous] rather than the kind of carefully researched and planned 'ovíparo' [oviparous] composition exemplified in his first published novel *Paz en la guerra*. See also the discussion of this division in Chapter 2 of this volume.

are taken from *Don Quixote*. In Part II, chapter 3, Don Quixote, Sancho and the graduate Sansón Carrasco discuss the many flaws that cause Part I to be an unreliable story. Don Quixote protests:

> que no ha sido sabio el autor de mi historia, sino algún ignorante hablador, que a tiento y sin ningún discurso se puso a escribirla, salga *lo que saliere* [emphasis added]
>
> (Cervantes 2005: 469)

> [The author of my story was not a wise man, but instead some ignorant charlatan who recklessly and clumsily started writing it without any plan about how it might turn out].

Unamuno borrows Cervantes's words literally, updating the archaic form *saliere* to *salga*. The method of writing a narrative told by an unreliable or otherwise questionable narrator is common to both Cervantes and Unamuno, as we see in *Niebla*, *San Manuel Bueno, mártir* and *La novela de Don Sandalio, jugador de ajedrez*.[5]

Unamuno also found the chapter in which Don Quixote encountered Maese Pedro and his puppet show (Part II, Chapter 26) particularly fertile and suggestive for his own ideas about literature, and the process of creative writing. For example, in a prologue to the 1934 edition of his play *El hermano Juan* (1929), he explains his reasons for rewriting the myth of Don Juan. Having made his case, Unamuno concludes:

> No más comentarios críticos al paño, no hacer más de Maese Pedro, que predica desde detrás de bastidores
>
> [No more critical commentaries from behind the curtain, no more Maese Pedro preaching from behind the scenes]
>
> (OCE V, 724; OCA XII, 882).

Distancing himself from the figure of the author/dramatist as all-knowing and all-controlling, Unamuno asks:

> Porque estas reflexiones metafóricas, estas disertaciones al paño, de Maese Pedro, ¿precedieron o siguieron al drama? ¿Le engendraron o fueron engendradas por él?

---

5   For further discussion in relation to *Niebla*, see Ardila (forthcoming 2015).

[Because these metaphorical reflections, this speech from behind the scenes by Maese Pedro, did they precede or follow the drama? Did they give birth to the drama or were they engendered by the drama itself?]

(OCE V, 724; OCA XII, 882)

Although the Cervantine narration centres on the question of verisimilitude (Don Quixote doubts the verisimilitude of the story he sees played out, and Maese Pedro justifies himself by responding that there are many stories told and published that do not conform to the principle of verisimilitude), Unamuno is more interested in the question of what comes first: the story or the author's ideas about it. Questions about the 'ontology' of literature occupied Unamuno for his entire career: we saw above the questions he asked in 1896 in 'El caballero de la triste figura'; as this prologue demonstrates, he is still ruminating on the relationship between the author and his creations towards the end of his life.

This metafictional technique whereby a character tells a story and the story is criticised as unrealistic by another character was replicated in Unamuno's *Niebla*. In chapter 17, Víctor tells the story of don Eloíno, which Víctor intends to include in the novel he is writing, just as Cervantes – Víctor claims – included interpolated stories in *Don Quixote* (OCE II, 615; OCA II, 894). Once Víctor has told the story, Augusto exclaims: 'This is all fantasy!', and Víctor replies: 'No, it's history!' (OCE II, 614; OCA II, 893). Afterwards, Víctor says about don Eloíno's story: 'These are things that one wouldn't make up, that it is not possible to make up'. This discussion about fiction, reality and verisimilitude is very similar to what happens in Part II, Chapter 26 of *Don Quixote*. Of course in *Niebla*, Unamuno goes on to explore the claim that literature is as real as life, and vice versa, and the Cervantine story of don Eloíno is an initial articulation of this thesis.

Although there are obvious traces of Cervantes in works such as *El Cristo de Velázquez*, and resonances in titles such as his 1920 short-story collection *Tres novelas ejemplares y un prólogo*,[6] most studies of Unamuno's literary engagement with Cervantes have focused on *Niebla*.[7] Indeed so striking are the analogies between *Don Quixote* and *Niebla* that Willard King has claimed that 'perhaps *Niebla* was conceived as a Quixotic work, as a modern recreation of the greatest jewel in Spanish literature' (1967: 219). Indeed, many features of *Niebla* have been deemed to be inspired by *Don Quixote*: the parody of previous literary trends (in *Niebla*'s case the realist novel); literature as a topic for literature, and the metafictional elements; the interpolated stories; the Quixotic

---

6   The prologue to the collection also discusses Cervantes's *Novelas ejemplares* (OCE II, 971–977; OCA IX 413–423)

7   The most recent are Ardila (2010), Friedman (2006), Franz (2007), and Vauthier (1999).

protagonist Augusto, who lives in a world of his own and is in love with a young woman who differs markedly from his idealised view of her; the extensive use of dialogue; the use of more than one narrative voice; the tension between realism and idealism; the use of irony in the prologues and the death of the main character at the hands of the author.[8]

As suggested above, both Unamuno and Cervantes were particularly concerned with the concept of realism. Cervantes sought to transcend the ideal representation of reality given by the romances of his day; Unamuno was committed to establishing a new way to represent reality that transcended the limitations of nineteenth-century realism. Cervantes thus moves from idealism to verisimilitude; Unamuno discards empirical realism and adopts a form of psychological realism that delves into dreams and into the exaltation of literature. As Friedman, and Ardila (2010), have argued, the technique is identical – Cervantes parodies chivalry romances; Unamuno parodies nineteenth-century realism and, in particular, the novels of Spain's most prominent realist writer, Benito Pérez Galdós.[9] In sum, in *Niebla* Unamuno borrows a significant number of methods of literary composition from Cervantes. But although *Niebla* may be a Cervantine novel, Unamuno uses those Cervantine techniques to create something new and distinctly modernist.

Cervantes perhaps exerted almost as deep and comprehensive an influence on Unamuno as Ibsen and Kierkegaard, on his philosophy and on his literature alike. Don Quixote the character inspired Unamuno to explain Spain's decadence in *En torno al casticismo*, to develop his own *national* philosophy in the *Vida de Don Quijote y Sancho* and *Del sentimiento trágico de la vida*; and provided Unamuno with the compositional tools to develop a new form of literature, one that left nineteenth-century realism behind and established the foundations of the modernist novel in Spain.

Further Reading

Ardila (2010, 2015), Cerezo Galán (1996), Close (1978), Franz (2003, 2007), Friedman (2006), Ouimette (1974), Vauthier (1999).

---

[8]   See Friedman for a more detailed discussion of the last two features.
[9]   On the parody of Galdós in *Niebla* see Franz (2003).

11

Landscapes of the Soul: Unamuno's Travel Writing

RAMÓN F. LLORENS GARCÍA

The experience of travel in fin-de-siècle literature

The experience of travel in all its diverse forms – excursion or tour, adventure, day trip or walk – was a constant of nineteenth-century European literature. Spain did not escape scrutiny, though a glance at the bibliography shows that the major writers tended to be from the Anglo- or Francophone traditions: Borrow, Achard, Andersen, Ford, Irving, and Mérimée all focused their attention on Spanish customs, inhabitants and landscapes. Unamuno himself, and José Martínez Ruiz ('Azorín') championed the figures of Théophile Gautier and Alexandre Dumas, underlining their intimate sensitivity to the Spanish landscape and their ability to discover the 'essence' of the country. Azorín asserted that Gautier 'helped the youth of 1898 see the landscape of Spain ... in terms of poetic interpretation of the countryside. It is difficult to imagine that he will ever be surpassed, because the physical geography of the Peninsula is not just *narrated* in his work, but *seen*, with a rapt, disinterested and dazzling eye' (Martínez Ruiz 1998: 997).

Spanish literature, in contrast, produced relatively little travel writing. Emilia Pardo Bazán, Ortega Munilla and Benito Pérez Galdós contributed to the genre in the second half of the nineteenth century, but the culminating text was Pedro Alarcón's 1874 work, *La Alpujarra. Sesenta leguas a caballo, precedidas de seis en diligencia* [The Alpujarras. Seventy Leagues on Horseback, Preceded by Six in a Stagecoach], which he would subsequently publish in his *Viajes por España* [Travels Through Spain]. The most important influence on the so-called Generation of 1898 as far as travel was concerned came later, and not from literature, but from the La Institución Libre de Enseñanza (ILE: the Independent Institute of Education).[1]

---

[1] The progressive lay institute was established in 1876 by Francisco Giner de los Ríos and other liberal educationalists in order to train a new generation of leaders who would help modernize Spain culturally, spiritually and politically. For further details, see López Morillas (1981).

It was only with the Institute's appearance that the excursion as ideal means to discover and understand the physical terrain and landscape of the country began to be put into meaningful practice. Guided both by academic study and popularisation of the geographical sciences, Francisco Giner de los Ríos and his students were influential in spreading the practice of hiking and rambling as means of acquiring geographical and geological knowledge of the country: Giner undertook numerous excursions through central Castile, 'the physical and emotional centre of what was identified as the national spirit' (Pena 1982: 86). Those associated with the Institute applied new methodologies, observing the countryside through the prisms of positivism and the human sciences. For the Institucionistas, an excursion or journey put the individual in touch with nature, providing a priceless form of training: it promoted 'an *integral* education and the postulates of the [empirically-based] intuitive method that such thinking encapsulates' (Ortega 1988: 72). The ILE saw the landscape as both a proper object of scientific experimentation and as an expression of national history: in this sense, it was a perfect projection of the Institute's ethics and aesthetics (Pena 1982: 75). The synthesis of scientific knowledge and a feeling for natural terrain is evident in Giner's work. The growing interest in geography, fomented in part by the ILE's activities, and the need both for wider experience of travel and accessible writing on it, engaging with history and literature as well as geography, in order to open up Spain to its inhabitants, were factors that created a fertile breeding ground for a new type of travel writing on Spain. Although ILE writing on travel and the landscape was more scientific than literary, and although its terrain was fairly limited—the axis being the Guadarrama mountain range in Castile— this group undoubtedly left a mark on the travelling Generation of 1898.

Influenced by Krausist Institutionist currents regarding the Spanish countryside and its terrain, Spanish writers began to publish articles, chronicles and poems about their travels at the end of the nineteenth and first two decades of the twentieth century. Azorín, Unamuno, Ciro Bayo, Darío de Regoyos and Gutiérrez Solana all extolled the aesthetic qualities of the Spanish landscape, combining historical, cultural and psychological approaches in their meditations: '[t]o varying degrees, these authors' articles and books constituted – in addition to informative, first-hand testimonies – criticism of a wretched current situation, in which cultural ... political ... and religious factors all played an equal part' (Martínez Cachero 1984: 28). Azorín, a theorist of travel like Unamuno, considered in some depth and detail the practices that all good travellers should adopt: reflection at a temporal distance; the avoidance both of fatigue—an obstacle to the proper contemplation of the journey—and of spots recommended to tourists (whom he considered 'anti-travellers'); the seeking out of unexplored spaces; the careful consideration of the ideal time to undertake the journey, and the best modes of transport (cited in Llorens García 1986: 27). The 'globetrotter'

Ciro Bayo would publish a varied body of travel writing which tackled topics ranging from the discomforts of travel, the shunning of tourist routes and the advantages of travelling on foot or by horse to the search for a hidden Spain. Other writers of the time noted for their contributions to travel writing included Darío de Regoyos, with his anthropological optic of enquiry and the surprising Spain he depicted; Gutiérrez Solana and his caricatural, tragic vision; Julio Camba, whose foreign travels were captured in witty impressionistic sketches and Eugenio Noel, with his pessimistic, distorted representations.

The inhabitants – the 'peoplescape' – the cities, different ways of life and characters were all part of this new literary vision of the landscape. The journey was the most direct way of getting to know the country: it allowed writers to travel to the furthest and sometimes most forgotten places, making direct contact with the *patria* (fatherland) – both the landscape and the people in it – in its entirety. The writers of this time were rebelling against the historical and literary circumstances they had inherited, and it became essential for them to get to know their country as a preliminary step to establishing a strong emotional bond with it. 'To know' and 'to love' were considered essential watchwords. In order to carry out this urgent requisite, an intrahistorical interiorisation, dispensing with scientific methods, statistics or precise prior studies was what was needed; these writers focused their attention instead on thorough, deep observation and contemplation, offering a new perspective – the aesthetic – in contradistinction to the approach of the Institute. The old towns and villages, the landscapes, the inhabitants and Spain's intrahistory were the fundamental objects of the travel chronicles they produced for the press of the time, chronicles that explained the country's situation and its more hidden aspects. It was in this context that Unamuno's own travel writing first developed.

Unamuno's literary travels: preliminary remarks

When studying Unamuno's travel writing, it is helpful to bear in mind a number of factors which will help us situate and understand its importance in relation to his work as a whole. First, as was not uncommon for writers of his time, his early writings were journalistic, and only later collected as volumes of travel writing connected by theme. The articles had their origins in weekend excursions, in journeys to give public lectures, or in holidays. We should not look to Unamuno for description of intercontinental travel; his observations arise from contemplative peninsular journeying. He walked, discovered old towns and villages, and wrote articles connected only loosely to the terrain travelled – basically, Spain and Portugal. At times, particularly early on in his career, the articles were published in small-circulation periodicals, aimed at those who were not necessarily 'readers of Unamuno'; later, they tended to be published in more widely read journals and newspapers that followed Unamuno's work with interest. Aware of this, he made sure his writing bore his own distinctive imprint.

He granted extraordinary importance to the first impression a place produced in him:

> '...the first is the always the freshest and most spontaneous impression, the most profoundly truthful, piercing the feelings more than the intellect'
>
> (OCE I, 306; OCA I, 542–3).

He was a constant observer, initially noting everything which caught his attention in notebooks or pieces of paper, and only later setting out his meditations in more organised form. The importance he gave to conveying the first impression meant that he seemed to relegate reflection to a seemingly secondary position, the responsibility of the writer rather than the traveller:

> When one arrives at a place, one must suck the very marrow from it, especially those of us who have to write. It's a terrible thing to go and see something in order to write about it, rather than to write because one has seen something. But the demands of the profession... And, once there, one is not going to waste the journey
>
> (OCE, I, 238; OCA I, 436–7).

In his literary sojourning, Unamuno saw himself as undertaking a pedagogical task, offering an understanding of the country and its inhabitants, studying both the physical and human components of the fatherland, its intrahistory.[2] For Escobar, the travel article put at Unamuno's disposal 'a flexible, creative and entertaining vehicle in which theoretical reflections on intrahistory could be introduced into journalistic praxis' (2003: 105). We need to be attentive to the diversity of his travel writing, which ranged from a hybrid between the chronicle and journalistic article (sometimes in epistolary or quasi-epistolary form), short and addressed to a specific readership, through the essay format, which allowed him to reflect in a more erudite way on various matters, but always in an accessible style, to collected travel writings, with their personal or anecdotal experiences ordered chronologically. Such variety allowed Unamuno to develop his reflections and descriptions with the greatest possible freedom, 'to roll up the shirtsleeves of his soul' ['poner el alma en mangas de camisa'], 'to dive in', 'to roll around', and 'to throw off decorum' (Escobar 2003: 104).

We also need to bear in mind that, precisely because they had their origin as journalistic articles, and because Unamuno was an indefatigable traveller

---

[2]   See Jean-Claude Rabaté's chapter in this volume for a discussion of the concept of intrahistory.

and hardy excursionist, his work certainly chronicled his travels, but also functioned as an at times intimate diary of his personal adventures, and of his views on the social and political reality of Spain; it also reflected on the very experience of travel. The vicissitudes of his life, and his intellectual and affective preoccupations are prominent within his travel writing. Discussion of mankind's hunger for immortality, the writer's professional and social responsibilities, existential anguish, and a certain amount of irony all coexist with a rich theory of the experience of travel, including definitions of traveller and journey, all alongside practical recommendations for places to visit, routes, means of transport, guides and the necessity of fatigue as a kind of purgation. His travel books are always autobiographical: 'This is no book, it's a man!', wrote Walt Whitman, whom Unamuno quoted in his prologue to *Paz en la guerra*, and we could say the same about Unamuno's travel books: 'There are those who investigate the biochemical body; I investigate my 'self' —my concrete, personal, living and suffering 'self'' (OCE VIII, 300; OCA X, 243).

Finally, although, from *Paz en la guerra* onwards, landscape and detailed physical location are almost entirely absent from Unamuno's fictional narrative output, we should keep in mind that the themes of travel, the traveller or landscape are certainly not confined to the articles collected in what are usually categorised as his travel books proper. Such was the importance of travel to the author that we find discussion of it not just throughout his vast output of journalistic articles, but in prologues and epilogues to other books, for example *Paz en la guerra* and *San Manuel Bueno, mártir* (which had its origins in an excursion) or in his poetry.

Indeed, it is perhaps in some ways his travel writing that brings the reader closest to the ethics, aesthetics and personality of Unamuno. It is an aesthetic that prompted Azorín, one of Spanish literature's most noted stylists, to argue that travel led Unamuno to write perhaps the finest words his pen ever produced, or indeed that have ever been written in Spanish (1961: 119). Unamuno made the journey 'a literary, mystic and social experience – evoked most often in lyrical terms – even as he also attempted to communicate to his readers not only his own personal and unique experience, but also the therapeutic value of travelling and the role of the punishment of the body in bringing the self and its environment into closer and more complete relation' (Ouimette 1994: 434). Unamuno turned travel into a necessity and a source of inspiration.

The major collections

Paisajes (1902) was the first book Unamuno published on his experiences as a traveller. It is composed of five articles, previously published in Madrid and Basque Country newspapers between 1898 and 1900. All the pieces describe landscapes and places not far from Salamanca, the city to which Unamuno had moved in 1891 to take up a Chair in Greek at the University. But the articles are linked less by the geographical proximity of their settings than by the use of landscape (and changing 'skyscapes') to prompt wider meditations on time, on religious feeling, on the sublime and on the way that history is experienced in the countryside. So large do these wider considerations bulk that the title of the collection is almost misleading in its bald simplicity. For example, the first essay, 'La Flecha',[3] is less a description of the small town of that name than a commentary on the sixteenth-century Spanish theologian and Friar Luis de León's writings on it, and an analysis of how the Friar's theology was itself shaped by his local environs. For Unamuno, Fray León's vision of Christ as shepherd, mastering and roaming across the land (rather than being enslaved by it, like the landworker), moving amongst men in the process, had been formed partly by the transhumant pastoral life he himself had witnessed in and around La Flecha. Similarly, 'Brianzuelo de la Sierra' describes a brief overnight stay in a small town (in reality La Alberca), but is just as much a meditation on how its inhabitants experienced the passing of time and history. It focuses on the vast difference between city and countryside in Spain (a function of the extremely uneven economic and social development in Spain at the end of the nineteenth century), but eschews empirical or material analysis, drawing instead on the concept of *intrahistoria*. It is also an idealising paean to rural tranquillity.

The gulf between city and countryside is addressed again in another of the essays, 'Humilde heroismo' [Humble Heroism], and in this essay there is a focus on the need to bring social change, modern political movements, science and rational knowledge to the rural ambit. In order that this might happen, Unamuno argues, such change and such knowledge has first to be translated into the language and thought of the countryside, because, for Unamuno, 'the slow son of the soil converts all that he takes into his heart into religion'. Thus, Unamuno argues, 'It is necessary to turn the flower of laboratory science into religion, fertilising it with humanitarian fraternity' (OCE I, 81; OCA I, 83). This article demonstrates both the sincerity of Unamuno's desire to address the social and political problems assailing Spain at this time, and also the barriers to his progressiveness – he finds it difficult to imagine peasants' ability to be opened to and transformed by new forms of knowledge and understanding, instead calling for a translation of new forms into pre-existing frameworks. The educability of the rural masses is clearly limited for Unamuno and some of his fellow republican thinkers.

---

    [3]   Translator's note: throughout the chapter, where an English translation does not follow the title of an article by Unamuno, it is because the title consists entirely of a place name or the name of a person.

Religion in this brief collection is certainly not viewed only as an instrumental idiom for communicating social and political change to rural inhabitants. 'Puesto del sol' [Sunset] is suffused with religious feeling, and it is present also in 'Fantasía crepuscular' [Twilight Fantasy/Fantasia]. For Unamuno, contemplation of the rural landscape prompts both thoughts of the transcendence of time, and connection through time to ancestral bonds (Unamuno was keen to stress the etymological roots of the term 'religion' in the Latin 'ligere' – to bind). The sublime appears in 'Puesto del sol', as does the lyrical and synaesthetic representation of land- and cloudscape. What unites all the essays in *Paisajes* is the preoccupation with time and history: in this early collection, there is no contemplation of place without contemplation of time also.

The volume *De mi país: descripciones, relatos y artículos de costumbres* was published a year after *Paisajes* in 1903. The country referred to in the title is the Basque Country, where Unamuno had grown up, and the volume consists of fifteen early articles, dating from between 1885 and 1900, the majority of which had first appeared in the Basque press. *De mi país* is too eclectic to be categorised simply as a travel book: it contains, for example, a respectfully affectionate obituary piece for the influential Basque writer, critic and editor Antonio Trueba ('Antón el del pueblo' [Antón, Man of the People/ Man from the Village]), a fictional character sketch dating from 1887 rehearsing some of the themes and preoccupations of *Paz en la guerra* ('Solitaña'), wry articles on the inhabitants of Bilbao and on Basque customs and pastimes ('Bilbao al aire libre' [Bilbao in the Open Air], 'Un partido de pelota' [A Pelota Match], and 'Chimbos y chimberas'),[4] and a trenchant piece criticising what Unamuno saw as the negativity and bigotry of a certain type of early Basque nationalism ('La sangre de Aitor' [The Blood of Aitor]). There are a few scattered accounts of excursions and travels ('Guernica: recuerdos de un viaje corto' [Guernica: Memories of a Brief Trip], 'La romería de San Marcial en Vergara' [The San Marcial pilgrimage in Vergara] and 'La casa-torre de los Zurbarán' [Zurbarán Tower].

But the real interest of the collection—and what connects it to Unamuno's wider writings on travel and place—is the importance placed on history in any apprehension of locale: for Unamuno, as in his first collection, an awareness of time is intrinsic to any experience of place. At times this is a function of the positivism that marked Unamuno's early thought: the essay 'En Alcalá de Henares. Castilla y Vizcaya' muses on the role of the bare,

---

4   Translator's note: the title of this article is not neatly translatable. 'Chimbo' was a slang term for a native of Bilbao: it derived from the name given to several species of bird, including the redstart, which adapted to live at the heart of urban and industrial centres. Unamuno here plays on both meanings of the word.

empty Castilian landscape in forming the ideal or mystical visions of figures such as Cervantes and St Teresa of Ávila (a thesis that, as Unamuno notes here, was developed further in *En torno al casticismo*): environment and the historical development of mentalities are very closely interconnected in this piece. The imprint of history is present in most of the studies, both in terms of major events such as the siege of Bilbao during the last Carlist War, which features in 'Del arbol de la libertad al palacio de la libertad, o sea, el cuartito de vino' [From the Tree of Liberty to the Palace of Liberty, or rather, the Little Wine Cellar] and 'San Miguel de Basauri: en el Arenal de Bilbao', and as longer-term process and shifter of mentalities: the gently humorous 'Gigantes' [Giants] is a micro social history, recounting how changes in the giant figures processed through Basque streets during fiestas related to wider changes and apprehensions of the world over time.

The recurrent concern with the ways in which place connects us to history extends to critical reflection on how place is used to invoke and commemorate the past. In a 1902 footnote added to the 1885 article 'Guernica. Recuerdos de un viaje corto', Unamuno deprecates what he sees as the artificial preservation of the now-dead old Guernica oak, historic symbol of Basque distinctiveness and identity: rather than 'embalming' and 'entrapping' it in a glass structure, it should have been felled and ploughed back into the earth to fertilise its successor tree. A similar disdain for the symbolic ossification or freezing of the past is present in the 1900 article 'Mi Bochito' [My Lair], which is attentive to the charged and complex relationship between memory, place and social change. Noting at the beginning of the article that he is increasingly disinclined to visit Bilbao because the more it develops and grows, the less it resembles *his* Bilbao – the image fixed and preserved in his soul on the basis of his childhood memories. Although he maps his remembered city in fond and emotional detail, and notes that soon not a shred of this cartography will remain in the rapidly expanding and industrialising urban centre, this is no exercise in reactionary nostalgia: Unamuno ends the article calling for the continued transformation of the city: '¡viva Bilbao! [...] let it continue to change, to purge itself, to throw off the narrow confines of its prison-like pupa, and take off and fly over the forge of industry; those of us who make our souls pantheons of the dead gods, or heroes deified by a purifying death, will be left with the empty chrysalis' (OCE I, 173; OCA I, 222). This sense of ascending change, and the sublating incorporation and purification of the past into the future suggests that important elements of Hegelian thought, though they may be have been gently parodied in *En torno al casticismo* (published three years previously), remain in Unamuno's own understanding of history and human development.

The remembered cartography of Unamuno's childhood Bilbao laid out in 'Mi bochito' also illustrates a point that was fundamental to Unamuno's conception of travel as a means to acquire meaningful feeling for one's country ('sentir la patria' OCE I, 86; OCA I, 89). By this, Unamuno did not mean a narrow patriotism, but a profound and intimate engagement with national territory. In order to love a country deeply, one must experience it up close. Intellectual or emotional knowledge is not enough: one must not just regard or contemplate it, but *touch* it and immerse oneself in its physicality (OCE I, 86; OCA I, 89). One begins with one's most immediate environs – not just one's *patria chica* ('little homeland', the Spanish term used to describe one's particular region or area) but one's 'tiny' homeland ('la patria [...] menos que chica' OCE I, 86; OCA I, 89) – the ambit and environs explored and physically experienced during childhood. The principle remains valid as one's (physical and figurative) horizons expand: in order to love one's country profoundly, one must make what is felt emotionally into a physically experienced, sentient contact (OCE, I, 87; OCA I, 90).

Nine years after *De mi país*'s publication, *Por tierras de Portugal y España* appeared. This collected twenty-six articles written between 1906 and 1909. A little under half of the articles are dedicated to Portugal; the rest to various Spanish regions and territories including Galicia, Castile, the Canary Islands, Extremadura, Catalonia and the Basque Country. Quite a few of the pieces on Spain were written for an Argentinian readership, and had been published in *La Nación*; others had appeared in established Spanish periodicals such as *El Lunes del Imparcial* or *España*. Much of Unamuno's literary work was notable for pushing against the confines of the conventions of genre, and his writings on travel and place were no exception in this regard, as the wide-ranging meditations in *De mi país* had suggested. *Por tierras de Portugal y España* continues this tendency: for example, although some of the articles in the section dedicated to Portugal had their origins in a holiday Unamuno had taken there in August 1908, half are not studies of place or specific custom, but are broader meditations on Portuguese culture and history. The first three article of the volume, 'Eugenio de Castro', 'La literatura portuguesa contemporánea' [Contemporary Portuguese Literature] and ' "Las sombras" de Teixeira de Pascoaes' ["The Shadows" of Teixeira de Pascoaes] are devoted to Portuguese literature.

But he also familiarises himself with local tourist attractions, visits picturesque or panoramic scenes unknown to tourists, climbs mountains, visits cities that no one visits and is a *flâneur* in the urban landscape. ' "Las sombras" de Teixeira de Pascoaes' present a picture of local customs in a landscape that is dreamed and affectively experienced as well as observed. Here the reader can appreciate Unamuno's enthusiasm for the landscape, and his reflections on the fishermen's lives and on literature. The article is about the grandeur and the importance of small things. He reflects on the 'fishing, peasant, simple Portugal, father of the seafaring, heroic Portugal' (OCE I, 194; OCA I, 368). He also follows current events in the country in 'Epitafio' [Epitaph], 'Desde Portugal' [From Portugal] and 'Un pueblo suicida' [A Suicidal People]. His travel writings are also often political readings, and are further combined with other opinions and thoughts about religion, history, memories of the Basque Country, autobiographical details and literary quotations. Throughout, what interests him is the attempt to capture the *soul* of Portugal, the national character, Man reflected in the country's landscapes, in its literature, in its history, and in the landscape as reflected in its men.

Once the 1908 academic year was finished, Unamuno went to Extremadura, where he visited the monastery of Guadalupe, travelled on horseback to Yuste, crossed the river Tiétar by boat, hiked in the Vera region, and returned via Cuacos to Yuste: all these trips are recounted in the volume. It also contains broad criticism of the dramatically uneven economic, social and infrastructural development of the country. In 'Yuste', he notes 'this truly beautiful Vera de Plasencia languishes in sad backwardness because of a lack of communication routes with the outside world. Neither the riches of its fruits and its timber can be exploited, nor that of its countryside. Not to mention the moral and social backwardness!' (OCE I, 267; OCA I, 482) He goes on to mention how little human life seems to be valued there, the damage that alcohol abuse has caused in the area, and laments the state of sexual relations in the town. He notes that the abandonment of babies is frequent, and is particularly sensitive to the plight of the adolescent women; when not acting as very young wet nurses, having to hire their services out to the wider region, they are subject to the unpleasant scrutiny of the lazy male 'drones' [zánganos] (OCE I, 267; OCA I, 482).

Some articles ('Guadalupe', 'Excursión', 'De Oñate a Aitzgorri', 'Trujillo') develop his particular ideas about travel. They emphasise the importance of the traveller's (subjective) impression, the panoramic view from the summit, and Spaniards' ignorance about Spain – topics discussed further below. Others focus more closely on the Castilian landscape. In 'Yuste', he notes that:

> 'Those who speak of Castile, León and Extremadura as if they were nothing more than bare uplands, denuded of trees and burnt by both sun and arid, sad frosts have only had a very partial glimpse of these lands from a train window. [...] In the heart of the sierras lie valleys whose beauty and verdant freshness exceeds that of the most famous locales of the Cantabrian seaboard. For myself, though, I prefer the mountainous landscapes of Castile and Extremadura. They are graver, more serious, rougher and less like picture postcards. And they are less profaned by tourism and by the banal admiration of summer visitors.'
>
> (OCE I, 267; OCA, I, 481).

This disdain for 'easy' landscape and travel is apparent also in 'Excursión' and in 'El sentimiento de la naturaleza' [The Feeling for Nature], where he insists that: '[Nature's] most intimate and collected language is not within everybody's grasp, nor will one succeed in penetrating its mysteries of love without putting in some work' (OCE I, 336; OCA, I, 589). He also makes an argument here that recurs in his early work on landscape and place: he asserts that the feeling for nature, which he defines as the intelligent, and also heartfelt love for the countryside, is 'one of the most refined products of civilisation and culture. The peasant also loves it, but he loves it instinctively, almost animalistically, and his love is an instrumental love' (OCE I, 336; OCA, I, 589).

Throughout the collection, the attention to landscape and place is accompanied by a no less intensely felt interest in their human inhabitants. The pieces on Portugal are suffused with arguments about the national character of the Portuguese; the same is true of the article 'Barcelona', in which Unamuno gives vent to some unflattering stereotyping of the city's inhabitants, and the Catalans more generally, painting them in a clichéd manner as mean, and as vain, preoccupied with appearance. He acknowledges Barcelona's magnificent facades, but also notes that typhus rages through the city because it lacks an adequate sewage system: all the effort is put into the visible surface; what lies below is neglected.

In addition to Spain and Portugal, a third country—Argentina—makes its presence felt in the pages of the collection, even though Unamuno never visited it: several articles had been published originally in the Buenos Aires press. Unamuno is attentive to his Argentinian readers, seeking to contextualise his writings on the geography and history in Spain in ways that might resonate with them. He is also deeply sensitive to how contemporaneous events in Spain were being represented internationally, most notably in relation to the aftermath of 'Tragic Week' in Barcelona in the summer of 1909:[5] 'El sentimiento de la naturaleza' opens with a splenetic attack on the way that Spain's reputation was, in Unamuno's eyes, being unjustly impugned in the wider world (OCE I, 335; OCA I, 588). His transition to the main theme of the article—the beautiful mysteries of nature—is rather jagged.

Eleven years after *Por tierras de Portugal y España*, Unamuno published *Andanzas y visiones españolas* (1922). Although it was not a popular success, the book's critical reception was positive. For García Mercadal, '[t]he landscape

---

[5]   A general strike in protest at military conscription for colonial war in Morocco had led to serious civil disturbance and violence in Barcelona and industrial towns in Catalonia. The anarchist writer and educationalist Francisco Ferrer was judged to be 'intellectual author' of the violence, and was executed by the state shortly after the disturbances, prompting protest across Europe and beyond.

as described by Unamuno is not just something experienced visually, but also something that lives in the present, and even more so, in the past. It is suggested, evoked, and is full of substance, like everything Unamuno writes. It is a thought-provoking, meditative landscape. His travel writing at times bears no small resemblance to philosophical works' (1922). Candela Ortells argued that that the volume contained descriptions of 'lands and towns, mountains and valleys populated by those unknown to the sort of tourist who feels only a [superficial] aesthetic curiosity for things, and does not consider what emanates from them and how this might benefit and console the beholder' (1922). For Unamuno's fellow writer Azorín, 'Unamuno's landscapes are suffused with spirituality. Indeed, they are barely landscapes; we scarcely see what the author aims to portray. We see instead the moral, often mystical corollary that the author draws out by using cities, woods and mountains as a prop' (cited in Unamuno 1988: 9).

The volume consists of thirty-one articles, ordered chronologically and written between June 1911 and March 1922. The majority were published either in the Argentinian newspaper *La Nación* or the Madrid-based periodical *El Imparcial*. In them he recounts his travels, his moments of contemplation of the landscape, and his inner feelings when in the company of friends, to whom he dedicated a number of articles. They were written, as Unamuno noted in the prologue, 'as I was making the excursions or seeing the sights I describe' (OCE I, 346; OCA I, 601).

As in *Por tierras de Portugal y de España*, the volume consists of articles which collect sketches of travels undertaken for holidays or trips taken to deliver public lectures or talks. They record the first impressions of the traveller, his personal feelings and the particular situation he found himself in, as well as his preferences for certain types of landscape. Some of the articles were written to supplement Unamuno's income: González Egido notes that the texts 'often flew from Unamuno's pen only a short time after the trip was taken. This allows us to follow the organic birth of his ideas, which are then developed 'oviparously' by the vital logic of the connotations and personal resonances awakened in him by his travels (1988: 11).

Andanzas explores the lands of León, Zamora, Ávila, Galicia, Salamanca, Mallorca, Extremadura and Portugal. It is also notable for including a collection of eight 'Rhythmic Visions', poems and prose-poems about urban and rural locales across Spain. There are clear continuities with previous collections: the countryside is presented as a liberation from the oppressive pace and volume of information, news and chatter of urban life ('De vuelta a la cumbre' [A Return to the Summit]; 'El silencio de la cima' [The Silence of the Summit]); it is free of the city's vanity and envy ('Ciudad, campo, paisajes y recuerdos' [City, Countryside, Landscapes and Memories]); in this sense, the summits which Unamuno seeks out in the countryside are sites from which he can contemplate – not just physically but also morally – on the urban landscape. As in previous collections too, his observations on travel and landscape are intertwined with reflections on literature, the eclectic references ranging some way beyond what might be expected (for example, Rosalía de Castro in pieces on Galicia) to include Flaubert, Senancour, Georges Sand, Milton, Thomas Gray and the English lake poets. Also mirroring previous travel writing is the deep historical consciousness that suffuses the description of landscape, architecture and local character in articles such as 'Hacia el Escorial', 'En el Escorial' [To/In the Escorial respectively] and 'Extramuros de Ávila' [Beyond the City Walls of Ávila].

In two notable respects, *Andanzas* does not just reproduce, but expands or intensifies tendencies and features of previous collections. For Unamuno, the contemplation of landscape had always been intimately caught up with meditation on the spiritual self. He argues in 'Paisaje teresiano' [Landscapes of Saint Teresa] that '[t]he visible universe is a metaphor for the invisible, the soul, even though it seems to us the other way round' (OCE I, 496; OCA I, 842). The 'rhythmic visions' presented in this collection embody this belief/argument: they may be seen as heightened versions of Unamuno's previous lyrical responses to landscape, and his tendency to fuse perception of landscape/cityscape both with intimately emotional autobiography and fervent national sentiment. They also evince Unamuno's dislike of closed generic categories or oppositions: half the 'visions' are laid out as poems; the other half are formatted as continuous prose, but employ a syntax or metre closer to poetry.

The brief 'visions' address loss, time past, death and religious feeling, most often in the form of melancholic or nostalgic apostrophe to place, as this extract from 'Al Nervión' [To the Nervión] (the river running through Bilbao) illustrates:

> Una vez más, Bilbao, sobre tu seno
> maternal descansando mi cabeza
> vuelvo a soñar la vida de esperanzas
> y ensueños juveniles
> que me conservas
> esas nubes que embozan las montañas
> seto de mi primera visión del mundo
> las nubes son en que atisbé visiones
> de allende el valle humano…
> ¿serán de lágrimas?
>
> Once more, Bilbao, my head resting
> In your maternal lap,
> I dream again of the life of hopes and

Childhood reveries that you conserve for me
Those clouds that shroud the mountains,
Horizon of my first vision of the world,
The clouds in which I first glimpsed visions
Of what might lie beyond the vale of humans
Are they made of tears?

(Unamuno 1988: 279)

The socio-political also has a more visible presence in *Andanzas* than in the previous collections. This is hardly surprising given that the period covered by the anthology comprised events of cataclysmic international importance such as the First World War and the Russian Revolution. Both these events played a part in growing discontent and unrest in Spain as war-related inflation, workers' rights and the question of political representation and power within the anachronistic Restoration monarchy became more acutely pressing. The political also encroached dramatically on Unamuno's professional life too during this period: he was removed from his rectorship at Salamanca in 1914 on the orders of the government for his criticisms of the Restoration monarchy. The great sense of escape and antidote that Unamuno found in the countryside, and on the rural summits he scaled, are understandable in this context: the city was associated with turmoil and disturbance far beyond mere metropolitan bustle. Although Unamuno does not write of this episode directly, the attraction of the summits referred to in 'De vuelta de la cumbre' and 'El silencio de la cima', for example, may in part have been the vantage point they offered for the contemplation of a country beyond and, for Unamuno, morally and spiritually above the immediate political landscape that he was having to negotiate at this time. This is certainly what is suggested in 'La España que permanece' [The Spain that Remains], an article published in 1923:

Oh, how nice it was to be there, on the steep summit of Gredos, the dorsal column of Castile, besides the crests which slice into the sky, more than two and a half thousand kilometres above sea level, watching the sun set – and what sunsets! – at our feet, far from these plazas where the rumour of political fights break the day! Oh, how nice to be there, storing sun and air and serenity and solitude! But one must come down, one must cross these plains and valleys in which one escapes the battle

(OCE I, 637; OCA I, 1012).

Unamuno does not write at length about international issues, but references to war are woven into 'Coimbra', 'De Salamanca a Barcelona' and 'En la calma de Mallorca' [In the Tranquillity of Mallorca]. The prominent references to French and British literature throughout the collection may also in part be a reflection of Unamuno's sympathies for the Allied powers' cause during this period.[6] There is mention of post-1914/post-1917 domestic upheaval in 'Frente a Ávila', 'En Palencia', and in 'Camino de Yuste', where he argues for the incompatibility of socialism and communism with rural society. 'En la frontera lingüística' [On the Linguistic Frontier] addresses the growing demands for greater autonomy and officially recognised cultural identity in Catalonia and Valencia; Unamuno's liberalism ensured his enduring hostility to forces he saw as fissiparous to the notion of *españolidad* (Spanish nationhood), and injurious to state-wide democracy. This wariness towards other forms of political belonging and organisation within the Spanish state is accompanied by a vigorous defence of Castile, and the values which, in Unamuno's eyes, it has represented through Spain's modern history in, for example, 'Hacia el Escorial', an earlier article pre-dating the war. When considered alongside the number of articles devoted to the region (twenty-two out of a total of thirty-one), *Andanzas y visiones españolas* is a Castile-centric collection in more ways than one.[7]

The socio-political content of the collection ranges wider than these contexts: the pre-war articles bear clear traces of Unamuno's engagement with Regenerationist/post-1898 thought: 'Por capitales de provincia' [In the Provincial Capitals] is a call for schoolteachers in the provinces to be in the vanguard of cultural activism and re-invigoration of Spain; and if Unamuno is a staunch advocate of political centralism/unionism, he here presents himself as a champion of cultural de-centralisation, calling for a revitalisation of culture from outside Madrid. In this article too, as elsewhere in the collection, Unamuno uses his famous formulation 'me duele España' [Spain hurts me].[8] The phrase neatly encapsulates two of Unamuno's most enduring preoccupations: his country and individual subjectivity/consciousness.

Andanzas y visiones españolas also contains an account of Unamuno's 1913 visit to Las Hurdes, one of the most abjectly poor and isolated rural areas of western Spain, and an area probably most familiar to contemporary readers though Buñuel's 1933 documentary *Tierra sin pan* [Land without Bread]. He was accompanied by the distinguished French Hispanist Maurice Legendre, who would go on to study Las Hurdes in depth and advocate for greater state aid to alleviate its natural and infrastructural problems. Unamuno's article is concerned to praise the heroism and dignity of the inhabitants of the region; in

---

6   A selection of articles written by Unamuno about the First World War, accompanied by a useful contextualising introduction by Christopher Cobb, is found in Unamuno (1976).

7   For an at times polemically hostile, but worthwhile reading of Unamuno's representation of Castilian landscape, see Resina (2000).

8   Translator's note: the translation does not adequately capture the emotional force of the phrase, which implies that Spain is so much a part of the author that it pains him in the way that a body part or limb might hurt.

contrast to some commentators who had described Las Hurdes as shaming Spain, Unamuno argues that the stoicism and dogged persistence of the inhabitants to make a living from its inhospitable lands *honoured* the country. There is no doubting the sincerity of Unamuno's praise for the Hurdanos, but his apparent downplaying of the political aspects of their plight—the extreme unevenness of development and infrastructural modernisation within the country; the fiscal weakness of the state and its resultant inability to alleviate pockets of appalling poverty—can make for slightly uncomfortable reading today. Unamuno presents the Hurdanos as stubbornly attached to their poor, unproductive lands in the way that one might be attached to a sick child, and, referring to the infected waters of the region (a source of malaria to the Hurdanos), Unamuno points out that completely pure water is also undrinkable and unhealthy—a well-intentioned point, to be sure, but also one that might strike the contemporary reader as slightly jarring in the circumstances.

Unamuno the pilgrim; the Place of the Summit

As suggested above, for Unamuno, a journey often prompted a kind of diary-writing or autobiography, in which he mused on his public lectures and speeches, or on matters as diverse as his friendships, fears and uncertainties: the account of the journey, then, reflected also the man and the citizen. In the travel writing that was published outside Spain (for example in Buenos Aires in *La Nación*), the accounts of his excursions serve both as physical itinerary and spiritual guide, projecting an image of Spain and of himself to his foreign readers. Unamuno was conscious of the work he was carrying out when travelling: he was a keen hill-climber, rambling in order to discover the *patria* in its entirety and to forge a different view of it; he was also a pilgrim, travelling in order to explore both his own soul and the soul of Spain through its lesser-known areas and inhabitants.

On obtaining the Chair of Greek at its ancient university in 1891, Salamanca became the starting point for the journeys he undertook to get to know the physical terrain of Spain. His having visited more than three hundred Spanish locations – cities, towns and villages, lakes and valleys – and 'thirty of the forty-nine provincial capitals and many more cities' (OCE I, 435; OCA I, 742), is proof of his zeal for travel. According to Cardis (1951: 12–13), we can speak of three broad 'series' of journeys in Unamuno's work. The first series is represented mostly in early writings, and is focused on the Basque Country. It gives rise to writing that focuses on 'sensory assimilation' – spontaneous impressions, without contextualising background. The second series concerns travel within Galicia and Portugal; Spain as problem is the focus of the third series. Writing in this series is centred on Castile until Unamuno's exile (1924–1930) and on Castile, Catalonia and the Levante after his return in 1930.

Many of his travels were prompted by his work as an intellectual, and the destinations tended to be urban: every city wanted to host this fearless public figure who confronted dictators, kings and republics. The professional reasons for his urban journeys, however, did not mean that travel became a humdrum experience for him: he prepared carefully for his trips, consulting local histories, reading the writers and poets native to a place, and studying its characteristic monuments and sites. He thus composed a kind of 'guide' to his destination, and added to it during his visit, making use of conventional tourist guides when suitable, the press and popular pamphlets etc. But Unamuno also needed direct contact with ordinary, anonymous inhabitants, 'the little historians' of a place, those who knew its myriad irrelevant anecdotes. Unamuno did not limit himself to visiting tourist destinations, and tried to rewrite understandings of the places he visited.

Although it is evident that it was the countryside and the mountains that gave him most satisfaction, urban travel allowed Unamuno to make official contact with cultural associations, be hosted at banquets where he was the guest of honour, and gave him the chance to explore the towns and villages of the provinces that he visited. Travel, then, served various purposes: it was a means of escape, a way of discovering new places, a source of income and a way to make himself better known. Unamuno also famously hungered for immortality, and travel offered a form of enduring (after)life: whether in the local press which commemorated his visit, in the reception to speeches or public lectures he gave during his visits, or in his articles published in the local and national press. Travel offered a magnificent way of being present not just across geography but also time.

Coexisting with the urban sojourner was the pilgrim traveller, whose constant preoccupation was the search for the spirit and soul of Spain in its countryside and mountains. He travelled slowly, at the pace and in the fashion of the traditional pilgrim. During such trips, learning and creation were conjoined: a place visited, experienced and contemplated was the starting point of the literary creation: the external journey led to an internal journey, a path towards perfection.[9]

The intimately emotional and spiritual aspects of travel as pilgrimage are also considered by Unamuno in their literary, social and historical dimensions. When reflecting on the conditions which had given rise to Spaniards' ignorance about their own country, he attributed it in part to the lack of sufficiently good writers who had portrayed different areas of the country in their fictional writings, so leading to a lack of 'artistic pilgrimages'. This lack meant that it was difficult for Spaniards to get to love the *patria* consciously if they did not

---

[9]   The reference is to St. Teresa of Avila's reflections on spiritual progress in *Camino de perfección*.

know its diverse landscapes or people, and if they did not traverse the country, even if only in travel books:

> '[O]ur landscapes [...] remain raw, primary materials for pleasure and for spiritual solace because of the lack of travellers who might refine it through their vision with artistic descriptions. There is no doubt that much of the beauty of a landscape is in the eye of the beholder, and educated people who look at it take much more substance from its beauty than those uneducated'
> (OCE I, 617).[10]

For Unamuno, then, the population must be taught to *read* a landscape, and writers had a key role to pay in this educational process.

For Unamuno, inadequate transport infrastructure and uneven modernisation also contributed to Spaniards' ignorance of their country. Spain's railway system was highly radial, centring on Madrid, and a limited number of trunk roads exacerbated the unevenness of development:

> '[i]t has been the major routes which have abolished distance, and, with it, the restful enjoyment of restrained, contemplative journeying. This in turn has isolated certain regions, until they have effectively been returned to the wild'
> (OCE I, 479; OCA I, 814).

Excessive love of comfort was a further cause of Spaniards' ignorance about their country: in Unamuno's analysis, the tourist – target of the pre-fabricated advice and recommendations of the *Baedeker* guides, whose presence had given rise to 'annoying tourist guides, innkeepers and sellers of curios' (OCE I, 627; OCA I, 1001) – was the enemy of travel, interested only in consuming spectacles, or sampling different cuisines, or travelling for the sake of it—what Unamuno called 'topophobia'. The tourist differed from the Unamunian traveller essentially in the different importance each granted to the path travelled: while for the gastronome, the culture seeker or the topophobe the journey was a means to an end, the Unamunian traveller was attentive to the journey itself. Unamuno favoured the discomfort of the long hike, of home-cooked rather than restaurant food, and of natural spring water – everything tourists normally detested, worried as they were more about comfort than the experience of travel itself: 'these poor people will never know the world' (OCE I, 283; OCA I, 507).

The regeneration of the spirit and the fresh perspective that the summit provided for Unamuno's visions and thoughts made it one of his favourite terrains, and it was in his writings on mountains and summits that he developed

---

10   This article is not collected in the Aguilar *Obras completas*.

most fully his concept of travel as pilgrimage. The summit acted as a form of palingenesis, and offered the best place to be most sincere—both with his readers and with himself. It allowed a series of visions to be experienced, and the fatigue – understood as suffering – along with the repose which follows it, permitted him to achieve a state of peaceful contemplation and meditation, an adequate reward for his efforts.

Of course the mountain was one of the symbols which best served to represent the romantic soul: Rousseau, Chateaubriand and Senancour all made use of it as such in various ways, but it is Senancour's vision that is closest to Unamuno's. Both writers mystified the mountain peak, and saw it as the ideal site for the resolving of crises: the ascent to the summit was a way of conquering the mountain which dwarfed man and forced him to live in its shadow. From the summit, 'everything looks like a map, lying humbly at our feet' (OCE I, 284; OCA I, 509). And it was the summit which most clearly revealed the nuanced exchange between the state of the soul and the state of the landscape: it was not possible to hide when high up:

> There, alone with the mountain, the summits of my soul came back into view, and the plains at my feet allowed me to see the depths of my spirit. And it was necessarily an examination of conscience. The sun of the summit illuminated the most hidden folds of my heart. It had risen, furthermore, alongside a restrained anguish, a piercing preoccupation that had its origin in concerns about my family; above my hopes as a father hung a wisp of cloud that my apprehension turned into a thick mass of cloud
>
> (OCE I, 356; OCA I, 616–7).

At times, such illumination and transparency cast uncomfortable light on Unamuno's conscience and will: 'There, on the peak, shrouded by silence, I dreamt about everything that I could have been, but was not, in order to be what I am now: I dreamt of all the possibilities that I let slip' (OCE I, 357; OCA I, 618). As well as regarding the mountain as a site allowing better knowledge of oneself, Unamuno was interested also in acquiring 'scientific' knowledge of it also, and would pore over maps to understand the features of the terrain he was exploring, consulting books on botany, geography and biology, and making his ascents in the company of local experts—guides and shepherds.

As this chapter has attempted to demonstrate, Unamuno's travels, and his various travel writings served varied purposes at different times: therapeutic physical exercise; spiritual contemplation and self-examination; social or political analysis and also escape from the hurly-burly of politics and his growing fame in society; direct contact with a range of landscapes and people of Spain and Portugal as well as connection with an Argentinian readership. In addition to the writings published in the four volumes that appeared during his lifetime, Unamuno wrote many more articles on travel. Although some were subsequently collected in the *Obras completas*, more remain uncollected, and there is work to be done both in analysing his travel writing as a whole, and in focusing further on particular aspects, such as his travels and reflection on landscape while in exile. Research that engages with recent theorising of travel writing would also be a very welcome addition to Unamuno scholarship.

Further Reading

González Egido (1988), Llorens García (1986), Ouimette (1994).

Bibliography

Álvarez Castro, Luis. 2005. *La palabra y el ser en la teoría literaria de Unamuno.* Salamanca: Ediciones Universidad de Salamanca.

Alvarez Junco, José and Adrian Shubert (eds.). 2000. *Spanish History since 1808.* London: Arnold.

Andrews, Jean, and Stephen G.H. Roberts (eds.). 2009. *Obra en marcha. Ensayos en honor de Richard A. Cardwell.* Nottingham: Critical, Cultural and Communications Press.

Arranz, Luis. Mercedes Cabrera and Fernando del Rey. 'The Assault on Liberalism'. In Alvarez Junco and Shubert 2000: 191–206.

Ardila, J.A.G. 2008. 'Nueva lectura de *Niebla*: Kierkegaard y el amor', *Revista de Literatura* 70: 83–115.

——. 2010. 'Unamuno y Cervantes: narradores y narración en *Niebla*', *Modern Language Notes* 135: 348–368.

——. 2015. *La construcción modernista de Niebla.* Barcelona: Anthropos.

Azaola, José Miguel de. 1996. *Unamuno y sus guerras civiles.* Bilbao: Ediciones Laga.

Azorín (José Martínez Ruiz). 1961. *La generación del 98.* Salamanca: Anaya.

——. 1984. *La ruta de Don Quijote* [1905]. Madrid: Cátedra.

——. 1998. *Obras escogidas, II. Ensayos.* Coord. M.A. Lozano. Madrid: Espasa.

——. 1941. 'Unamuno', *Unidad.* 31 dic. n.p.

Bacarisse, Pamela. 1991. 'Will the Story Tell? Unamuno's *San Manuel Bueno, mártir*', in Bacarisse 1991: 55–72.

——. (ed.). 1991. *Carnal Knowledge: Essays on the Flesh, Sex and Sexuality in Hispanic Letters and Film.* Pittsburgh: Ediciones Tres Ríos.

Barea, Arturo. 1952. *Unamuno.* Cambridge: Bowes & Bowes.

Batchelor, R.E. 1972a. *Unamuno, Novelist: a European Perspective.* Oxford: Dolphin Books.

——. 1972b. 'Form and Content in Unamuno's *Niebla*', *Forum for Modern Language Studies* VIII (3): 197–214.

Bazán, Armando. *Unamuno y el marxismo.* 1935. Madrid: Imprenta de Juan Pueyo.

Bennett, Simon and Rachel B. Blass (eds.). 1991. 'The Development and Vicissitudes of Freud's Ideas on the Oedipus Complex' in Neu 1991: 161–74.

Bermúdez-Cañete Fernández, Federico. 1976. 'Giner de los Ríos y la Generación del 98'. *Cuadernos Hispanoamericanos* 317: 414–424.

Biggane, Julia. 2000. 'Yet Another Other: Unamuno's *El otro* and the Anxiety for Influence'. *Bulletin of Spanish Studies* 77: 479–91.

——. 2009. '*Cómo se hace una novela*: Confession, Abjection, Religious Economy'. *Modern Language Review*, 104 (4): 1018–1037.

——. 2013. 'La agonía de Don Juan: exilio, política y género en *El hermano Juan, o el mundo es teatro*', *Anthropos* 238: 205–24.

Bioy Casares, Adolfo (ed.). 1977. *Antología de la literatura fantástica*. Barcelona: Edhasa.

Blanco Aguinaga, Carlos. 1954. *Unamuno, teórico del lenguaje*. Mexico DF: Colegio de México.

——. 1964a. 'Unamuno's *Niebla*: Existence and the Game of Fiction'. *MLN* 79: 188–204.

——. 1964b. 'Aspectos dialécticos de las *Tres novelas ejemplares*', *Revista de Occidente* 19 (2ª época, Año II): 51–70.

——. 1974. 'Sobre la complejidad de *San Manuel Bueno, mártir*', in Sánchez Barbudo 1974: 273–296.

——. 1975. *El Unamuno contemplativo*. Barcelona: Laia.

——. 1978. *Juventud del 98*. Barcelona: Editorial Crítica.

Blanco Aguinaga, Carlos, Julio Rodríguez Puértolas and Iris M. Zavala. 1979. *Historia Social de la Literatura Española*. Madrid: Castalia.

Blanco Aguinaga, Carlos. 1981. 'Relectura de San Manuel Bueno, mártir—para Sánchez Barbudo', in Brancaforte 1981: 109–115.

Blasco, Javier. 2009. 'La *Vida de Don Quijote y Sancho* o lo que habría ocurrido "si don Quijote hubiese en tiempo de Miguel de Unamuno vuelto al mundo"'. In Andrews and Roberts 2009: 77–97.

Bolaño, Roberto. 1997. *Llamadas telefónicas*. Barcelona: Anagrama.

Borzoni, S. and A. Marocco. (ed). 2008. *Añorando a Miguel de Unamuno 1936–2006*. Morolo: If-Press.

Borzoni, Sandro. 2009. 'Fajismo y fascismos. Miguel de Unamuno frente a las ideologías totalitarias en la década de los 30'. PhD thesis. Universidad de Salamanca.

——. 2012. 'Il falso vangelo pragmatista di Miguel de Unamuno', in Pozzoni 2012: 135–156.

Bradbury, Malcolm and James McFarlane (eds.). *Modernism: a Guide to European Literature 1890–1930*. Harmondsworth: Penguin.

Brancaforte, Benito, Edward R. Mulvihill and Roberto G. Sánchez (eds.). 1981. *Homenaje a Sánchez Barbudo: ensayos de literatura española moderna*. Madison: University of Wisconsin.

Bretz, Mary Lee. 1993. 'The Role of Negativity in Unamuno's *La tía Tula*', *Revista Canadiense de Estudios Hispánicos* XVIII (1): 17–29.

——. 2001. *Encounters Across Borders: the Changing Visions of Spanish Modernism, 1890–1930*. Lewisburg: Bucknell University Press.

Brewer, Derek. 1980. *Symbolic Stories*. Woodbridge: Brewer.

Browning, Robert. 2009. *The Major Works*, ed. Adam Roberts. Oxford: OUP.

Butt, John. 1981. *Miguel de Unamuno: San Manuel Bueno, mártir*. Critical Guides to Spanish Texts. London: Grant & Cutler/Tamesis.

Calzada, Jerónimo de la. 1952. 'Unamuno paisajista', *Cuadernos de la Cátedra Miguel de Unamuno* 3: 55–80.

Campos Marín, Ricardo, José Martínez Pérez and Rafael Huertas-Alejo. 2000. *Los ilegales de la naturaleza: Medicina y degeneracionismo en la España de la Restauración (1876–1973)*. Madrid: CSIC.

Candela Ortells, Vicente, 1922. 'Recensión de *Andanzas y visiones españolas*', *El Mercantil Valenciano*, 16 octubre.

Cánovas del Castillo, Antonio. 1997. *Discurso sobre la nación* [1882]. Introducción de Andrés de Blas. Madrid: Biblioteca Nueva.

Cardis, Marianne. 1951. 'El paisaje en la vida y obra de Miguel de Unamuno'. Unpublished PhD thesis. University of Leeds.

——. 1953. 'El paisaje en la vida y en la obra de Miguel de Unamuno: Castilla y lo intelectivo', *Cuadernos de la Cátedra Miguel de Unamuno* 4: 71–83.

Carducci, G. 1902. *Poesie di Giosué Carducci (1850–1900)*. Bologna: Zanichelli.

Cardwell, Richard. 1988. 'Modernismo frente a noventayocho. El caso de las andanzas de Unamuno', *Anales de Literatura Española* 6: 87–107.

Casanova, Julián and Paul Preston (eds.). 2008. *La guerra civil española*. Madrid: Pablo Iglesias.

Cascardi, Anthony. 2005–6. "'Comi-tragedia' in Cervantes: *Don Quixote* and the Genealogy of the 'Funny Book'", *CIEFL Bulletin* 15–16: 19–37.

Cerezo Galán, Pedro, 1996. *Las máscaras de lo trágico. Filosofía y tragedia en Miguel de Unamuno*. Madrid: Trotta.

——. 2003. *El mal del siglo: el conflicto entre Ilustración y Romanticismo en la crisis finisecular del siglo XIX*. Madrid: Biblioteca Nueva.

Cervantes, Miguel de. 2005. *El ingenioso hidalgo don Quijote de la Mancha* [1605]. Madrid: Espasa-Calpe.

Chaguaceda Toledano, Ana (ed.). 2005. *Miguel de Unamuno: estudios sobre su obra*. Salamanca: Ediciones Universidad de Salamanca.

Chicharro de León, J. 1941. 'Unamuno', *Unidad*. 31 dic.

——. 1956. 'El sentimiento de la naturaleza unamuniana', *Quaderni Ibero-americani* III (18): 122–127.

Cifo González, Manuel. 2005. '*Amor y pedagogía* o el problema de la educación visto por Miguel de Unamuno' in Chaguaceda Toledano 2005: 329–48.

Close, Anthony J. 1978. *The Romantic Approach to* Don Quixote. *A Critical History of the Romantic Tradition in* Quixote *Criticism*. Cambridge: Cambridge University Press.

——. 2000. *Cervantes and the Comic Mind of his Age*. Oxford: Oxford University Press.

——. 2008. *A Companion to Don Quixote*. Woodbridge: Tamesis.

Collins, Marsha S. 2002. 'Orfeo and the Cratyline Conspiracy in Unamuno's *Niebla*', *Bulletin of Spanish Studies* LXXIX: 285–306.

Comín Colomer, Eduardo. 1968. *Unamuno, libelista. Sus campañas contra Alfonso XIII y la Dictadura*. Madrid: Colección Siglo Ilustrado.

Conde Gargollo, E. 1964. 'Unamuno, viajero', *Extremadura*. 15 de julio.

Craig, Edward. 1998. *Routledge Encyclopaedia of Philosophy*. London: Routledge. Electronic resource: http://www.rep.routledge.com/article/N020SECT1. Accessed January 10, 2012.

Davies, Catherine. 1998. *Spanish Women's Writing 1849–1996*. London: Athlone Press.

Díaz, Elías. 1968. *Revisión de Unamuno: análisis crítico de su pensamiento político*. Madrid: Tecnos.

Di Febo, G. 1988. *La santa de la raza*. Barcelona: Icaria.

Doménech, Ricardo. 1998. 'Buero Vallejo y el camino de la tragedia', in Leyra 1998: 109–18.

Douglas, M. 1966. *Purity and Danger: an Analysis of the Concepts of Taboo*. New York: Praeger.

Doyaga, Emilia, 1967. *La mujer en los ensayos de Unamuno*, unpublished PhD thesis. New York University.

Echavarri, Luis. 1928. 'El sentimiento de la naturaleza en Unamuno', *La Nación*. 27 de mayo.

Ereño Altuna, José Antonio. 2002. 'Un texto inédito de Miguel de Unamuno y Jugo: 'Los arribes del Duero' (1898), *Cuaderno Gris* 6: 117–128.

Escobar Borrego, Federico Javier. 2003. 'El concepto de intrahistoria como praxis periodística en *Andanzas y visiones españolas*, de Miguel de Unamuno', *Anuario de Estudios Filológicos* XXVI: 103–116.

Evans, Jan E. 2005. *Unamuno and Kierkegaard: Paths to Selfhood in Fiction*. Lexington MD: Lexington Books.

Fagoaga, Concha. 1985. *La voz y el voto de mujeres. El sufragismo en España 1877–1931*. Barcelona: Icaria.

Ferrater Mora, José. 1985. *Bosquejo de una filosofía* [1944]. Madrid: Alianza editorial.

Filer, Malva, Dominick Finello and William Sherzer (eds.). 2004. *A Celebration of Brooklyn Hispanism*. Newark: Juan de la Cuesta.

Fox, Arturo A. 1991. 'Lo imaginario en Unamuno. El caso de *El otro*', *Revista canadiense de estudios hispánicos* 16: 61–72.

———. 2001. *El edipo en Unamuno y el espejo de Lacan*. Lewiston; Lampeter: Edwin Mellen Press.

Franco, Andrés. 1971. *El teatro de Unamuno*. Madrid: Insula.

Franz, Thomas. 2003. *Niebla inexplorada: midiendo intersticios en el maravilloso texto de Unamuno*. Newark: Juan de la Cuesta.

———. 2007. '*Niebla* y el *Quijote* (otra vez)', *Cuadernos de la Cátedra Miguel de Unamuno* 44. 13–26.

Frénal, Simone. 1955. 'Recherches sur le style de Miguel de Unamuno dans les descriptions du paysage'. Unpublished PhD thesis. Universidad de París.

Friedman, Edward H. 2006. *Cervantes in the Middle. Realism and Reality in the Spanish Novel from Lazarillo de Tormes to Niebla*. Newark: Juan de la Cuesta.

Freud, Sigmund. 1991. 'The Instincts and their Vicissitudes' [1915], in *On Metapsychology: The Theory of Psychoanalysis*. The Penguin Freud Library. Vol. 11. Ed. A. Richards. Harmondsworth: Penguin Books. 13–38.

Gabe Coleman, Dorothy and Gillian Jondorf (eds.). 1987. *Words of Power: Essays in Honour of Alison Fairlie*. Glasgow: University of Glasgow.

Gagen, Derek. 1989. 'Unamuno and the Regeneration of the Spanish Theatre', in Round 1989: 53–79.

García Blanco, Manuel. 1964. 'Unamuno y el profesor francés Jacques Chevalier', *Revista de la Universidad de Madrid*, XIII [número homenaje a Unamuno]: 7–76.

García Lorca, Federico. 2008. *Four Major Plays*. Trans. John Edmunds. New York: OUP.

García Mercadal, José. 1922. Reseña de *Andanzas y visiones españolas*, *Información*: 14 de julio.

Gómez Mendoza, Josefina, *et al*. 1988. *Viajeros y paisajes*, Madrid: Alianza.

García Morejón, Julio. 1971. *Unamuno y Portugal*. Madrid: Gredos.

Gómez Molleda, María Dolores. 1966. *Los reformadores de la España Contemporánea*. Madrid: CSIC.

———. 1978. *Unamuno socialista. Páginas inéditas de d. Miguel*. Madrid: Nercea.

———. 1989. *Actas del Congreso Cincuentenario de Unamuno, Universidad de Salamanca 10–20 diciembre 1986*. Salamanca: Universidad de Salamanca.

García de la Concha, Víctor. (Dir.) 1998. *Historia de la Literatura Española*. Madrid: Espasa Calpe.

Gibson, Ian. 1998. *Federico García Lorca*. 2 vols. Barcelona: Crítica.

Gilmore, David D. 1987. *Aggression and Community: Paradoxes of Andalusian Culture.* New Haven: Yale University Press.

González Egido, Luciano. 1988. 'Introducción', in Unamuno 1988: 7–46.

Guignon, C.B. 1998. 'Existentialism', in Craig 1998: n.p.

Gullón, Ricardo, 1964. *Autobiografías de Unamuno.* Madrid: Gredos.

——. 1965. 'Imágenes del otro', *Revista Hispánica Moderna* 31: 210–21.

——. 1987. 'Introducción'. In Unamuno 1987: i-xviii.

Gordon, M. 1986. 'The Elusive Self: Narrative Method and its Implications in *San Manuel Bueno, mártir*', *Hispanic Review*. 54. 147–161.

Guereña, J-L and Mónica Zapata (eds.), *Censure et manipulations dans les mondes ibérique et latino-américain.* Tours: Presses Universitaires François-Rabelais.

Hannay, A. and G.D. Marino. 1998. *The Cambridge Companion to Kierkegaard.* Cambridge: Cambridge University Press.

Harrison, Joseph and Alan Hoyle. 1998. *Spain's 1898 crisis.* Manchester: Manchester University Press.

Hegel, G.W. 1952. *Hegel's Philosophy of Right* [1820], trans. T.M. Knox. Oxford: Clarendon.

Heil, Katrina M. 2009. '*La esfinge*: Unamuno's Tragic Sense on the Stage', *Anales de la literatura española contemporánea* 34: 479–504.

House Webber, Ruth. 1964. 'Kierkegaard and the Elaboration of Unamuno's *Niebla*', *Hispanic Review* 32: 118–34.

Howells, C. 1988. *Sartre: The Necessity of Freedom.* Cambridge: Cambridge University Press.

Hudson, Ofelia M. 1991. *Unamuno y Byron: la agonía de Caín.* Madrid: Pliegos.

Huertas García-Alejo, Rafael. 1987. 'Psiquiatría forense', in Huertas García-Alejo et al 1987: 161–176.

Huertas García-Alejo, Rafael, Ana L. Romero and Raquel Alvarez. 1987. Eds. *Perspectivas psiquiátricas.* Madrid: CSIC.

Ilie, Paul. 1961. 'Unamuno, Gorky, and the Cain Myth: Toward a Theory of Personality', *Hispanic Review* 29: 310–23.

——. 1987. 'Language and Cognition in Unamuno', *Revista Canadiense de Estudios Hispánicos* 11: 289–314.

Inman Fox, E. 1976. *La crisis intelectual del 98.* Madrid: Cuadernos para el diálogo.

Jacobson, Stephen, and Javier Moreno Luzón. 'The Political System of the Restoration, 1875–1914'. In Alvarez Junco and Shubert 2000: 111–120.

Johnson, Roberta, 1989. 'El problema del conocimiento en Unamuno y la composición de *Niebla*', in Neumeister 1989: 303–8.

——. 1993. *Crossfire: Philosophy and the Novel in Spain 1900–1934.* Lexington, Ky.: University Press of Kentucky.

——. 2003. *Gender and Nation in the Spanish Modernist Novel.* Nashville: Vanderbilt U.P.

Juaristi, Jon. 1987. *El linaje de Aitor. La invención de la tradición vasca.* Madrid: Taurus.

——. 2007. *La caza salvaje.* Barcelona: Planeta.

——. 2012. *Miguel de Unamuno.* Madrid: Taurus.

Jurkevich, Gayana. 1990. 'Archetypal Motifs of the Double in Unamuno's *Abel Sánchez*', *Hispania* 73: 345–52.

Kierkegaard, Søren. 1968. *Concluding Unscientific Postscript* [1846]. Trans. David F. Swenson and Walter Lowrie. Princeton: Princeton University Press.

——. 1987. *Either/Or* [1843]. Princeton: Princeton University Press.

King, Willard F.1967. 'Unamuno, Cervantes y *Niebla*', *Revista de Occidente* 47: 219–231.

Labanyi, Jo. 2010. *Spanish Literature: a Very Short Introduction*. Oxford: OUP.

Lacan, Jacques. 1977. Écrits: *A Selection*. Trans. Alan Sheridan. London: Routledge.

Laertius, Diogenes. 1925. *Lives of the Eminent Philosophers*. Trans. R.D. Hicks. London: Heinemann. 2 vols.

Lannon, Frances. 1987. *Privilege, Persecution, and Prophecy: the Catholic Church in Spain 1975–1975*. Oxford: Clarendon Press, 1987.

Larraín, Sergio Fernández (ed.). 1965. *Cartas inéditas de Miguel de Unamuno*. Santiago de Chile: Zig-Zag.

Lee, Dorothy H. 1979. 'Joaquín Monegro in Unamuno's *Abel Sánchez* Thrice Exile – Cain/Esau/Satan', *Journal of Spanish Studies: Twentieth Century* 7: 63–71.

Leyra, Ana María (ed.). 1998. *Antonio Buero Vallejo: Literatura y filosofía*. Madrid: Editorial Complutense.

Livingstone, Leon, 1967. 'The Novel as Self-Criticism'. In Rubia Barcia and Zeitlin 1967: 92–115.

Llorens García, Ramón F. 1986. 'Azorín y Unamuno: teoría y práctica del viaje", *Anales Azorinianos* 3: 265–273.

——. 1992. *Los libros de viajes de Miguel de Unamuno*. Alicante: CAP.

Longhurst, C.A. 1981. 'The Problem of Truth in "San Manuel Bueno, Mártir", *Modern Language Review* 76 (3): 581–597.

——. 1989. 'Para una interpretación de *La tía Tula*', in Gómez Molleda 1989: 143–152.

——. 2009. 'Unamuno y su problemática visión de la familia ibérica', *Revista de Lenguas y Literaturas Catalana, Gallega y Vasca* (UNED) XIV: 343–353.

——. 2011. 'Unamuno, Schleiermacher, Humboldt: A Question of Language', *Hispanic Review* 79 (4): 573–591.

——. 2014. *Unamuno's Theory of the Novel*. Oxford: Legenda.

Lopez-Morillas, Juan. 1981. *The Krausist Movement and Ideological Change in Spain, 1854–1874*. Cambridge; New York: Cambridge University Press.

Luby, Barry J. 2008. *The Uncertainty in Twentieth- and Twenty-first Century Analytic Thought: Miguel de Unamuno the Precursor*. Newark: Juan de la Cuesta.

Machado, Antonio. 1989. *Campos de Castilla* [1912]. Ed. Geoffrey Ribbans. Madrid: Cátedra.

Macklin, John. 1993. 'Competing Voices: Unamuno's *Niebla* and the Discourse of Modernism'. In Macklin 1993: 167–190.

——. (ed.). 1993. *After Cervantes: A Celebration of 75 years of Iberian Studies at Leeds*. Leeds: Trinity and All Saints College.

——. 1999. 'Introduction', in Unamuno 1999: 1–18.

Magnus, B. and K. Higgins. 1996. *The Cambridge Companion to Nietzsche*. Cambridge: Cambridge University Press.

Malefakis, Edward. 1970. *Agrarian Reform and Peasant Revolution in Spain: Origins of the Civil War*. New Haven: Yale UP.

Marbán, Jorge. 1976. 'Unamuno y Lord Byron: dos tratamientos distintos de un tema bíblico', *South Atlantic Bulletin* 41: 34–42.

Marías, Julián. 1966. *Miguel de Unamuno*. Trans. Frances M. López Morillas. Cambridge MA.: Harvard University Press.

Martín, Rebeca. 2007. '«El que se enterró», germen de *El otro*, o el misterio del doble en Miguel de Unamuno', *Cuadernos de la Cátedra Miguel de Unamuno* 44: 113–24.

Martín Gaite, Carmen. 1978. *El cuarto de atrás*. Barcelona: Destino.

——. 1987. *Usos amorosos de la postguerra española*. Barcelona: Anagrama.

Martínez Cachero, José María. 1984. 'Introducción' in Azorín 1984: 13–71.

Martínez Nadal, Rafael (ed.). 2001. *Miguel de Unamuno y José María Quiroga Pla. Un epistolario y diez 'Hojas Libres'*. Madrid: Editorial Casariego.

McFarlane, James. 1991. 'The Mind of Modernism'. In Bradbury and McFarlane 1991: 71–93.

Mermall, Thomas. 1990. 'The Chiasmus: Unamuno's Master Trope', *PMLA*. 105 (2): 245–255.

——. 1993. '*En torno al casticismo* and Unamuno's Rhetorical Revolution', *Anales de la Literatura Española* 18(2): 281–94.

Minter, Gordon. 1998. '*Amor y pedagogía*: an object lesson in biography', in Harrison and Hoyle 1998: 81–90.

Mitchell, Timothy. 1988. *Violence and Piety in Spanish Folklore*. Philadelphia: University of Pennsylvania Press.

Molas, Joaquim *et al.* (eds.). 2000. *1898: Entre la crisi d'identitat i la modernització*. Montserrat: Publicacions de l'Abadia de Montserrat.

Moreau, Joseph. 1956. 'Miguel de Unamuno ou le paysage et l'ame espagnole', *Bulletin de l'Association Guillaume Budé*, XV (4): 122–138.

Morón Arroyo, Ciriaco. 1966. '*Niebla* en la evolución temática de Unamuno', *MLN* 81: 143–58.

Müller, Max. 2002. *The Essential Max Müller. On Language, Mythology and Religion*. Ed. Jon R. Stone. New York: Palgrave Macmillan.

Navajas, Gonzalo. 1985. 'The Self and the Symbolic in Unamuno's *La tía Tula*', *Revista de Estudios Hispánicos* 19: 117–137.

Navarro, Alberto. 2005. 'Introducción'. In Unamuno 2005d: 13–129.

Neu, Jerome. (ed.) 1991. *The Cambridge Companion to Freud*. Cambridge: Cambridge University Press.

Neumeister, Sebastian (ed.) 1989. *Actas del IX Congreso Internacional de Hispanistas*. Frankfurt-am-Main: Vervuert.

Nozick, Martin. 1971. *Miguel de Unamuno*. Boston: Twayne.

Olson, Paul. 1984. *Unamuno: 'Niebla'*. Critical Guides to Spanish Texts. London: Grant and Cutler.

——. 2003. *The Great Chiasmus: Word and Flesh in the Novels of Unamuno*. West Lafayette, Ind.: Purdue University Press.

Orringer, Nelson. 1986. 'Civil War Within: The Clash Between Sources of Unamuno's *Abel Sánchez*', *Anales de la literatura española contemporánea* 11: 295–318.

Ortega Cantero, Nicolás. 1988. 'La experiencia viajera en la Institución Libre de Enseñanza', in Gómez Mendoza et al. 1988: 67–88.

Ortega y Gasset, José. 1983. *Obras completas*. 12 vols. Madrid: Alianza/Revista de Occidente.

Ouimette, Victor. 1974. *Reason Aflame: Unamuno and the Heroic Will*. New Haven: Yale University Press.

——.1976. 'Unamuno, Blasco Ibáñez and *España con Honra*', *Bulletin of Hispanic Studies* LIII: 315–22.

——.1977. 'Unamuno and *Le Quotidien*', *Revista canadiense de estudios hispánicos* 2 (1): 72–82.

——.1983. 'El destierro de Unamuno y el ataque a la inteligencia', *Cuadernos de la Cátedra Miguel de Unamuno* XXVII-XXVIII: 25–41.

——. 1987. 'Paz en la guerra y los límites de la ideología', Revista canadiense de estudios hispánicos 11: 355–76.

——. 1994. 'Los libros de viajes de Miguel de Unamuno', Hispanic Review. Summer 62 (3): 434–435.

——. 1998. Los intelectuales españoles y el naufragio del liberalismo (1923–1936), 2 vols. Valencia: Pre-Textos.

Pascal, Blaise. 1952. The Provincial Letters, Pensées, Scientific Treatises. Trans. Thomas M'Crie, W.F. Trotter and Richard Scofield. Chicago: William Benton.

Pascal Mezquita, Eduardo, (ed.) 2003. La política del último Unamuno. Salamanca: Globalia Anthema.

Pena, Mª. Carmen. 1982. Pintura de paisaje e ideología. La Generación del 98. Madrid: Taurus.

Prado Herrera, María Luz de. 2007. 'Patria y dinero. La contribución salmantina a la financiación de la guerra civil española: suscripciones e impuestos especiales', in Robledo, 2007: 189–214.

Pozzoni, Ivan (ed.). 2012. Pragmata. Per una ricostruzione storiografica dei Pragmatismi. Morolo: IF-Press.

Quinones, R.J. 1991. The Changes of Cain: Violence and the Lost Brother in Cain and Abel Literature. Princeton, NJ: Princeton University Press.

Rabaté, Jean-Claude. 2001. Guerra de ideas en el joven Unamuno 1880–1900. Madrid: Biblioteca Nueva.

Rabaté, Colette y Jean-Claude. 2009. Miguel de Unamuno: Biografía. Madrid: Taurus.

Radcliff, Pamela. 'The Emerging Challenge of Mass Politics'. In Alvarez Junco and Shubert 2000: 138–154.

Rambaud, G. 'José Antonio Primo de Rivera (1903–1936)' in www.larousse.fr/enclyclopedie. Accessed June 2011.

Regalado García, Antonio. 1968. El siervo y el señor: la dialéctica agónica de Miguel de Unamuno. Madrid: Gredos.

Reig Tapia, Alberto. 1999. Memoria de la Guerra Civil. Los mitos de la tribu. Madrid: Alianza.

Renshaw, Layla. 2011. Exhuming Loss: Memory, Materiality and Mass Graves of the Spanish Civil War. Walnut Creek, CA: Left Coast Press.

Resina, Joan Ramón (ed.) 2000. Disremembering the Dictatorship: the Politics of Memory in the Spanish Transition to Democracy. Amsterdam: Rodopi.

Ribas Ribas, Pedro. 2002. Para leer a Unamuno. Madrid: Alianza.

Ribbans, Geoffey. 1971. Niebla y soledad: aspectos de Unamuno y Machado. Madrid: Gredos.

——. 1987. 'A New Look at La Tía Tula', Revista Canadiense de Estudios Hispánicos. 11(2): 403–20.

——. 1989. 'Dialéctica de lucha y ambigüedad en la novelística unamuniana'. In Actas del Congreso Cincuentenario de Unamuno, Universidad de Salamanca 10–20 diciembre 1986. Ed. D. Gómez Molleda. Salamanca: Universidad de Salamanca. 153–64.

Ricapito, Joseph. 2004. 'Cervantes and the Funny Book Syndrome'. In Filer et al 2004: 13–44.

Rivero Gómez, Miguel Angel. 2006. 'Cuaderno XXVI. Notas íntimas y reflexiones políticas del joven Unamuno. Un texto inédito', Cuadernos de la Cátedra Miguel de Unamuno, 42: 189–221.

———. 2010. 'Unamuno y el euskera. Aproximación a las raíces de una relación conflictiva', in *La filosofía y las lenguas de la península ibérica. Actas de las VIII y IX Jornadas de Hispanismo Filosófico*. Madrid: Fundación Ignacio Larramendi. 535–559.

Roberts, G. 1986. *Unamuno: afinidades y coincidencias kierkegaardianas*. Colorado: Society of Spanish and Spanish-American Studies.

Roberts, Stephen G.H. 1986. 'Unamuno contra Primo de Rivera: 10 artículos de 1923–24', *Sistema* 75: 83–112.

———. 2000a. 'Unamuno, Spanishness and the Ideal *Patria*: An Intellectual's View', *Journal of the Institute of Romance Studies* 8: 125–136.

———. 2000b. 'Unamuno, 1898 y la crisis de la Restauración', in Joaquim Molas *et al.* 2000: 239–48.

———. 2000c. 'El exilio como una experiencia temporal: Unamuno y *Cómo se hace una novela*', *Hispanística XX, 17: Le XXème Siècle: Parcours et Repères. Culture Hispanique*: 329–38.

———. 2004. 'Hispanidad: El desarrollo de una polémica noción en la obra de Miguel de Unamuno', *Cuadernos de la Cátedra Miguel de Unamuno* 39: 61–80.

———. 2007. *Miguel de Unamuno o la creación del intelectual español moderno*. Trans. María José Martínez Jurico. Salamanca: Universidad de Salamanca.

———. 2011. 'Rescatando a Don Juan: *El hermano Juan o el mundo es teatro* de Unamuno', *Hecho teatral* 11: 193–218.

———. 2013. 'Censura, auto-censura y traducción en los artículos publicados por Miguel de Unamuno durante su exilio voluntario en Francia (1924–1930)', in Guereña and Zapata 2013: 253–72.

Robertson, David. 1985. 'Una guerra de palabras: Primo de Rivera y Unamuno en *Le Quotidien*', *Cahiers du C.R.I.A.R.* 107: 107–21.

———. 1996. *Miguel de Unamuno's Political Writings*, 3 Vols. Lewiston, N.Y: Edwin Mellen Press.

Robledo, Ricardo. (ed.) 2007. *Esta salvaje pesadilla. Salamanca en la guerra civil española*. Barcelona: Crítica.

Rogers, Gayle. 2012. *Modernism and the New Spain: Britain, Cosmopolitan Europe and the New Spain*. Oxford: OUP.

Round, Nicholas. 1974. *Unamuno: Abel Sánchez*. London: Grant and Cutler.

———. (ed.). 1989. *Re-reading Unamuno*. Glasgow: University of Glasgow Press.

———. 1989. '"Without a City Wall": *Paz en la guerra* and the End of Realism', in Round 1989: 101–20.

———. 1992. 'Tragic Sense of *Niebla*'. *Bulletin of Hispanic Studies* Special Homage Volume: Hispanic Studies in Honour of Geoffrey Ribbans. Liverpool: University Press. 171–83.

Rubia Barcia, José and Phyllis Zeitlin (eds.). 1967. *Unamuno: Creator and Creation*. Berkeley: University of California Press.

Ruiz Ramón, Francisco. 1989. *Historia del teatro español. Siglo XX*. Madrid: Cátedra.

Russell, P.E. 1953. 'English Seventeenth-Century Interpretations of Spanish Literature', *Atlante*. 1: 65–77.

Salcedo, Emilio. 1964. *Vida de don Miguel. Unamuno en su tiempo, en su España, en su Salamanca; un hombre en lucha con su leyenda*. Salamanca: Anaya.

———. 1998. *Vida de don Miguel. Unamuno en su tiempo, en su España, en su Salamanca; un hombre en lucha con su leyenda*. (Edición corregida). Salamanca: Anaya.

Salinas, Pedro. 1970. *Literatura española. Siglo XX*. Madrid: Alianza.

Sánchez Barbudo, Antonio (ed.). 1974. *Miguel de Unamuno: el escritor y la crítica.* Madrid: Taurus.

Sartre, Jean-Paul. 1943. *L'Etre et le néant: essai d'ontologie phénoménologique.* Paris: Gallimard.

Shaw, D.L. 1975. *The Generation of 1898 in Spain.* London: Ernest Benn.

——. 1977. 'Three Plays of Unamuno: a Survey of his Dramatic Technique', *Forum for Modern Language Studies.* 13: 253–264.

——. 1979. 'Imagery and Symbolism in the Theatre of Unamuno: *La esfinge* and *Soledad*', *Journal of Spanish Studies: Twentieth Century* 7: 87–104.

Shubert, Adrian. 1990. *A Social History of Modern Spain.* London; New York: Routledge.

Simon, Bennett, and Rachel B. Blass. 1991. 'The Development and Vicissitudes of Freud's Ideas on the Oedipus Complex'. In Neu 1991: 161–74.

Sinclair, A. 1987. 'Definition as the Enemy of Self-Definition: A Commentary on the Role of Language in Unamuno's *Niebla*', in Gabe Coleman and Jondorf 1987: 187–225.

——. 1989. 'Concepts of Tragedy in Unamuno and Kierkegaard' in Round 1989: 121–138.

——. 2001. *Uncovering the Mind: Unamuno, the Unknown and the Vicissitudes of Self.* Manchester: Manchester University Press.

——. 2004. 'Interior and Internal Spain: Visions of the Primitive at the Cultural Interface', *Romance Studies* 22(3): 209–221.

——. 2008. 'Social imaginaries: the literature and discourse of eugenics', *Studies on the History and Philosophy of Biological and Biomedical Sciences* 39(2): 177–272.

Smith, Gilbert. 1972. 'Unamuno, Ortega and the *Otro*', *Revista de Estudios Hispánicos* 6: 29–39.

Sobejano, Gonzalo. 2004. *Nietzsche en España.* Madrid: Gredos.

Spires, Robert C. 1986. 'From Augusto Pérez to Alejandro Gómez to Us', *Revista de Estudios Hispánicos*, 20: 39–49.

——. 1988. *Transparent Simulacra: Spanish Fiction 1902–1926.* Columbia: University of Missouri Press.

Storm, Eric. 2001. *La perspectiva del progreso: pensamiento político en la España del cambio del siglo (1890–1914).* Madrid: Biblioteca Nueva.

Summerhill, Stephen J. 1985. '*San Manuel Bueno, mártir* and the Reader', *Anales de Literatura Española Contemporánea* 10: 67–79.

Teira, Javier. 2008. 'El descubrimiento de Kierkegaard y la lectura de *Enten-Eller*' in Borzoni and Marocco 2008: 69–124.

Tuñón de Lara, Manuel. 1974. *Costa y Unamuno en la crisis del fin de siglo.* Madrid: Edicusa.

Tuñón de Lara, Manuel, *et al* (eds.). 1985. *La guerra civil española 50 años después.* Barcelona: Labor.

Turner, David. 1974. *Unamuno's Webs of Fatality.* London: Tamesis.

Unamuno, Miguel de. 1910. *Mi religión y otros ensayos breves.* Madrid: Biblioteca Renacimiento.

——. 1916–1919. *Ensayos.* Madrid: Residencia de Estudiantes.

——. 1923. 'Fiesta de la raza', *El Socialista.* 18-X.

——. 1932. '¿Partido único?'. *El Día*, Palma de Mallorca, 26 de abril.

——. 1933 'La ciudad de Henoc'. *Ahora*, Madrid, 3 January, 1933.

——. 1954. *Tragic Sense of Life.* Trans. J.E. Crawford Flitch. New York: Dover.

——. 1959. *Teatro completo*. Ed. Manuel García Blanco. Madrid: Aguilar.

——. 1974. *The Agony of Christianity and Essays on Faith*. Ed. and Trans. Anthony Kerrigan and Martin Nozick. Selected Works of Miguel de Unamuno (Bollingen Series), 7 Vols. (Vol. 5). Princeton, N.J.: Princeton University Press.

——. 1976. *Artículos olvidados sobre España y la Primera Guerra Mundial*. Ed. Christopher Cobb. London: Tamesis.

——. 1976b. *Our Lord Don Quixote*. Ed. and Trans. Anthony Kerrigan. Selected Works of Miguel de Unamuno (Bollingen Series), 7 Vols. (Vol. 3). Princeton, N.J.: Princeton University Press.

——. 1979. *República Española y España república*. Ed Vicente González Martín. Salamanca: Almar.

——. 1981. *De Fuerteventura a París*, prólogo de Gregorio San Juan. Bilbao: Ediciones El Sitio.

——. 1983. *Peace in War: a Novel*. Ed. and Trans. Anthony Kerrigan and Martin Nozick. Selected Works of Miguel de Unamuno (Bollingen Series), 7 Vols. (Vol. 1). Princeton, N.J.: Princeton University Press.

——. 1985. *Niebla* [1914]. Barcelona: Plaza y Janés.

——. 1985b. *The Private World: Selections from the Diario Intimo and Selected Letters, 1890–1936*. Ed. and Trans. Anthony Kerrigan and Martin Nozick. Selected Works of Miguel de Unamuno (Bollingen Series) 7 Vols. (Vol. 2).

——. 1986. *Dos artículos y dos discursos*, ed. David Robertson. Madrid: Espiral Hispanoamericana.

——. 1987a. *Vida de Don Quijote y Sancho*. Madrid: Alianza.

——. 1987b. *La tía Tula*. Ed. Carlos Longhurst. Madrid: Cátedra.

——. 1988. *Paz en la guerra*. Ed. Juan Pablo Fusi. Madrid: Alianza.

——. 1988b. *Andanzas y visiones españolas*. Madrid: Alianza.

——. 1991a. *El resentimiento trágico de la vida*. Ed. Carlos Feal. Madrid: Alianza, 1991a.

——. 1991b. *Epistolario inédito*. 2 vols. Ed. Laureano Robles. Madrid: Espasa Calpe.

——. 1993. *Miguel de Unamuno en las 'Noticias' de Barcelona, 1899–1902*, ed. Adolfo Sotelo Vázquez. Barcelona: Lumen.

——. 1994. *Nuevo mundo* [c.1897]. Ed. Laureano Robles. Madrid: Trotta.

——. 1996a. *La agonía del cristianismo*. Ed. Víctor Ouimette. Madrid: Espasa Calpe.

——. 1996b. *Political Speeches and Journalism*. Ed. Stephen G.H. Roberts. Exeter: Exeter Hispanic Texts.

——. 1996c. *Miguel de Unamuno's Political Writings 1918–1924*. Ed. G.D. Robertson. Lewiston/Queenston/Lampeter: The Edwin Mellen Press.

——. 1997a. De patriotismo espiritual Miguel de Unamuno, «Un forjador de cultura», en *De patriotismo espiritual. Artículos en La Nación de Buenos Aires 1901–1914*. Ed. Víctor Ouimette. Salamanca: Universidad de Salamanca.

——. 1997b. *Crítica del problema sobre el origen y prehistoria de la raza vasca*. Ed. José Antonio Ereño Altuna. Bilbao: Beitia.

——. 1998a. *Diario íntimo*. Madrid: Alianza.

——. 1998b. *Alrededor del estilo*. Ed. Laureano de Robles. Salamanca: Ediciones Universidad de Salamanca.

——. 1999a. *Paz en la guerra*. Ed. Francisco Caudet. Madrid: Cátedra.

——. 1999b. *Abel Sánchez*. Trans. John Macklin. Oxford: Aris & Phillips.

——. 2002. *Amor y pedagogía; Epistolario Miguel de Unamuno y Santiago Valentí Camp*. Ed. Bénédicte Vauthier. Madrid: Biblioteca Nueva.

——. 2005a. *Manual de quijotismo. Cómo se hace una novela. Epistolario Miguel de Unamuno/Jean Cassou.* Estudio preliminar de Bénédicte Vauthier. Salamanca: Ediciones Universidad de Salamanca.

——. 2005b. *Del sentimiento trágico de la vida en los hombres y los pueblos y Tratado del amor de Dios.* Ed. N. Orringer. Madrid: Tecnos,

——. 2005c. *En torno al casticismo* [1902]. Ed. Jean-Claude Rabaté. Madrid: Cátedra.

——. 2005d. *Vida de Don Quijote y Sancho.* Ed. Alberto Navarro. Madrid: Cátedra.

——. 2005e. *Nuevo Mundo.* Ed. Paolo Tanganelli. Caserta: Saletta dell'Uva.

——. 2007. *Saint Manuel Bueno, Martyr.* Trans. Paul Burns and Salvador Ortiz Carboneres. Oxford: Aris and Phillips. Oxford: Aris and Phillips.

——. 2009. *Abel Sánchez.* Trans. John Macklin. Oxford: Aris and Phillips.

——. 2012a. *Diario íntimo.* Ed. Etelvino González. Salamanca: Ediciones Universidad de Salamanca.

——. 2012b. *Cartas del destierrro.* Ed. Colette y Jean-Claude Rabaté. Salamanca: Ediciones Universidad de Salamanca.

——. 2013. *Aunt Tula.* Trans. Julia Biggane. Oxford: Aris and Phillips.

——. 2014. *Mist.* Trans. John Macklin. Oxford: Aris and Phillips.

Urrutia Jordana, Ana. 2003. *La poetización de la política en el Unamuno exiliado.* Salamanca: Ediciones Universidad de Salamanca.

Urrutia León, Manuel. 1997. *Evolución del pensamiento político de Unamuno.* Bilbao: Universidad de Deusto.

——. (ed.). 2007. *Miguel de Unamuno desconocido. Con 58 nuevos textos.* Salamanca: Ediciones de la Universidad de Salamanca.

——. 2009. 'Miguel de Unamuno y *España con Honra* (1924–1925)', *Cuadernos de la Cátedra Miguel de Unamuno* 47 (1): 193–234.

Valdés, Mario J. 1982. *Shadows in the Cave: A Phenomenological Approach to Literary Criticism Based on Spanish Texts.* Toronto: Toronto U. P.

Vauthier, Bénédicte. 1999. *Niebla de Miguel de Unamuno: a favor de Cervantes, en contra de los "cervantófilos". Estudio de narratología estilística.* New York: Peter Lang.

Vicente Rodríguez, José. 2005. *Miguel de Unamuno, proa al infinito.* Madrid: B.A.C.

Wright, Sarah. 2004. 'Ethical Seductions: A Comparative Reading of Unamuno's *El hermano Juan* and Kierkegaard's *Either/Or*', *Anales de la literatura española contemporánea* 29:2. 489–504.

Wyers, Frances. 1976. *Miguel de Unamuno: The Contrary Self.* London: Tamesis.

——. 1990. 'Unamuno and 'The Death of the Author''. *Hispanic Review* 58: 325–346.

Zavala, Iris. 1963. *Unamuno y su teatro de conciencia.* Salamanca: Ediciones Universidad de Salamanca.

Zubizarreta, Armando F. 1958. 'Desconocida antesala de la crisis de Unamuno: 1895–6', *Insula* 142: 13.

——. 1960. *Unamuno en su nivola.* Madrid: Taurus.

Zulueta Artaloytia, J.A. de. 1988. 'Vocación viajera y entendimiento del paisaje en la generación del 98'. En Gómez Mendoza *et al* 1988: 89–106.

Index

CPSIA information can be obtained
at www.ICGtesting.com
Printed in the USA
LVHW082356311018
594737LV00007B/123/P